Points for the Meditations and Contemplations
of St. Ignatius of Loyola

Points
for the Meditations and Contemplations of St. Ignatius of Loyola

by

FRANZ VON HUMMELAUER, S.J.

Translated by V. J. HOMMEL, S.J.
Second Revised Edition by H. ROPER, S.J.

THE NEWMAN PRESS
WESTMINSTER, MARYLAND
1955

Imprimi potest: Gulielmus F. Maloney, S.J.
Praepositus Provincialis
Provinciae Marylandiae

Nihil obstat: Eduardus A. Cerny, S.S., D.D.
Censor Librorum

Imprimatur: Franciscus P. Keough, D.D.
Archiepiscopus Baltimorensis

die 27 mensis Septembris, 1954

Library of Congress Catalog Card Number: 54-12084
Copyright, 1955, by The Newman Press
Printed in the United States of America

Preface to the Second English Edition

★

IN ADDITION to the points for meditation, this edition contains Father von Hummelauer's most valuable introduction to and analysis of the *Spiritual Exercises,* together with his occasional notes showing the significance of each exercise in relation to the work as a whole. Father Hommel did not live to see his complete translation published. He died in 1948, a year after keeping his golden jubilee in the Society of Jesus. But he left the unpublished portions of the book in manuscript. These, as well as the part already published, have been either rewritten or carefully revised for this edition.

H. ROPER, S.J.

Bombay, June, 1949

Preface to the First English Edition

★

THAT THE Latin original of this Retreat has gone through several editions is palpable proof of its excellence. *

This English edition gives the points " cut and dried " for direct practical use by directors and retreatants; only a very few of the copious theoretical and historical explanations are included: this gap will be filled up in the second edition, and we trust the indulgent reader has that much patience.

A few biographical details about the well-known author may be welcome.—Franz von Hummelauer was born August 14, 1842, at Vienna (Austria). His father belonged to the diplomatic service; his mother (née Karolinas von Suini) is still remembered for her charities to young students.

From 1856 to 1860 Franz studied, as a boarder, at the *Stella Matutina,* Feldkirch, a hill-school conducted by the German Jesuits, and including an Austrian as well as a German section. This early connection with the German Fathers brought Franz, at the age of 18, to the noviceship at Gorheim, in preference to his native Austria.

The training of a Jesuit is a slow and lengthy process, and by 1872, the year of Father von Hummelauer's or-

---

* The descriptive Latin title runs as follows:
Meditationum et Contemplationum S. Ignatii de Loyola Puncta, Libri Exercitiorum Textum diligenter secutus explicavit.

Franciscus de Hummelauer, S. J.

Editio tertia.   Friburgi Brisgoviae, 1925.
Herder & Co. Typographi Editores Pontificii.
Imprimatur, Friburgi Brisgoviae, 19 Nov. 1924.
CAROLUS, Archiep.

dination to the priesthood, the members of the German Province were living in exile. The professors and students had found a hospitable home at Ditton Hall, England. Here it was that the full-fledged Jesuit, the proficient classical and Oriental scholar, began for good his life-work, exegesis and Biblical research; the catalogue for 1877 gives the status of Father von Hummelauer as Scriptor.

The transfer from England to Trevueren (Brussels), and in 1895 to the newly opened St. Ignatius College at Valkenburg (Holland), meant no change in the primary task of our exegete; his books were his inseparable companions. Year after year saw the contributions of Father von Hummelauer swell the voluminous *Cursus S. Scripturae* published by Lethielleux, Paris. Eight portly volumes are signed by our author, and his name became a household word in Catholic circles; Protestants had to take account of the sound and solid learning. Ere long the highest official acknowledgment was forthcoming: in 1903 Father von Hummelauer was appointed Consultor to the newly established Pontifical Biblical Commission, Rome.

Mention should also be made of essays of a general nature on the fundamental and burning questions of the day: Inspiration, the Hexaemeron, Pre-Mosaic Priesthood. Translations into French and Italian spread his ideas, which were both conservative and progressive, to larger circles; at the same time criticism tended to become sharp, and for the sake of peace—it was now a winning battle—Father von Hummelauer was able to anchor his boat in more retired waters. It was during this period of apostolic work at Berlin, 1908-1910, that he sent the *Points* on their second round. The peaceful preface of the second edition is reproduced here. No better recommendation seemed required for the third edition, when the book set out to bring to the war-weary world the old teaching of humility and true penance: "But your sorrow shall be turned into joy." (John 16:20)

Father von Hummelauer never lost touch with living realities: he used to be a popular examiner of theological students; his moral cases in particular were taken from experience, and his interest in the monthly debates of budding philosophers and theologians was an encouragement to the most easy-going candidates. Many a humorous anecdote about him was current in our student world.—As a rest from the learned studies the great writer used to spend his holidays giving retreats, especially to priests. The fruit of these responsible labors is gathered up in the *Points*; they will long survive and continue his apostolate: like the booklet of St. Ignatius, they will be ever new and up-to-date, precious metal that will not rust; the gold-standard of humility has every chance long to serve as sure measure of values.

It was only when life's forces were all spent that Father von Hummelauer found a quiet retreat in the noviceship at 's Heerenberg (Gld. Holland). Like his brother in religion, St. Robert Bellarmine at S. Andrea, Rome, the fearless champion of Catholic truth passed away peacefully in the kiss of the Lord, on 12 April 1914.—Well done, thou good and faithful servant!

V. J. HOMMEL, S.J.

Bombay, August 20, 1937

Author's Preface to the Second Latin Edition

★

Berlin, 21st. June, 1909

DEAR READER,

While preparing the second edition of this booklet, I thought I must take care not to change the book so as to make it appear different from the first publication, which met with the approval of many. I have made a few additions and several corrections; and the publishers have taken pains to give a yet more suitable shape to the little volume. In this, as in the previous edition, I felt in conscience bound to be merely the interpreter of St. Ignatius, to unfold the meaning of the Book of the *Exercises,* not to saddle it with my own views.

Farewell!

FRANZ VON HUMMELAUER, S.J.

Author's Preface to the Second Latin Edition.

Berne, 21st June, 1909.

DEAR READER,

While preparing the second edition of this booklet, I thought I must take care not to change the book so as to make it appear different from the first publication, which met with the approval of many. I have made a few additions and several corrections; and the publishers have taken pains to give a yet more suitable shape to the little volume. In this, as in the previous edition, I felt in conscience bound to be merely the interpreter of St. Ignatius, to unfold the meaning of the book of the Exercises, not to meddle it with my own views.

Farewell.

FRANZ VON HUMMELAUER, S.J.

Contents

★

THIRD WEEK

FOURTH WEEK

Points for the Meditations and Contemplations
of St. Ignatius of Loyola

Preliminary Remarks

*

THE *Spiritual Exercises* of St. Ignatius contains chiefly meditations and contemplations. St. Ignatius' book embraces both the points of these meditations and contemplations, which he calls the *matter* of the exercises, and instructions regarding meditation and contemplation, which he calls the *form* of the exercises. With the exception of The Contemplation to attain Love only the exercises on the mysteries of our Lord's life and passion are usually spoken of as contemplations; the other exercises are called meditations.

How the Meditations are United

According to the first " preliminary remark," " every way of preparing and disposing the soul to rid itself of all inordinate attachments, and, after their removal, of seeking and finding the will of God in the disposition of our life for the salvation of our soul" (Sec. 1) * is a spiritual exercise. The title of the book runs: *Spiritual Exercises which have as their purpose the regulation of one's life in such a way that no decision is made under the influence of any inordinate attachment.* (Sec. 21) It is thus clear that

* Throughout this book all quotations from the text of the *Exercises* will be taken from *The Spiritual Exercises of St. Ignatius,* a New Translation by Louis J. Puhl, S.J., published by the Newman Press, Westminster, Maryland, 1953. All references will be to sections. All quotations from the New Testament will be taken from the Confraternity Edition, published by St. Anthony Guild Press, Paterson, New Jersey, 1947. Where Father Puhl uses another translation the text of the Confraternity Edition will be substituted.

the ultimate end or purpose of the exercises is the ultimate end of human life itself, namely, the salvation of one's soul; the proximate end, or the means whereby one saves his soul, is the re-ordering and disposing of one's life for the future. For the latter the correction of past faults is required.

If such is the aim of the exercises, we shall naturally find it expressed in what St. Ignatius calls the Principle and Foundation of the whole spiritual edifice. Indeed, the nature of this re-ordering of one's life is distinctly stated there in the words: " Our one desire and choice should be what is more conducive to the end for which we are created." (Sec. 23) The search for, and discovery of, God's will in our regard, and the disposal and re-ordering of our future life accordingly, is the main task of the whole series of exercises, to which all else is subordinate.

In the preparatory prayer of the first exercise, a prayer preceding all subsequent exercises, we discover the motif unifying the entire work. That prayer asks " that all my intentions, actions, and operations may be directed purely to the praise and service of His Divine Majesty." (Sec. 46) It gives to all the exercises a common direction toward the orientation of one's life and work. Although the " intentions, actions and operations " sought embrace directly only those which occur in the course of the exercise preceded by the prayer, they include as well those subsequent to the meditation, directed and sanctified by it.

A term of note is *choice*. For Ignatius, *choice* comprises not only the embracing of a state of life but also of the means necessary for perfecting oneself in that state. The main task of the *choice* is the actual choice of a state of life, as is evident from the words: " One considers first for what purpose man is born, that is, for the praise of God our Lord and for the salvation of his soul. With the desire to attain this before his mind, he chooses as a means to this end a kind of life or state within the bounds of the Church that will help him in the service of God our Lord and the salvation of his soul." (Sec. 177) We can safely assert that the immediate purpose of the *Exercises* is that we should either choose a state of life or perfect ourselves in a state already chosen.

In his Introduction to the Consideration of Different States of Life Ignatius teaches us explicitly how contemplation on Christ's life can help us make our choice. (Cf. Sec. 135) Christ is the living example for us of both ordinary and evangelical perfection. Indeed, in the two mysteries of the Hidden Life and the Finding in the Temple, He sets an example of the contemplative and active lives, and in other mysteries He shows Himself a model of virtues to be practiced. It is " whilst continuing to contemplate His life " that we can " investigate in what kind of life or in what state His Divine Majesty wishes to make use of us." (Sec. 135) Why? Because in contemplating His life we become deeply penetrated by His spirit, which will preserve us from the deceits of the Devil in making our own election, and enable us to choose a state of life " not because of any sensual inclination " (Sec. 182), but " for the praise of God our Lord and for the salvation of my soul." (Sec. 169) Contemplation on the life of Christ enables us to see how we should use our intellect, and especially our will, in the choice of our way of life.

For those about to make their choice of life St. Ignatius

proposes the meditation on the Kingdom of Christ, whose title states: " The call of an earthly king . . . will help us to contemplate the life of the eternal king." (Sec. 91) We can say that this meditation prepares for the mysteries to follow, those dealing with the life of Christ. However this meditation has not the same place as the Principle and Foundation in regard to the entire work. The Principle and Foundation is the root giving nourishment and strength to the other meditations and contemplations. The meditation on the Kingdom of Christ is not so essential; it is primarily meant to be a valuable help to us in the choice of a state of life. The Principle and Foundation is so essential that without it the whole structure of the *Exercises* and the actual choice of a state of life would collapse. We cannot conceive the *Exercises* without it; whereas it is possible to make the *Exercises* without the meditation on the Kingdom of Christ, since the helps it provides for the contemplation of the life of Christ could be conveniently and effectively suggested by the one giving the exercises when proposing different mysteries. Nevertheless the meditation on the Kingdom of Christ is not merely a preface to the mysteries of Christ's life, nor does it merely summarize or repeat them in shorter form. It gives us positive help for the subsequent contemplations, enabling us at the outset to take in at a single glance all the main considerations which urge us to follow Christ, explaining concisely and clearly the conditions of Christ's call, conditions set forth more explicitly in the meditations and contemplations to follow. Above all, this meditation accounts fully for the third prelude to the contemplations on Christ's life: " to ask for what I desire

. . . . an intimate knowledge of our Lord, who has become man for me, that I may love Him more and follow Him more closely." (Sec. 104)

Again, the choice of a state of life is the sole reason for the insertion of the meditations on the Two Standards and the Three Classes of Men. The former meditation is intended as an introduction to the matter of choosing a state of life, and the latter tells us " to beg for the grace to choose what is more for the glory of His Divine Majesty and the salvation of my soul." (Sec. 152)

The above analysis shows us that the choice of a state in life is the principal task of the whole retreat and that all other exercises are related to it. It now remains for us to examine more closely the connection of each of the meditations with this task.

The Foundation and The Choice of a Way of Life

By an examination of the Introduction to Making a Choice of a Way of Life and other passages we find that St. Ignatius insisted that the choice must be made in a due and orderly manner, sincerely and purely. In order to insure the proper choice " I must consider only the end for which I am created, that is, for the praise of God our Lord and for the salvation of my soul . . . Nothing must move me to use . . . means, or to deprive myself of them, save only the service and praise of God our Lord, and the salvation of my soul." (Sec. 169. Cf. also Secs. 175-180) In making the choice we must keep ourselves " indifferent, without any inordinate attachment." (Sec. 179)

The last words quoted indicate what St. Ignatius meant by an inordinate and crooked choice. It is the choice made by those who " do not go directly to God, but want God to come straight to their inordinate attachments." Consequently, " they make of the end a means, and of the means an end." (Sec. 169) It is a choice based not on reason, but on sentiment or emotion. It is one which lacks detachment or indifference.

From this it is clear how closely connected are the Foundation and the Choice of a Way of Life. The choice is so based and built on the two truths of the end of man and the necessity of detachment that the rules for making it in an orderly way could be given immediately after the Foundation, without missing any logical link. Not only are the suggestions relative to the choice based entirely on the Foundation, but the Foundation itself contains matter properly pertinent to the choice in the words: "Our one desire and choice should be what is more conducive to the end for which we are created." (Sec. 23)

The First Week and the Choice

According to Loyola the choice is concerned only with the selection between things good or indifferent, not with the rejection of things evil: " It is necessary that all matters of which we wish to make a choice be either indifferent or good in themselves . . . and not bad." (Sec. 170)

The meditation on the Three Sins is wholly concerned with arousing a sense of shame, to make us not only detest our past sins but also regulate our life for the future: " What have I done for Christ? What am I doing for Christ? What ought I to do for Christ? " (Sec. 53) These words of the colloquy evidently suggest not only the sincere admission of past sins but also the will to do something in the future. The meditation on Personal Sins leads finally to a petition whereby we resolve with God's grace to make amends in the future. (Cf. Sec. 61) The whole purpose of this meditation and the exercise following it is to make us rid ourselves of those attachments which make our choice inordinate and worthless and stir up within ourselves the desire for firm amendment of our lives.

The Kingdom of Christ and the Choice of a Way of Life

The meditation on the Kingdom of Christ dwells chiefly on three points: the plan of Christ the King for those who wish to follow Him, the motives for following Him, and the degrees of that following. Plan, condition, and motives all prepare the way for embracing the more perfect degree of the following of Christ in the choice of a way of life and thus subserve that choice.

The plan of Christ is stated in the words: " It is my will to conquer the whole world and all my enemies, and thus to enter into the glory of my Father." (Sec. 95) In penning these words, St. Ignatius no doubt had in mind Our Lord's saying: " Did not the Christ have to suffer these things before entering his glory." (Luke 24:26) The enemies are " sensuality and carnal and worldly love." (Sec. 97) Knowing the enemies we know the battlefield. Not tracts of country but the hearts of men, our own hearts, are the field of battle. It is our duty to drive these enemies from our hearts and prepare an abode for Christ the King. Christ is ready to help us, but we must use our own free wills. Christ cannot conquer the enemies in our hearts unless we so will. Hence the second part, and essential part, of His plan is that we must submit ourselves to

His leadership in order to conquer these enemies. His plan can be summed up in one word: *Following.*

The condition imposed on Christ's followers is clearly stated in the following passages: " whoever wishes to join with me . . . must be content with the same food, drink, clothing, etc. as mine. So, too, he must work with me by day, and watch with me by night . . . that as he has had a share in the toil with me, afterwards, he may share in the victory with me." (Sec. 93) *

Motives for following Christ are indicated partly in the first point of the meditation and partly in the last point. In the former only the motives of equity and uprightness are stressed, corresponding to the motive of shame first proposed in the consideration of sin. Equity and uprightness are shown both by an external argument, bringing in the comparison of a temporal king—" If such a summons of an earthly king to his subjects deserves our attention, how much more worthy of consideration is Christ our Lord, the Eternal King, before whom is assembled the whole world " (Sec. 95)—and by internal arguments, drawn from the person who invites us, Christ Himself, who is the Second Person of the Blessed Trinity, from His kindness which invites us, rather than commands us, from His personal braveness. The last point proposes the higher motive of " greater proof of . . . love " for Christ. (Sec. 97) From this motive arises the desire " to distinguish [ourselves] in whatever concerns the service of the eternal King and the Lord of all " and to imitate His patience in adversity and to follow Him as closely as possible. (Secs. 95-98) The meditation seeks to arouse in us unselfish, disinterested love in Christ, love of Him for His own sake.

The purpose of Christ's call is to make us go with Him, work with Him, follow Him in sufferings and ultimately enjoy with Him the glory of heaven. However there are two degrees in this following of Christ. The first is attained by those who " will offer themselves entirely " for Christ's work; the second by those who, going beyond this, are desirous " to distinguish themselves in whatever concerns the service of the Eternal King and the Lord of all." (Sec. 97)

It is unnecessary to say that the meditation on the Kingdom of Christ supposes we have made advancement during the first week and already have sincere hatred of sin, both mortal and venial, and of the enticements of the world. It is supposed that we have acquired a resolve to be detached. In Ignatian terminology we have been established in the first and second kinds of humility, at least in desire. The call of Christ urges us to embrace the third kind of humility, which, in the mind of Ignatius, constitutes the summit of all perfection. This is undoubtedly expressed in the final point of the meditation and in the colloquy, where we pray that we may freely imitate Christ our Lord " *in bearing all wrongs and all abuse and all poverty, both actual and spiritual, should Thy most holy majesty deign to choose and admit me to such a state and way of life.*" (Sec. 98)

The third kind of humility is thus set before us in the meditation on the Kingdom of Christ, and this perhaps explains why later St. Ignatius does not propose the three kinds in the form of a separate meditation. Since the meditation on the Kingdom of Christ is designed to help us throughout our contemplation of the mysteries of Christ's life and to show us what we should seek therein, it follows that each contemplation should lead us not to any kind of imitation, but to that of the third kind of humility. In this wise the Kingdom of Christ is linked to the three kinds of humility, which in turn are linked to our choice of a way of life, for in considering the three kinds we are told that " Before entering upon the Choice of a Way of Life, in order that we may be filled with love of the true doctrine of Christ our Lord, it will be very useful to consider attentively the following Three Kinds of Humility. These should be thought over from time to time during the whole day." (Sec. 164)

One may ask whether the apostolic following of Christ is not also suggested here, so that we should work with Him not only in subduing our own hearts but also in winning others to Him. Implicitly this is suggested. Not so much in the solemn offering of oneself, an offering made also by those who follow Christ in the contemplative life, as in the desire to distinguish ourselves in entire service of Christ. The main purpose, however, is not to speak to all indiscriminately about the apostolic life, but to establish all in a generous love of Christ and a general determination to follow Him.

The Two Standards and the Choice

The meditation on the Two Standards is given expressly as an introduction to the choice of the way of life. (Cf. Sec. 135) St. Ignatius wants us to see " how we ought to prepare ourselves to arrive at perfection in whatever state or way of life God our Lord may grant us to choose." (Sec. 135) To do this he sets before our eyes as one stand-

ard that " *of Christ, our supreme leader and lord; [as an]
other [that] of Lucifer, the deadly enemy of our human
nature.*" (Sec. 136)

The plan of Christ has as its end that Christian perfection which can be attained by doing His will on earth. The
meditation on the Two Standards is by no means solely
concerned with the state of evangelical perfection. On the
contrary " Christ calls and wants all beneath His standard." (Sec. 137) Christ wills us to be perfect, to possess
all supernatural qualities or virtues, possessed, not in their
lowest degree, but already augmented by diligent exercise.
Christ wants us to rise to the summit of perfection by
three stages: " the first, poverty as opposed to riches; the
second, insults or contempt as opposed to the honor of this
world; the third, humility as opposed to pride." (Sec.
146) The poverty spoken of here is spiritual poverty,
which, however, must become actual poverty should God's
sovereign Majesty so desire. (Cf. Sec. 146)

In short Christ's plan is this: acts of poverty and humiliation must be made, as they lead the way to the ac-
quisition of habitual humility and every virtue. This is
the general plan. We must, however, allow for divine grace,
which can proceed in other ways. Humility is not necessarily always present before every other virtue, nor does
one necessarily always reach the other virtues through humility. Otherwise in the spiritual life everyone would be
obliged to aim first and before all else at humility. But
this is not the case, since the first thing of all for us to do
is root out our predominant vice and acquire the contrary
virtue. This meditation therefore aims: (1) to show us
the usual way in which Lucifer sets about the ruin of souls

(by tempting men " to covet riches " [Sec. 142]) and Jesus Christ their sanctification (by attracting men " to the highest spiritual poverty " [Sec. 146]); (2) to induce us, in our choice of a way of life, to keep the spirit of Christ before our eyes and be on guard against the deceits of Lucifer. Christ's plan is set before us that in all things we should esteem poverty and humiliations and eagerly embrace them when they present themselves. Such is the disposition this meditation seeks to give us.

The call of Christ in this meditation is identical with His call in the Kingdom of Christ, but it is much more explicit. There we were invited to follow Christ in general terms, the choice of poverty being left a matter for spontaneous and generous offering; here the profession of poverty, at least of spiritual poverty, is explicitly suggested by Christ our leader. The reasons in this meditation point not to any kind of following but to the following of Christ in His poverty and humility.

We are taught to view riches and honors with mistrust as the deceits of the evil leader, nets set out to trap us; we are shown the practical connection between humility and taste for poverty and humiliations, a connection bringing about true life. The necessity of this connection is still more evident by the counsels and example of Christ, who is presented to us, in contrast with Lucifer, as infinitely loveable, as the friend of men, and as generously extending to all the invitation to follow Him in the highest poverty and humility.

The Three Classes of Men and the Choice of a Way of Life

The meditation on the Three Classes of Men is immediately concerned with the choice of a way of life. It sets before us three dispositions and endeavors to raise us to the third of these. We must analyze these dispositions accurately.

We must first note in all three cases five points of similarity: (1) the money was not acquired unjustly, otherwise it would be merely a case of restitution; (2) the possession of the money immediately gives rise to an inordinate attachment to it; (3) all three classes "wish to save their souls and find peace in God our Lord by ridding themselves of the burden" (Sec. 150); (4) their inordinate attachment to this money constitutes an obstacle to their salvation; (5) all three classes agree in having some desire to "rid themselves of the attachment" (Sec. 155), but in the way in which they try to accomplish this desire they differ widely.

The first class wish to find God in peace and to be rid of their inordinate attachment, but "the hour of death comes, and they have not made use of any means." (Sec. 153) From this inactivity we see the hollowness of their resolve; it is only a velleity, not a volition. At the hour of death this class still has its burden and faces all the consequence of laziness.

The second class wish to find peace and be rid of their attachment, and even to take some means toward the realization of both these ends, but at the same time they are altogether bent on keeping the money. Consequently they are ready to take any means except that of giving up the money, even though they realize that this is the best and perhaps only efficacious means. This class want salvation, but only conditionally. They want the money and salvation. If salvation cannot be had except by giving up the money, they do not want salvation. They subordinate God and the salvation of their souls to the money. They want God to save them on their own conditions. Although they do take some means they lack sincerity; in a word, they are dishonest. Their attitude is quite contrary to the spirit of the entire retreat.

The third class wish to find peace, and consequently to be rid of their attachment. Indeed they wish this absolutely. They do not hold back. They do not make God accept them on their own terms. They are truly detached, wishing solely " to will and not will as God our Lord inspires them, and as seems better for the service and praise of the Divine Majesty." (Sec. 155) Until God's good pleasure is made known to them they resolve and strive to give up their attachment to the money. Indeed they have already given it up in intention. They no longer are attached to it. If God wills them to have it, good; if not, good. Theirs is the disposition referred to by St. Ignatius in the title of this meditation: " *to choose that which is better.*" (Sec. 149)

The scope of this meditation is to make us realize (1) that the choice calls for positive action on our part, (2) that ineffective means do not suffice, because they are really not means at all, and (3) that only a generous giving up of our attachments will suffice. Understanding this we must examine our feelings in regard to the choice of the means. If we find that we are not in the best disposition we must strive with all our might and by persistent prayer to obtain it. The first point attacks sloth in this matter, the second self-deceit, and the third puts in place of both sloth and deceit true generosity.

Kinds of Humility and the Choice of a Way of Life

The three kinds of humility are not, says Ignatius, to be given as a meditation but are to be "thought over from time to time during the whole day." (Sec. 164) In fact, they do not present new matter for meditation but sum up and give more concise expression to the main lessons taught in the preceding exercises, chiefly the Kingdom of Christ and the Two Standards, and in the contemplations on the mysteries of our Lord's life.

One new point should be noticed. The Kingdom of Christ and the Two Standards set before us the third kind of humility as an excellent thing, recommended by the example and counsel of Christ. This exercise explains it by a comparison, showing how the third kind of humility is the greatest. In this exercise we say: " I desire and choose poverty with Christ poor, rather than riches; insults with Christ loaded with them, rather than honors; I desire to be accounted as worthless and a fool for Christ, rather than to be esteemed as wise and prudent in this world. So Christ was treated before me." (Sec. 167)

St. Ignatius desired that the consideration of the three kinds was to serve as a leaven which should pervade all the following contemplations and so, by means of these, to inspire the choice of a way of life. Its scope is to help us "be filled with love of the true doctrine of Christ our Lord." (Sec. 164)

The kinds of humility are states, not acts, as is clear from the words: "if my attitude of mind is such." (Sec. 166) They are called "kinds" because they are different manifestations of the same virtue. This virtue, humility, may be defined as a disposition to see oneself as God sees him, and not exalt oneself. It is to be exercised to superiors, equals, and inferiors. First of all it is to be exercised to superiors, primarily to God Himself. In Loyola's mind man's subjection and obedience to the Divine Will is a part of humility; indeed, it is its first and most genuine characteristic.

The first kind consists in the habitual will to obey God so that I would never " consent to violate a commandment . . . that binds me under pain of mortal sin." (Sec. 165) This says more that not committing mortal sin, since it excludes even " the thought " of so doing. It also extends to *all* things.

The second kind is the same humility raised to greater perfection and requires detachment. The disposition to serve God has its root in the truth concerning the end of man; but the necessary corollary of that truth is detachment or self-control. Consequently humility infused with detachment is more perfect that the first kind of humility. When we possess this kind we would never " consent to commit a venial sin." (Sec. 166)

The third kind consists in still more perfect obedience or subjection to God, obedience not only of His Law but a willingness to do whatever is pleasing to Him, even though no obligation by way of sin is present. In the first place this implies a full imitation of Christ, an imitation not only in a general way, but in all that we do. In this third kind we have a disposition to sacrifice our own well-being, accept poverty and reproaches, and all for the love of Christ.

Throughout the meditation it is assumed that we desire to obtain the highest degree of humility, regardless of what our final state in life may be. In the concluding paragraph of the meditation St. Ignatius speaks of the way whereby humility assists us in choosing our state of life. We are asked to beg our Lord to choose us for the highest kind of humility. Possessed of this humility we can then choose our state of life in a manner most pleasing to God. (Cf. Sec. 168)

The three kinds of humility are distinguished both by their object and by their motive: the first has as its object obedience necessary for salvation from the motive of fear; the second has obedience from the motive of justice; the third has perfect conformity to God's good pleasure from the motive of love. The kinds are closely connected; indeed, they are degrees of humility, of which the lower is not just a state but also an efficacious means to reach the higher states.

The first two kinds are absolutely necessary for salvation and must be asked for from God. The third, however, is to be asked only on the condition that God wills us to have it and that equal praise and service be given to the Divine Majesty. (Cf. Sec. 168) The third kind is not imposed on us as a command as are the first two; it is a counsel of our Lord.

The purpose of the consideration of the three kinds of humility is to lead us to the third, which gives us the most favorable disposition for choosing our state in life. We are to arouse in ourselves the disposition to follow God's grace in all things; even if we do not seek the third kind of humility, we must be disposed to beg God's grace to accept it if He honors us by giving it to us.

By means of the meditations on the Kingdom of Christ, the Two Standards, the Three Classes and the Three Kinds of Humility, St. Ignatius seeks to build in us the dispositions needed for choosing our state in life in a way conformable to God's will. Never does St. Ignatius try to push us into the religious life. He is quite emphatic and clear in showing us what is a matter of precept and what of counsel. It is his constant fear that we should rush hastily into the religious life. That life is only for those called by Christ. What we must do is seek Christ's will and make ourselves ready to follow it when found. But, no matter what our state of life may be, the third kind of humility can be sought. Contrary to popular belief all Christians, lay as well as religious, can aspire to perfection. Perfection requires first of all detachment from things of this world. The spirit of detachment had been placed before us in the Principle and Foundation. Secondly perfection requires conformity of the highest kind with Christ. That conformity is to be found in the third kind of humility. Though we need not have such humility in order to save our souls, we can ask God for it, and we must be ready to accept it if He gives it. All the meditations we have considered thus far have emphasized the need for detachment. Now, in the meditation under consideration, perfect conformity to Christ's will is emphasized. From these considerations we can see the unifying theme of the exercises, and we must note well that all the meditations thus far considered are directed to the ultimate purpose of the exercises, namely the choice of a way of life.

How the Contemplations are connected with the Meditations

The general connection between the meditations and the contemplations is indicated by the statement that the meditation on the Kingdom of Christ " *will help us to contemplate the life of the eternal King.*" (Sec. 91) Consequently all the mysteries of Christ's life, or contemplations, are directly linked to the meditations on the Kingdom, and at least indirectly to the other meditations. St. Ignatius explicitly points out the connection between two mysteries—the Hidden Life and the Finding in the Temple—and the choice of a way of life. Inasmuch as St. Ignatius states: " Whilst continuing to contemplate His life, let us begin to investigate in what kind of life or in what state His Divine Majesty wishes to make use of us " (Sec. 135), we can be certain that all the contemplations on the mysteries of Christ's life bear an intimate relation to the meditations, since all have as their common goal the choice of a way of life. Christ's life is taken as the criterion of our life. Throughout the retreat St. Ignatius never proposes for simultaneous consideration matters which do not effectively contribute to the single end he has in view. The contemplations on the mysteries of Christ's public life have an intimate relation to the choice of a way of life. St. Ignatius says: " The treatment of the matter dealing with the Choice of a Way of Life will begin with the contemplation of our Lord's departure from Nazareth for the Jordan." (Sec. 163)

As the whole life of Christ is related in a general way to the meditation on the Kingdom of Christ, so the different weeks are related to the different parts of that meditation. In the second week we see Christ the King calling by word, by teaching, and by example; in the third week we see Him laboring by day and watching by night, content with the food and drink of tribulation and the dress of ignominy; in the fourth week we see Him in the glory of the Father.

Then too, according to St. Ignatius' own words, the

mysteries of the second week are arranged in groups, each of which has its special connection with the task of making a choice in life. Since the Hidden Life and the Finding in the Temple illustrate two states of life, and the whole contemplation of Christ's life is adapted to the choice of a way of life, we can rightly classify the mysteries of the second week as follows: from the Incarnation to the Return from Egypt the choice is being prepared; in the Hidden Life and the Finding in the Temple the states of life available for the choice are shown; the remaining mysteries of the second week are meant to help us make our choice; finally, the mysteries of the third and fourth weeks are to confirm the choice made.

The question now arises whether, in addition to this general connection, there is or is not a special connection between particular contemplations and the meditations and the choice. If we examine the series of contemplations on the mysteries as given by St. Ignatius, we cannot fail to notice that not a little of what is narrated in the Gospel is omitted; not merely incidents like the angel's appearance to St. Joseph or the suicide of Judas, but mysteries of the Public Life itself. There would not be time, we may argue, to contemplate all the mysteries. Yet on what principle did St. Ignatius make his selection of just a few mysteries out of so many? Surely he did not make his choice arbitrarily or by whim; the very idea is unworthy of such a man. Did he then select the mysteries to which the Gospel seemed to give greater importance? Surely the Gospel does not give greater importance to the Miracle at Cana than to the Confession of St. Peter, nor to the Supper at Bethany than to the rich and salutary teaching of the Parables. There must then be a reason other than the Gospel itself which guided St. Ignatius in making his selection. What that was can easily be seen: he selected the mysteries from which he himself had drawn most profit, on account of their closer connection with the entire scope of the retreat and the task of the choice.

Note now the arrangement of the points in the contemplations. Usually, that arrangement is the obvious one. For example, in the mystery of the Presentation, the three points are: (1) the Presentation, (2) the part of Simeon, (3) the part of Anna. Or again, in the Last Supper we have: (1) the eating of the Paschal Lamb, (2) the washing of the Disciples' feet, and (3) the institution of the Holy Eucharist. But sometimes the choice is not so obvious. For example, in the contemplation of the Cleansing of the Temple, our Lord's saying about the destruction of the temple of His own body is omitted. Many useful lessons indeed could be drawn from that saying, but St. Ignatius is more interested here in the lesson to be drawn from the distinction to which he so carefully draws attention between the " rich " money-lender and the " poor " sellers of pigeons.

Not only are mysteries abbreviated; the order is sometimes changed. Thus the " Glory to God in the highest " is given as the third point in the contemplation on the Nativity, while the shepherds make their first appearance in the next contemplation; in the Flight into Egypt, we are first told of the slaughter of the Innocents and then of the departure of the Holy Family. Other contemplations offer similar remarks.

It may be objected that all these points are not so important as to warrant any solid conclusions. There are, however, some rather striking inversions of order. The first is placing the contemplation on the Hidden Life before the Finding in the Temple. This certainly shows that the inversions are not always accidental. It is clear from the Introduction to the Consideration of Different States of Life that the reason for the inversion here is that we are first to contemplate Christ giving an example of the common life, and only afterwards to contemplate Him giving an example of a more perfect state of life. In the public life the order of some mysteries differs so noticeably from that of the Gospel, that it will be useful to set them side by side:

ORDER IN THE GOSPELS	ORDER IN THE *Exercises*
1. Conversion of Magdalene	2. Calming of the Tempest
2. Calming of the Tempest	5. Walking on the Sea
3. Mission of the Twelve	3. Mission of the Twelve
4. Feeding of the Five Thousand	1. Conversion of Magdalene
5. Walking on the Sea	4. Feeding of the Five Thousand
6. The Transfiguration	6. The Transfiguration

What is the reason of all these anomalies? Clearly all of them were not due to inadvertence on St. Ignatius' part, especially as he was always most prudent in what he said or wrote and treated Holy Scripture with the greatest reverence. To say that he could not possibly have made even a slight error would be going too far, and in fact there are scattered inaccuracies in the mysteries. E.g., after saying " I thirst," Jesus was given " gall and vinegar." One inversion of order, too, for which there does not appear to be any reason, may have been due to inadvertence. It occurs in the meditation for the tenth day when the preaching in the Temple (during Holy Week) is placed before the raising of Lazarus, especially as later these are given in the Gospel order. While in this single case it is possible that the order of events was changed inadvertently, there is no doubt at all that the change in the order of the mysteries of the Hidden Life and the Finding in the Temple was made deliberately. We must be on our guard against two dangers: (1) attributing all departures from the Gospel narrative as due to inadvertence, thereby doing St. Ignatius an injustice and failing to catch his meaning; and (2) suspecting some deep significance in every trifling discrepancy, thereby doing violence to the text and introducing our own ideas in place of those of St. Ignatius. In order to counter these dangers we shall not marshall our notes on the mysteries here but attach them to each of the mysteries as we come to them. The points which follow not only form a commentary on the text of St. Ignatius but also show how in our opinion it should be developed according to his mind. In particular, we have developed those points of the mysteries which are given only summarily in St. Ignatius' book. We have in fact endeavored to explain all the meditations and contemplations according to the mind of St. Ignatius, faithfully adhering to his text and carefully comparing his remarks made in different places.

A prudent man will hardly need be told that in order to give the exercises of St. Ignatius properly, it is necessary to keep closely to his thought even in minor details, not indeed by following slavishly the opinion set down in this book, but as the result of one's own research. Of course, the main principles of the exercises, which we have already explained, must be followed; otherwise the exercises will not be those of St. Ignatius. His book was given to his sons to be for them a living rule, not a dead one, to be adapted to the circumstances of time and place as well as to the talents of the retreat-master. In his own lifetime the Saint allowed his sons great liberty in giving the exercises. Does not Father Luis de la Palma, a notable interpreter of the exercises, follow up the punishment of the angels and of our own first parents with the punishment inflicted on men by the Flood? Nevertheless, it must be held as certain that one who proposes to give an Ignatian retreat must strive with all his might to understand thoroughly what Ignatius himself taught and said in his book, lest in seeking to adapt the form, he should change or even spoil the substance.

First Week

DURING the first week of an Ignatian retreat we must come to a realization of the purpose and scope of such a retreat. Consequently the meditations of the first week are centered about The Principle and Foundation, which, for practical purposes, Father Hummelauer has divided into three separate meditations, namely, the meditations on The Creation and End of Man, The Creation and End of the World, and Detachment. In addition to these meditations the first week also contains meditations on The Three Sins, My Personal Sins, The Vanity of Worldly Things, and Hell.

The Principle and Foundation

★

THIS IS not proposed by St. Ignatius in the form of a meditation; it is not divided into points, neither has it colloquies or preludes. It is preliminary to all these. The preparatory prayer flows from it; the necessity of prayer and of colloquy with God in prayer are its natural corollaries. It seems that this exercise is proposed by St. Ignatius as an earnest consideration to be made in God's presence.

The Foundation treats directly of man, not of God. It is taken for granted that God is the foundation of the

Foundation. Thus are assumed: (1) His existence; (2) His omnipotence; (3) His sovereignty, on which the world created by Him and man's free will wholly depend; (4) His wisdom, by which all His creatures are united in a single plan and purpose; (5) His goodness, which seeks not only service from His creatures but also the " salvation " of these servants; (6) His liberality, which provides men with so many means of serving Him and obtaining their salvation; (7) His unchangingness, which can be seen in the steadfastness of the order established by Him, allowing us to say absolutely " it follows that . . ."; (8) His perfection, majesty, and authority, which must be acknowledged respectively by praise, worship and service.

The Foundation is made up of two parts. The first states a fact and the second draws conclusions therefrom. The fact asserted is twofold: the creation of " man " and " the other things on the face of the earth." (Cf. Sec. 23) From this twofold fact follows first a rule, then a condition, drawn from the same fact and from the rule, but as applied to the fallen state of man.

In explaining the creation of man and other things two points are stressed, creation itself and its purpose. Since creation is the work of God alone, it can have only one purpose, a purpose rooted in the very nature of God, and His creature. It is not, however, the objective end of man (the glory of God) which is stressed, but the subjective end, and that both the immediate end to be attained in this life and the ultimate end to be attained in the life to come. The necessary connection of these two ends is implied in the phrase " therefore " (Sec. 23). In general the end of all creatures other than man is man; in particular it is " to help him in attaining the end for which he is created." (Sec. 23)

Why does St. Ignatius say that man is created " to praise, reverence, and serve God," rather than " to know, love and serve God "? The latter terms express man's duty to God in the manner of philosophy, going from cause to effect, since service follows from love, and love from knowledge. St. Ignatius has in mind the account of creation given in Holy Scripture, in which the duty of praise is stressed in the oft-repeated words, " and God saw that it was good," the duty of worship in the sanctification of the Sabbath, and the duty of obedient service in the command given Adam. Elsewhere Holy Scripture orders not so much the bare knowledge of God as that knowledge which breaks out in the praise of God. However, St. Ignatius, here as elsewhere, has adapted the inspired narrative to the matter in hand, in placing the creation of man before the creation of other things. The scriptural account places man last, but the main theme in the *Exercises* is man's obligations to God His Creator.

From man's end follows the rule of human action: " Hence, man is to . . . ." To correspond fully with what has gone before the rule should run: " Man must pursue the service of God and his own salvation with his whole soul and all his strength, using creatures only in so far as they help him . . . ." In fact, St. Ignatius omits the first part. Practically speaking, the service of God consists in the right use of creatures, just as the love of God consists in keeping His Commandments. Moreover " use " implies choice, and choice denotes man's free will. We must use the things of this world only so far " as they help " us to reach God. (Sec. 23) The fact that the exercises are primarily directed to helping us choose our state of life is shown by the words: " Our one desire and choice should be what is more conducive to the end for which we are created." (Sec. 23) Thus, in the Foundation is laid the basis for the entire exercises.

The Foundation also emphasizes the need for detachment as a disposition of the soul if we are to follow the rule of life. We are obliged to " make ourselves indifferent to all created things, . . . health . . . riches . . . honor." (Sec. 23) Detachment is limited in the sense that we can exercise our free choice only as " far as we . . . are not under any prohibition." (Sec. 23) To the question " What is detachment? " we answer: Knowledge of our end necessitates a twofold disposition in the will: to pursue our end, God, for His own sake; and to choose means for the sake of that end. The end must be sought with all our heart and strength; the means with a moderation imposed by the rule of the end. In the moderation of our use of means consists the essential feature of detachment. Detachment is temperance in regard to food and drink, chastity in regard to sex, humility in regard to self-esteem, spiritual poverty in the use of things, modesty in outward behavior. All difficulty of spiritual life lies here; once we have made detachment our own nothing can keep us from serving and loving God. Practically, not theoretically, this is the climax of the Foundation.

In St. Ignatius' mind detachment must be linked to the desire to serve God. Detachment moderates all our desires for created things, but by what standard does it moderate them if not by the desire to serve God? It follows that those who wholly desire to serve God in all things and are completely detached will always desire in their hearts and will always effectively choose those things which will better lead them to God.

Since we have divided The Principle and Foundation into three separate meditations, we suggest the following preludes:

First Prelude. See Paradise, planted with fair trees, and among them the tree of life, a type of eternal life, and the tree of knowledge of good and evil, also known as the tree of the divine command.

Second Prelude. Ask for knowledge of the duty to serve God and for grace to serve Him perfectly in all things.

CHAPTER I

The Creation and End of Man

★

Man is created to praise, reverence, and serve God our Lord, and by this means to save his soul. (Sec. 23)

FIRST POINT: The Creation of Man

I. *Man was created* by God, who alone can create.

1. *Who* was created?

Man, that is to say, the first man Adam, as to both the body and the soul; for God formed his body of the slime of the earth, and breathed into his face the breath of life. (Gen. 2:7) And God built the rib which He took from Adam into a woman (Gen. 2:22), and to her too He gave a spiritual, immortal soul.

Man, i.e., all human beings whose bodies are derived, by generation and birth, from our First Parents, whose souls are created directly by God.

Man, i.e., I, too, am a creature of God.

2. *To what extent* was man created?

The whole of man: all the faculties of his soul, all the properties and parts of his body; not only the acts of those faculties and parts but also every potentiality both natural and supernatural, so that whatever can be developed from them, whatever can come to them from elsewhere, must necessarily be also created.

The whole of man in duration, that is to say, as long as man exists: for the first creation is continued uninterruptedly by divine conservation and providence.

Consider here what in you is God's, and what yours. God made you a *man*, and He continually exerted Himself by His helps to perfect human nature in you; He made you a *Christian*, and endeavored continually, by so many gifts, to increase grace in you; He bestowed on you so many *particular benefits*, and continually invites you to make progress.

With these gifts of God you have partly been co-operating faithfully, and you have partly, *by sins*, delayed those gifts or made them void: so that whatever good there is in you is chiefly God's, and whatever evil is wholly yours.

3. Make *interior acts* of adoration and humiliation, of thanksgiving for benefits received, and of trust for benefits yet to be received.

II. Man was created *for some end*.

1. God in creation, conservation and providence must, of course, have had, and must still have, *some* end in view, for to act without any purpose is unreasonable.

2. This end must be *in harmony* with my nature and all my faculties, and so must be attainable through the exercise of my free will, since it is the part of wisdom to adapt the means to the end.

3. It is of the greatest importance for me to *know* this end in order that I may henceforth freely co-operate with it.

This truth is the *most worthy* of all to *be known*: for what is of more consequence than to know the end for which I was created?—This knowledge is *most useful*: for what will it profit to know everything else if I do not know this one thing?—It is *most necessary*: for this end is my own, that of my whole self, mine exclusively; if I neglect this, I am *useless*.

4. Make *interior acts* of eager desire to understand this end, of generous offering to co-operate with it faithfully.

SECOND POINT: The Proximate or Immediate End of Man

I. *The case of Adam.*

A thing's purpose is known from its nature, since the one must correspond to the other. To both nature and end are adapted the faculties which the Creator has given to nature for attaining its end. Accordingly the end is known from these faculties as well as from the very nature.

1. Now Adam was by nature endowed with intellect and free will. So gifted, he was able to reach out, beyond all created things, to God, and to seek God; it was therefore Adam's end to embrace God with his whole intellect and will.

In particular Adam perceived God's existence from the existence of creatures, God's wisdom from their nature, God's omnipotence from their power, God's loveliness from their beauty, God's providence from their activity; and by all this Adam was moved to proclaim the *praises* of God.

Adam also acknowledged the perfection of God by comparison, in so far as it surpasses every perfection of man, and every perfection of things visible or invisible, of things actually existing or merely possible. God's perfection is absolutely *infinite* or of supreme majesty, claiming for itself the greatest *reverence* to be shown with the body as well as with the soul.

Adam also acknowledged the essential *unity* and *simplicity* of the same perfection, and consequently its *divinity* and authority over himself, with a claim to his *service,* both internal and external.

Scripture states this end explicitly: Adam, placed in paradise, where all things were "very good," was moved to *praise* the divine goodness; by the prescribed rest on the seventh day he was led to *reverence* and worship; by the commandment which he received he was taught to *serve* God.

2. Adam was, by nature, created *to the image of God;* therefore his end was to express the image of God's life in his own life by the use of all his faculties.

What life, then, are the three Persons of the Blessed Trinity living? Their intellect is ever replete with the fulness of divine knowledge, and the mutual praise that flows from it: Adam was to imitate them by endeavoring to understand ever more deeply God and things divine, and to *praise* them more profusely.

The mind of the divine Persons is ever animated with infinite mutual reverence, not such as is shown to a superior by an inferior, but such as is shown among equals of surpassing dignity: Adam was to vie with them in this, by *doing reverence* to God through interior and exterior worship, such as the creature is bound to offer to the Creator.

The will of the divine Persons ever agrees in perfect harmony, nay, by very identity of nature; for the will of the three Persons is physically one and the same: Adam was to imitate this by conforming and subjecting his will as much as possible to the divine will in *serving* God. By doing these things Adam was to lead a perfect life, to imitate the divine life, as much as lies in the power of a creature.

II. *My own case.*

1. I have received the same nature as Adam, and have the same end as he.

Therefore I will *praise* God by acknowledging His perfections, by accepting the dispositions of His providence, and by offering prayers.—I will *do reverence* to God by performing the worship instituted by Him.—I will *serve* God by doing His holy will. I will do so, *whatever be the manner* by which God's will is made known to me, whether by the voice of conscience which even pagans hear (Rom. 2:14), or by the word of God in both the Testaments, and above all by the mouth of His Son (Hebr. 1:1), or by the voice of the Church to whom Christ has delegated His authority (Luke 10:16).

I will serve God equally *as to each and every commandment,* since each and every one is based on the same divine authority: "whoever keeps the whole law, but offends in one point, has become guilty in all." (James 2:10)

2. Consider the conditions of the end of God's service.

It is *most necessary* in its obligation, since it is founded on the very nature of the creature; therefore it is immutable, indispensable, universal, supreme, and exclusive: everything in man must at all times be subordinated to it. Whatever is done according to the standard of this end is useful, wise, right and fair; whatever is done in opposition to it is vain and useless, nay, it is ruinous, foolish, evil and unbecoming.

The end of God's service is also *most noble* as regards its excellency; nothing higher can be imagined for creatures; man has it in common with the angels, with the Blessed Virgin who was the "handmaid of the Lord," with Christ, whom the prophet called "the servant" of God. (Is. 42:1)

Ponder what a sacred thing it is *to be under an obligation*: The order of the world requires that every one fulfils his own duties. What do you think of one who is faithless? of a husband, a soldier, a servant who deliberately neglects really serious duties? What do you think of him who rejects the most serious of all obligations, and in effect says to his Creator: "I will not serve"?

3. Make *interior acts* of acknowledgment of God's supreme lordship, of offering and of desiring faithfully and perfectly to co-operate with so excellent an end.

THIRD POINT: The Last End of Man

I. *Man has a more remote end.*

1. *Nature* bears witness that a *reward* is due to every service, and a *punishment* to the neglect of service.—God has engraved

it deep in our mind that, in serving God, we are at the same time taking the best care of ourselves. We are, then, drawn to the service of God not only because it is an obligation to do one's duty, but also because it is for one's own good.

2. *Revelation* confirms the same truth.—The reward held out to Adam for fulfilling his duty was life; the punishment for neglecting his duty was death: both dependent on the fruit of the tree. This life in Paradise was not meant to be the whole reward, nor was that death the whole punishment; another life was in store for Adam, and consequently also an end or aim in the other life. According to Scripture these two lives stand in the relation of way and goal, journey and destination, labor and rest, work and pay, seed and plant, sowing and harvest.

3. The reward for the service is absolutely *certain*, since it rests on God's omnipotence, liberality and fidelity.

II. *This more remote end of man consists in the salvation of his soul.*

1. Ponder the excellence of this end *from without*:

The question is about the *soul*, the most noble part of our being by reason of its nature, its faculties, its derivation: far more noble than the material, corruptible body; far more noble and precious than any possession of mine, which is added to self and derives its value from the advantage it procures for myself. Listen to Christ, who warns you: "What does it profit a man, if he gain the whole world, but suffer the loss of his own soul?" (Matt. 16:26) As much as to say: it does not profit him anything at all. Ponder how much God and Christ have done for the salvation of that soul, how persistently they exhort you to secure its safety.

2. Ponder the excellence of this end *from within*:

Negatively it means freedom from all evil, for all time, with the exclusion of any interruption, fear or danger.

Positively it means a good that is eternal, ineffable, and divine.

a. Eternal: for it means the good of the next life, and that life is eternal.

b. Ineffable: St. Paul says of this good, " Eye has not seen nor ear heard, nor has it entered into the heart of man, what things God has prepared for those who love him." (1 Cor. 2:9) And St. John: "Beloved, now we are the children of God, and it has not yet appeared what we shall be. We know that, when he appears, we shall be like to him, for we shall see him just as he is." (1 John 3:2) The Apostles, therefore, confess that colors cannot paint, nor sounds express, nor the mind comprehend how excellent that good is. Scripture faintly illustrates the matter with comparisons borrowed from everything that is desirable, in order to suggest that the salvation of the soul not only includes, but exceeds, the excellence of all things desirable: it is light or rest eternal, glory, the kingdom, the wedding-feast, the banquet, etc.

c. Divine: The more remote end is divine because it consists in the eternal enjoyment of God; heaven will be our abode, and we enter it, not as strangers, but as sons; we shall rest in the arms of our Father, and there will be unceasing praise, filial reverence, and the delightful union of the will.

d. This good is the soul's unique happiness, since it alone is eternal and suited to the nature of an immortal soul; it is all-sufficient, because it alone satisfies the spiritual and supernatural longing of the soul; it is therefore necessary, and it must be obtained at any cost, however great.

3. Measure the excellence of this end by a comparison:

Survey the world and consider how strong is the motive of *reward or gain* everywhere and at all times. Yet all these earthly gains are insecure; they last but a short time, and they are nothing in comparison with heaven. How foolish is he who does not strive earnestly and constantly to obtain the eternal reward!

III. *The condition for salvation is the service of God.*

1. By praising God, doing reverence to Him, and serving Him, by doing nothing but this, which in comparison to other things is so simple and easy, by doing this constantly during the whole of this short life, I shall save my most precious soul, I shall be able to enjoy such surpassing and enduring happiness.

2. *By not doing this*, whatever else I am doing will profit me nothing; by setting this aside, even once only in a grievous matter—from fickleness, sloth, passion—I shall perhaps suffer the loss of my most precious soul, and exclude it forever from so great a happiness.

The *loss of the soul* means the privation of the highest good. This good alone answers the need of nature elevated by grace, it produces in the soul an insatiable desire or craving. Since there was first offered the possibility of fulfilling this desire, and that with relative ease, its loss produces a proportionate *sadness*; and since it was lost through one's own fault, there arises a proportionate *remorse*. Moreover, since every possibility of recovering that highest good or of receiving some substitute for it is altogether excluded, this causes absolute *despair*. This *pain of loss* is joined to a proportionate *pain of sense*: both of these pains are eternal, immutable, and do not admit of any relief.

3. *I will, therefore, do these things*, (*viz.* praise, reverence, and serve God, and thus save my soul).

Compare the labor this involves with the gain to be secured thereby. St. Paul writes: "For our present light affliction, which is for the moment, prepares for us an eternal weight of glory that is beyond all measure." (2 Cor. 4:17)—And again to the Romans: "For I reckon that the sufferings of the present time are not worthy to be compared with the glory to come that will be revealed in us." (Rom. 8:18)—Or, as St. Luke puts it: "Good measure, pressed down, shaken together, running over, shall they pour into your lap." (Luke 6:38)

CHAPTER II

The Creation
and End of the World

★

The other things on the face of the earth are created for man to help him in attaining the end for which he is created. (Sec. 23)

FIRST POINT: The Creation of the World

I. *The fact of creation.*

1. *"The other things on the face of the earth"* is a Biblical expression designating all the other material creatures as distinguished from man.

2. Heaven and earth, the firmament and the stars, plants and animals, other human beings *have been created* by God. He not only first created them, but He also preserves them continually in existence, and He operates directly in all their activities. God gave to all things their being; He also put into them the *laws* of their activity, and, in the case of living beings, the *power to increase and multiply.* Accordingly God's *providence* is continually ruling everything, not only each creature separately but also all their combinations, relations, and effects.—In particular, there come under God's providence the things which influence "our health or sickness," such as the weather, the distribution of "riches or poverty," the prosperity or adversity of a man in his dealings with his fellow-men, and "the honor or ignominy" that result therefrom, and, lastly, "a long life or a short life."

II. *God creates with a purpose.*

1. God has certainly *some* purpose in view, when He creates, preserves, and governs all things in the world; for it would be unreasonable to act without an end in view.

2. I must, by all means, know this purpose or end of God.

Next to the end of man, the end of creatures is *most worthy of being known:* first, in itself, seeing that the question is about the world of such vast extent, so great variety, and so skillfully constructed; secondly, owing to its bearing on the duty to praise God, a duty which man will fulfil far more perfectly, when he understands the aim and end of the world.

Moreover, this knowledge is *most necessary,* since man is all the time surrounded by "these other things," and involved in them; were he not to know their end, he would be in constant danger of making a wrong use of things, and of violating the right of the Creator over them: as a consequence man would stain his conscience with manifold guilt.

3. Make *interior acts* of eager desire to know the purpose of the world, and of generous offering to keep the same in view in everything.

SECOND POINT: The End or Purpose of the World

I. *All other things are created for man's sake.*

1. Though not made exclusively for man, the outer world is certainly in a true sense made for him: it is man's dwelling-place; in it he finds matter to supply the needs of his body, food and clothing, work and recreation, and practice for virtue; connected with this are health or sickness, a long life or a short life, consolation or desolation.

2. Of course all things were not created immediately for every individual, but according to God's providence and man's activity there is available for every one a definite supply of things: if

these are plentiful, there is *wealth*, if scanty, *poverty*; with wealth come, as a rule, *honors*, with poverty comes *ignominy*, and this implies harder work and fewer amusements.

3. Make *interior acts* of admiration at God's great wealth and liberality, of gratitude, and of shame.

II. . . . *to help him in attaining the end for which he is created.*

1. Consider that God could not give creatures to man for any other use: for then they would be *useless* for man, not helping him to his only end; nay, they would be *harmful*, withdrawing man's mind from this only end of his. On the other hand, as means to that end, creatures are *useful, precious,* and, in a sense, *sacred*, since they are destined to be the instruments of God's praise, reverence and service; they are like *rungs of a ladder* leading man from earth to heaven, provided he uses them in the right manner; but by a wrong use of them one would be led down to hell.

2. Consider *how* creatures help man in fulfilling his threefold duty: of *praising* God, whose existence, power and other perfections are manifested both by prosperity and adversity; of *doing reverence* to God, when they are used directly in divine worship; of *serving* God, by use, or abstention, or endurance of things and happenings. Accordingly creatures also help in obtaining the last end, *viz.*, in securing the *reward* of happiness, in avoiding the *punishment* of damnation and *saving one's soul.*

3. Consider that creatures are not gifts that man may use arbitrarily or for fun; no, they are *a trust*, which must be administered according to the master's mind, in a certain manner, and for a certain purpose: they carry with them a true *obligation.* The keeping of this obligation produces *merit*, and gives a right to a *reward;* its neglect brings *guilt,* and involves liability

to *punishment*. God, as a most wise Master, observes carefully what His servant is doing. He knows the deeds of all. At the time fixed by Himself He will *demand an account* of these deeds. He will then pass *judgment,* and either give a *reward* or inflict *punishment.*

4. Consider lastly what is man's true condition here on earth! *God* is always the *Master,* both of man and of things, by an inalienable right. *Creatures* are always a *means* for man, never an end; this is founded on the same necessity of nature as that by which man is destined for God's service. *Man* remains always God's *servant;* he must use creatures not as a master, but as a servant.

CHAPTER III

Detachment

★

Hence, man is to make use of them [creatures] *in as far as they help him in the attainment of his end, and he must rid himself of them in as far as they prove a hindrance to him.*

Therefore, we must make ourselves indifferent to all created things, as far as we are allowed free choice and are not under any prohibition. Consequently, as far as we are concerned, we should not prefer health to sickness, riches to poverty, honor to dishonor, a long life to a short life. The same holds for all other things.

Our one desire and choice should be what is more conducive to the end for which we are created. (Sec. 23)

First Point: We Must Be Detached.

I. *The nature of detachment.*

1. *It follows* that man's whole life must be ruled by a twofold tendency or inclination of the will: the one towards the *end*, which is the love of God, whether interested or disinterested love; there is no limit to this love, but it must be "with the whole heart, the whole soul, and with all our strength." The other tendency is towards the *means;* these are not sought for their own sake, nor with the whole heart, but with a view to the end, according to the laws and limits required by the end.

This second inclination is made up of two elements: a positive one, by which the means are sought as means, and it is one and the same virtue that seeks both end and means. The other element is a negative one; by it the means are not sought except in so far as they are means, and this constitutes the habit of detachment or self-control.

2. The first tendency implied by detachment, and completed by it, is none other than the *love* expressed in the first and greatest commandment: "Thou shalt love the Lord thy God with thy whole heart, and with thy whole soul, and with thy whole mind." (Matt. 22:37) Here the word love means not only the sentiment of love, but the worship of God in general, and every kind of service to God. The *law* of this love is rooted in the very fact of *creation*.

Now this law is *universal*: God is to be loved in all things, at all times, and with all our strength. It is the *highest* law, because God must be loved above all things, and all else must be loved only in so far as it helps to love God. It is the *rule* of all other laws: these are such only in so far as they conform to this law. Accordingly, "the law of sin" mentioned by St. Paul (Rom. 7:23) is no law, but a rebellion against this law.

3. Detachment, then, means that the will has no inclination towards any creature, and no aversion from any creature as such. Yet this detachment is far removed from an apathy which would seek nothing, and not care for anything. In fact, it has definite limits; it is regulated by the desire of the end and the means: "as far as we are allowed free choice and are not under any prohibition."

4. Detachment, therefore, does not exclude a partiality, however eager, for the objects prescribed by God, nor an aversion, however intense, from objects forbidden by God. Rather, since this detachment follows from the teaching about man's end or aim, we cannot think of it but as joined to entire devotion concerning the divine service. Thus the two aspects taken together mean not a state of inertia, but the perfect freedom of a mind not entangled in any lower inclination, and the undivided energy of a will embracing God, and all other things in God.

II. *The extent of detachment.*

1. *It follows that* this detachment must extend to all created things. In particular it must extend to *external goods:* riches and poverty, honor and ignominy, company and loneliness, pleasant or unpleasant character of companions, etc. It extends to the *goods of the body:* a long or a short life, strength or weakness, beauty or ugliness, health or sickness, etc. It extends to *natural goods of the soul:* talent, knowledge, character. It extends to *spiritual goods:* consolation or desolation, temptations, prayer, penance, etc.

2. *It follows that* detachment must extend to each and every degree of the things already mentioned and to their circumstances, so that each and every thing be sought or rejected *as much as* it helps or hinders our pursuit of the end; also as long as it does so, etc.

3. Consider that such a disposition is quite *as necessary as* the end of man itself. It is *wise:* without it our actions would be tainted with foolishness; it is *worthy* of man: without it human dignity would be lowered; it is *useful* and produces ample reward; it makes man happy and holy.

III. *The practice of detachment.*

I must make an earnest *resolution* to act always with a view to my end by observing all the commandments. I must *ask for grace,* without which I cannot carry out this resolution. I must *exact an account* of myself, how I have kept this resolution, like a servant who gives an account of his stewardship. And I must do all these things, not once or twice, but steadily and at fixed times. I will do this by means of the *General Examination of Conscience.*

SECOND POINT: We Are Not Detached.

I. In a perfect state detachment would be joined with a complete subjection of the sensual nature to the will; nevertheless detachment resides *in the will,* and there may be true detachment even along with a certain repugnance in the lower part of nature. As a matter of fact common experience shows that all of us are pitifully lacking in detachment, both in the lower nature and in the will. "For the imagination and thought of man's heart are prone to evil from his youth." (Gen. 8:21) The chief reason of this is a human nature corrupted by Adam's fall.

II. In particular every one has some *predominant disorderly inclination*; this is the root of every disorder in his life; it can be traced in all kinds of sin, and it comes to this, when all is said, that a person is not detached as regards certain creatures.

THIRD POINT: We Must Make Ourselves Detached.

I. *It is necessary.* We must be detached. Since we are not now detached, our one desire must be to make ourselves detached!

1. *The objections of fallen nature against detachment.* To make ourselves detached means the rooting out of likes and dislikes which have possessed our very hearts. Imagine a plant that has spread its roots in all directions in the ground; imagine how unpleasant it is to uproot such a plant by digging up the ground! Now reflect that your disorderly affections are such plants, and that the ground in which they have spread their roots is your own living and feeling heart. To make ourselves detached means a constant fight against an ever watchful enemy, namely, our own disorderly nature; therefore we ourselves must feel the

wounds we inflict on the enemy; it means an internal fight, and therefore one that is removed from the sight and praise of men.

2. *Arguments of reason supported by grace in favor of detachment:*

We must make ourselves detached, because we shall never become so, if we do not will it ourselves. If we are not detached, we shall not keep the rule of the end; if we do not keep this rule, we shall make a wrong use of creatures and shall be worthless servants and shall not be saved.

It is necessary; therefore it is possible, for God gives His grace to men of good will.

It is necessary; therefore if we neglect this we shall not be able to find true peace either in this life, or in the life to come.

II. *Then let it be done!* Let it be done without delay: with every delay the evil inclinations become stronger. Let it be done perseveringly: it is not the task of a single day to uproot them. Let it be done thoroughly: it is no use resisting one inclination, if you foolishly cherish another one. Let it be done systematically, by means of the Particular Examination of Conscience.

CHAPTER IV

The Three Sins

★

THE WHOLE purpose of this meditation is to arouse in the exercitant " shame and confusion . . . . because of the many grievous sins that I have committed." (Sec. 48) The reason for being ashamed is the foulness and malice of sin. Its foulness can be justly measured by the fearful punishment which is its due. We can either consider this punishment in itself or gauge it by conjecture and comparison from the punishments inflicted on others. St. Ignatius follows this latter twofold way in proposing points for the meditation, and reserves the former, and by far the more efficacious, consideration for the concluding colloquy.

Thus, he first sets before us the sin and punishment of the angels, and then invites us to consider what punishment must be due to our sins, and consequently how great must be their foulness. This is indeed a convincing argument. Nevertheless, it might be objected that a sin of angels is not a human sin and that it involves a special degree of malice on account of the greater perfection of the angelic nature, which is not found in human sin. St. Ignatius, however, forestalls this objection by setting before us the sin of our First Parents. Yet again it might be objected that this sin was committed by Adam and Eve while they were in the state of original justice, which was also far superior to our own condition. So St. Ignatius also sets before us the punishment inflicted on sins committed

by men in exactly the same state of fallen nature as ourselves. These sins are very like those which we commit,
and indeed are more or less the same, but they are not precisely our own personal sins. Hence finally, as the climax
of his argument, St. Ignatius brings us face to face in the
colloquy with the punishment which our own personal
sins did in fact bring upon the Son of God. What better
way could be found of making us realize profoundly the
foulness of our sins and be overwhelmed with " shame and
confusion "?

This argument, so forceful in itself, is still further
strengthened by the twofold consideration of " how many
have been lost on account of a single mortal sin " (Sec.
48) and how " countless others . . . have been lost for
fewer sins than I have committed." (Sec. 52) The first
occurs in the second prelude: " because I see how many
have been lost on account of a single mortal sin, and how
many times I have deserved eternal damnation, because of
the many grievous sins that I have committed." (Sec. 48)
The emphasis here is on the severity of the law, which admits of no exception, and is not moved to indulgence by
the great number of the guilty. The other consideration
occurs in the third point: " countless others . . . have
been lost for fewer sins than I have committed." (Sec. 52)
This argument is far weaker in that it deals with those
who were damned for more sins than one, but it is also
stronger in that these are " countless " and that all their
sins were fewer than mine.

These same considerations also occur in the course of
the points. St. Ignatius does not indeed expressly state that
the number of the fallen angels was immense, as we know

from Scripture that it was, but that this was in his mind is clearly shown by the words of the second prelude quoted above and by the second point of the first part of the meditation on the Two Standards. Among the evil consequences of the sin of our First Parents, the last mentioned is " that . . . so many [were] lost in hell." (Sec. 51) Then in the third point we are asked to consider the sin, not of any particular individual, but of any one out of all those have gone to hell for a single mortal sin. It is not indeed stated that the number of these is great, because that is not known, but it is immediately added that " countless others . . . have been lost for fewer sins than I have committed." (Sec. 52)

That the number of their sins was comparatively small is affirmed of the angels: " When I compare the one sin of the angels with the many sins I have committed, I will consider that they went to hell for one sin, and the number of times I have deserved to be condemned forever because of my numerous sins." (Sec. 50) The same is said of our First Parents: " By their sin they lost original justice, and for the rest of their lives, lived without it in many labors and great penance." (Sec. 51) Again, in the case of the one condemned to hell for but one mortal sin: " who went to hell because of one mortal sin." (Sec. 51) Finally we are told of those " countless others who have been lost for fewer sins than I have committed." (Sec. 52) This last aptly leads the argument from those who were cast into hell for a single sin to the many sins of mine, atoned for by the wounds of Jesus Christ.

St. Ignatius calls the present exercise a meditation " *employing the three powers of the soul*." (Sec. 45) He explains the meaning of this phrase in the course of the meditation. The first point "will consist in using the memory to recall the first sin, which was that of the angels, and then in applying the understanding by reasoning upon this sin, then the will by seeking to remember and understand all to be the more filled with shame and confusion when I compare the one sin of the angels with the many sins I have committed." (Sec. 50) The second and third points of the exercise illustrate the matter further.

Now, since these three powers are to be used in all the exercises, the question arises why this exercise in particular is called a meditation "employing the three powers"? Is the reason only because the application of the three powers is explained here? Or is there a further reason, namely, that each of the points falls naturally into three parts, in the first of which the use of the memory predominates, in the second that of the understanding, and in the third that of the will? This is actually the case.

The application of the memory is given in greater detail in the first two points: "I said we should apply the memory . . ." In the first point three things are separately mentioned for recollection: (1) the condition of the angels before their fall, (2) the fall itself which consisted in a proud use of God-given liberty, and (3) the punishment of the fall. Three facts are likewise mentioned in the second point: (1) the original state of our First Parents, (2) their fall, due to disobedience, and (3) the punishment given them and their children. (Cf. Sec. 51) The work of the understanding is described as "reasoning" upon the matter brought to mind by the memory. The aspect to which this mental effort should be directed primarily is clearly explained in the third point: " Use the understanding in considering that because of sin, and of acting against the Infinite Goodness, one is justly condemned forever." (Sec. 52) In this exercise, then, we must especially ponder on the justice of the punishment given us by God. Finally the work of the will is explained in the first point: " the will by seeking to remember and understand all to be more filled with shame and confusion when I compare the one sin of the angels with the many sins I have committed." (Sec. 50) Thus, the sense of shame is aroused not only by the punishment of the angels, nor only by a consideration of the justice of that punishment, but by a comparison between my own guilt and the punishment proportionate to it with the guilt and punishment of the angels. From what has been said, it will now be sufficiently clear how each point of this meditation falls naturally into three parts, in the first of which the work of the memory predominates, in the second that of the understanding, and in the third that of the will.

Indeed, traces of a similar arrangement may be observed even in the colloquy, the order only being somewhat different. In the first place, we are told to consider the state of Christ before His Incarnation (" though He is the Creator " [Sec. 53]), then His state on the cross, or rather from the Incarnation to the cross (" He has stooped to become man, etc."), and lastly the reason the change of state, namely, " for our sins." This part of the colloquy corresponds to the work of the memory described in the points. While recalling these things we should at the same time note the justice of the divine condemnation passed on

Christ, and consequently we should be overwhelmed with the shame that was asked for as the special fruit of the meditation in the second prelude. This sentiment will be further increased by asking ourselves, " What have I done for Christ? " hitherto, " What am I doing for Christ? " now, and " What ought I to do for Christ? " in the future, and so the mind is led gently to form an efficacious purpose of amendment.

A. The Sin of the Angels

The first meditation *will consist in using the memory to recall the first sin, which was that of the angels, and then in applying the understanding by reasoning upon this sin, then the will by seeking to remember and understand all to be more filled with shame and confusion when I compare the one sin of the angels with the many sins I have committed. I will consider that they went to hell for one sin, and the number of times I have deserved to be condemned forever because of my numerous sins.* (Sec. 50)

First Point: The Fact of the Sin of the Angels

I. *The condition of the angels before their sin.*

Consider *God*, the Creator and Lord of the angels, the Supreme and Eternal King, seated on the throne of His Majesty in heaven, as it were in a spiritual Paradise leading to the palace of eternal glory: all the *angels* stand before His throne.

1. View their *number*: they are countless.

2. View their *condition*:

(a) By *nature* they are pure spirits, and therefore they are immortal, independent of matter for existence, movement, knowledge and desire; they are far superior to the wisest of men in their natural knowledge, which is most lofty, comprehensive, penetrating and lasting; they excel also in power of will, which is proportioned to the nobility of their knowledge; they are endowed with strength that altogether surpasses the material order.

(b) By *grace:* from the very first the angels were clothed with sanctifying grace and made children of God; they were enriched with infused knowledge; they were adorned with infused virtues, the chief of which is charity.

3. Lastly, consider their *destiny:* " to pay reverence and obedience to their Creator and Lord."

Consider how they *praise* God unceasingly, singing: Holy, Holy, Holy!; how they *do reverence* to God, falling down in adoration before His throne; how they *serve* God, being ministering spirits, ever ready for any kind of service.

Consider how this purpose of the angels is necessary, since it follows from their nature as creatures; how noble, both as to its object, God, and as to the manner of obtaining this object, *viz.*, the supernatural state to which the angels were freely elevated; how fruitful this end is for giving honor to the supremely good God, their Creator and Lord, for securing peace that overflows into the angelic mind, for acquiring merit that is completed in glory, when their time of probation is over.

II. *The sin of the angels.*

1. Consider that all these angels had to pay homage of some kind to God. Very many angels, including St. Michael and St. Gabriel, gladly paid this homage to God: " Thee alone will I serve." And God, in return, showered on them His peace: " Peace be with you! " As a result, abundant peace filled their hearts. The Holy Spirit dwelt in them, uniting them to God and to each other, consecrating the very place so that it became the heavenly *Jerusalem*, the City of Peace.

2. But lo! Lucifer, when called upon, refused to do homage and cried out: " I will not serve." He is already lifting his foot to climb the steps of the throne, and to take his seat near the Most High. (Cf. Is. 14:13) Very many other angels join the rebellious leader, filling heaven with confusion and din, making it a *Babylon*, the City of Confusion.

Reflect on the *wickedness* of that declaration " I will not serve." It comes from a creature destined for the service of God, from a mind so much enlightened both by nature and by grace, from a mouth consecrated to the praise of God; it is uttered in the midst of the assembly of the holy angels, and in the very presence of the All-Holy Divinity, like filthy spittle or a pestilential breath.

III. *The punishment of the sin of the angels.*

1. They were changed from grace to malice.

Their love of God is immediately changed into implacable hatred; the rebels are stripped of sanctifying grace and deprived of actual grace; obduracy takes the place of charity, darkness of mind that of wisdom; and from this follows perversion in the pursuit of the end, and cunning in the choice of means; their exalted position turns into degradation and foulness; on their foreheads appears the seal of divine reprobation.

2. They were cast down from heaven to hell.

From the throne rings out a voice: " Depart from me, ye cursed! " Immediately the rebellious angels are thrust back from the throne of the Divinity by the invisible power of God; heaven is rent under their feet, and before their gaze yawns the abyss of hell, now opened for the first time.

Contemplate the *distance* of hell from heaven: the one is called simply height, the other simply depth, "Who hath measured the height of heaven, and the breadth of the earth, and the depth of the abyss? " (Eccl. 1:2) Contemplate the *difference* between hell and heaven: the one is a palace, the other a prison; the one is a spiritual paradise, the other a place of torment; the one is a home, the abode of glory and blissful light, the other a place of exile, of shame and tormenting fire; they are Jerusalem and Babylon.

Reflect that there is one thing common to both heaven and hell, *viz.*, their *eternity* and *immutability*.

Contemplate finally how by the power of God and the help of the faithful angels the wicked spirits were instantly cast headlong from heaven into hell, uttering groans of despair; as the abyss closed its mouth upon them, the victorious angels sang a canticle of triumph before the throne of God.

SECOND POINT: The Punishment of the Angels Is Examined More Closely.

I. *Consider that all this concerns—*

1. *Angels,* who were the first and most perfect creation of the infinitely loving God; the very perfection bestowed on them by God became the occasion of their pride and ruin. This was their first and only sin; one of them was the ringleader of the rebellion; the rest were only followers; so great was their number!

2. The punishment was inflicted by *God* who is infinitely *just:* He is not carried away by anger, nor does He punish beyond desert; by God who is infinitely *merciful:* He always punishes less than is due; His mercy always prompts Him to grant the guilty time for repentance, and to offer the grace of reconciliation; in the very instant and act of punishing them He was by no means unmindful of His mercy.

3. *For a single mortal sin:* The rebellion of the angels was a sin, for it was a free refusal of the reverence and obedience due to God. It was a mortal sin from its object, from its full deliberation, and from the rejection of so many graces freely offered. It was their first and only mortal sin.

4. Reflect that all this was done *instantly,* and *irrevocably!*

II. *Consider the justice of this condemnation.*

It comes from the just mouth of God; the hand of God justly wipes out from the Book of Life the names of the rebellious angels and confirms the decree of damnation with the ever ineffaceable seal of the Blessed Trinity. The faithful angels approve of that sentence; and the devils, in the very depth of hell, acknowledge its justice: " Thou art just, O Lord: and Thy judgment is right." (Ps. 118:137) All angels and men, the elect as well as the damned, will likewise acknowledge that verdict on the day of the Last Judgment, and throughout the whole of Eternity.

This judgment is just because mortal sin is a rebellion against the Sovereign Majesty, a turning away from the infinite Goodness, a challenge to the absolute Holiness; and therefore it is justly punished with eternal exile, eternal reprobation, and eternal curse.

THIRD POINT: A Practical Application

I. This exceeding great punishment of the rebellious angels yet falls short of the malice and deformity of even a single mortal sin, nay, even a *single mortal sin of mine.*

As often as I deliberately transgressed one of the Commandments of God, I said in effect: " I will not serve." The matter of my offense was different from the sin of the angels, but the formal aspect of rebellion was the same. I become guilty of an offence, the abomination of which in the eyes of God and of the saints is so great that nothing but the punishment of hell is sufficient for it. If God had deprived me of life, when I was committing sin, I should have fallen under the sentence of eternal damnation, heaven and earth proclaiming: " Thou art just, O Lord."

II. What punishment is then in store for *so many* mortal sins of mine, seeing their number, and the special malice of repeating a sin, especially after obtaining again and again pardon of my sins? How great is consequently the filth of my soul, defiled with those sins! God and the angels loathe it; the very devils, if one may say so, consider it unworthy of their company!

III. What if my sin or many sins *have been forgiven* already? The remission of sin is the effect of God's free mercy; the fact of having committed sin remains: it is, and ever will be, my own responsibility, though the guilt has been pardoned.

IV. What if, with the help of God's grace, I have *never committed* a mortal sin? Have I not, perhaps for some length of time, neglected prayer, which is so necessary to overcome temptations? Have I not let myself go rather freely into some kind of venial sin? By doing so I exposed myself to evident danger of mortal sin: it was due to the mercy of the Lord, and not to any merit of mine, that I did not fall into the depths to which the corruption of human nature must necessarily have dragged me. I have, then, ample reason for shame.

V. What is my position as to *keeping sin from others*, especially from those who were entrusted to my care? What is my condition as regards *giving scandal* to others?

VI. Reflect whither the neglect of detachment may lead a man!

B The Sin of Our First Parents

FIRST POINT: The Fact of the Fall in Paradise

I. *The condition of our First Parents before sin.*

" After Adam had been created on the Plain of Damascus and placed in the Garden of Paradise, and Eve had been formed from his side . . ." (Sec. 51) (St. Ignatius here quotes from Lud. de Saxonia: *Vita Christi*, I, 2.)

1. The body of Adam was formed by God; it was most beautiful, most perfect; the soul came forth from the mouth of God, as the most perfect image of the divine nature; it was endowed with knowledge and virtue and supernatural gifts of grace.

2. Adam was placed in the earthly paradise, where he could enjoy preternatural gifts. Consider the beauty and fertility of his first home, the sweetness and variety of its fruits, it health-giving springs of water, the animals in their variety and tameness, and lastly the tree of life which gave immortality and impassibility to the body. Consider that all this material happiness was but a shadow of the inner spiritual peace, due to the union with God and that complete subordination of all the lower inclinations which we call the state of original justice.

3. Eve, formed from a rib of Adam, was like him in every kind of perfection; she was destined to be his helpmate for the intimate union of their whole life, and in particular for the begetting of offspring and the institution of human society. " And Adam called the name of his wife Eve: because she is the mother of all the living." (Gen. 3:20)

4. Now all this was done with the one end in view, that both, together with their whole offspring, should praise God, do reverence to Him, and obey Him; thereby they were to attain to the perfection of a human being, and to complete the image

of God in themselves: thus paradise was consecrated as an earthly Jerusalem (City of Peace), the image of the heavenly one.

II. *The sin of our First Parents.*

" Being forbidden to eat of the tree of knowledge. . . ."

1. Consider how *just* this commandment was: certainly God, the Lord of all, was entitled to make such a prohibition.

It was *easy* to observe; for there was only one commandment, and it referred to one object only out of so many, and this so easy to keep.

Yet it was of *grave* importance from the very fact of being the only one; also from its purpose of putting them to the test, and from the added warning of heavy punishment.

It was *useful:* by it God would test the faithfulness of His servants, and man would fulfil his duty as regards his end and save his soul.

2. Reflect on the sanction that was added: if Adam obeyed the commandment, he would keep for himself and his posterity grace and the preternatural gifts; but if he did not obey, he would bring sin and death on himself and his descendants. He was given a choice between *life* and *death:* true life, including the fulness of natural life, joined with the supernatural life; and death of the soul as well as of the body.—A choice between *freedom* and *bondage:* perfect freedom, with the will fully free in itself, and nowise subject to the disorderly inclinations of lower nature; bondage, with the will dragged down by the baser appetite, and enslaved by the wiles of the devil.—A choice between *peace* and *misery* . . . .

" They ate and thereby sinned."

1. Consider the *serpent, i.e.,* Lucifer: from an angel he had become God's enemy, and also the enemy of all those who are created by God to obtain the places originally meant for the un-

faithful angels; the devil is, therefore, the enemy not of one human individual only, but of human nature itself.—But now Lucifer assumes a friendly appearance, that of an insinuating, cunning, ingratiating serpent. Yet he comes from the infernal Babylon, to lay the cornerstone of the *earthly Babylon*.

2. Consider with what *cunning* he tempts our First Parents: he allures them first with desire for the forbidden fruit, then with a desire for their own excellence, in order thence to rush them headlong into the extreme presumption of setting at nought the divine prohibition. Consider how at the same time he is undermining their trust, by suspicion, and how he abuses even conjugal affection for his evil end.

3. Consider lastly the *eating of the forbidden fruit*: it is a single act of very short duration, but it is sinful, because it violates the divine prohibition. The whole malice of the angels' rebellion is also found in this disobedience. Taste, as it were, this fruit of sin: its badness, loathsomeness and bitterness; compare these with the sweetness for the mouth from the eating of the forbidden fruit, and for the mind from indulging vanity.

III. *The punishment of our First Parents' sin.*

" Thereafter, they were clothed in garments of skin and cast out of Paradise. By their sin they lost original justice, and for the rest of their lives, lived without it in many labors and great penance." (Sec. 51)

1. *The personal punishment.*

Our First Parents lost that original righteousness in which all the faculties of soul and body were mutually subject in harmonious order, and which made up the fulness of peace and liberty. They were cast out of paradise, far from the tree of life, on the earth that was under a curse, and now brought forth thorns and thistles. They were without the original justice, which they had lost when losing grace and supernatural life, with all the gifts connected therewith. Thenceforth they lived in many labors, tilling the soil, bringing up their children, being exposed to sickness in the body and temptation in the soul. Theirs was "great penance," interior and exterior. Thus they spent their whole life, which was long if compared with the punishment and penance they had constantly to endure, but short if compared with the lasting life granted them at first. And it was to end with the unavoidable fate of death.

2. *The punishment of Adam's posterity.* " And what great corruption has come over mankind."

Every individual has lost original righteousness; there followed darkness of the mind and promptness to sin; every one lost access to paradise with the tree of life, as well as the privilege of immortality and immunity from suffering; every one lost grace and the supernatural gifts; every one is subject to continual " travails and pains " throughout life.—The consequence of this was *universal* and complete corruption: of the body, hastening to dissolution through sickness and death; of the soul, falling into sin through ignorance and error; of the whole social life in the family, the state, and religion, and in all nations. This condition prevailed in spite of the many efforts of physicians, pious parents, religious kings, magistrates, lawgivers, and philosophers; nay, in spite of the efforts of God Himself, first in choosing the children of Seth and protecting them by signal favors, then in choosing Noe and his descendants, Abraham and his seed, and finally two out of the twelve tribes.—Owing to this universal corruption it came to pass that the earth, which was at first a *Jerusalem*, a city of peace, was changed into a *Babel*, a city of confusion, where men, estranged from God and deprived of inward peace, are continually at strife one with another, and are finally laid low, caught in the snares of their enemy Lucifer, and pierced with his darts. Earth has become a vast *hospital* in which the whole human race is wasting away with numberless diseases of body and soul; it is changed into a vast *graveyard* where Death is ruling, where one scarcely finds, for setting the foot, a spot free from the dust of human rottenness.

3. " So many men are going to hell."

All these sins were a turning away from the praise, reverence and service of God; they were deliberate offences, and therefore liable to punishment: consequently they justly deserved the ruin of the soul, and the torments of the infernal Babylon.

Second Point: A Closer Examination of Our First Parents' Punishment

I. *Reflect on the circumstances of this punishment.*

1. The victims were *human beings,* not angels. Adam and Eve were altogether involved in the mean and weak condition of matter. Nevertheless, they had been created in the image of God, and so very liberally endowed with gifts by God. The first two were to be the parents of countless human beings, inheriting either blessing or curse; if the original gifts had been preserved, the rest of mankind would have been born free from sin, and by far the majority, it seems, would have persevered in good, while now they perish eternally; and they were enticed into sin by the deceit of Lucifer, the enemy of both God and man.

2. He who punishes is *God,* infinitely *just* and infinitely *merciful.*

3. *For a single mortal sin.* The action of our First Parents was a sin of deliberate, formal disobedience; it was a mortal sin not because of the outward palpable object, but because of the specific order given by God; it was the sin of a single person, for only the transgression of Adam constitutes original sin; it was a single sin, lasting but an instant, and soon afterwards it was most sincerely deplored. Although Adam committed some

other offenses, yet it is certain that not these, but the transgression of the divine prohibition constitutes original sin, which is the cause of the punishments we have enumerated.

II. *Consider the justice of the condemnation.*

God the Father is holding the balance in His hand: on one scale He places this one mortal sin; on the other scale He lays all the excuses we have mentioned, and He declares that the latter are of less weight. The Word of God accepts the justice of this sentence, together with the decree of Redemption based upon it. The Holy Spirit confirms the same sentence, which underlies the restoration of the whole order of grace. That sentence is also continually ratified by the countless verdicts passed at the particular judgment. The equity of that sentence was immediately acknowledged by the angels, by the devils, and by our First Parents; it will be acknowledged at the Last Judgment for all eternity by the whole creation.

THIRD POINT: A Practical Conclusion from the Case of Our First Parents

I. Great as was the punishment inflicted on our First Parents and their posterity, yet it falls short of the malice and foulness of even one mortal sin, and of even *one mortal sin of mine*.

The poison of the latter was such that of itself it would be sufficient to infect a whole world, supposing I had happened to be in a position like that of Adam. Therefore I too will weigh this single sin of mine on the scale. I will consider it closely and see whether it was not more grievous than that of Adam as to its material object or longer as to its duration. I will see whether I ought to have been deterred from committing it by a clear insight into the ruin of the angels, of my First Parents, and of countless others.

II. What punishment is then in store for my so many mortal sins? How great must be the foulness of my soul stained by those sins? I will place them once more on the scale; I will consider their number, their varied deformity, the disgrace of the several material objects, the urgency of God's prohibition, the special malice there is in committing sin again and again, especially after having received forgiveness.

III. What if my one sin, or my many sins have already been pardoned?

IV. What if, by the help of God's grace, I have till now been preserved from mortal sin? Consider Eve's loquacity, her eagerness for eminence and her vanity; consider moreover Adam's affection for his wife: although such feelings are not always sinful in themselves, they are worldly, to be sure, kindred to sin, and paving the way to sin. Compare now the *worldly affections* which you are wont to indulge; examine on the one hand their near approach to sin, and on the other hand their inner vanity. Express your sentiment of shame.

V. What is my position to *sharing in another's sin?* to *scandal?*

VI. Consider the manifold *neglect of detachment* in our First Parents, and apply the matter to yourself.

C. The Sin of Someone Damned for One Mortal Sin

N.B. Faith teaches us that anyone who dies with even one mortal sin unforgiven must infallibly go down to hell. Do we not find such people, who committed only one sin, and who died without that sin being pardoned, and who must therefore have gone to hell? No doubt these people were guilty, some of one kind of sin, others of another, so that at least the more common kinds of sin are to be found there. And so there will also be among them some who were damned on account of a single sin of the kind I myself have committed.

FIRST POINT: The Particular Sin of Someone Who Went to Hell on account of a Single Mortal Sin

I. *Considering the fact.* Picture some person damned for only one sin of a kind you too have committed, and see him before you in that infernal Babylon.

1. *Condition before sin.*—Ask him: " Who are you? " He will then tell you his difficulties of character, helps of grace, and circumstances of his youth very much like those in which you have grown up.

2. *The sin.*—Ask him: " How have you come hither? " He will then tell you the very sin which you too committed, and a similar progress of his temptation.

3. *The punishment of the sin.*—Ask again: " What are you suffering here? " He will answer (with the words of Dives): " I am tormented in this flame." (Luke 16:24)

II. *Examining the case more closely.* Ask that same person whether he thinks he is punished justly; he will reply:

1. *I got what I wanted.* I knew that God had threatened the

sinner with eternal punishment. I could have avoided the sin, but I did not. I committed the sin knowingly and willfully.

2. Now, as a sinner, I *justly* suffer the punishment threatened by God. Punishment is due to the offense against God, and such a punishment as corresponds to the offense: for turning away from God, there follows the pain of loss; for turning to the creature, the pain of sense; also in proportion to the dignity of God who is offended the punishment is endless, eternal!

3. The punishment, announced justly, was justly inflicted immediately after *a single sin*. Did not that mortal sin deserve punishment from the very first moment, and that, too, an eternal one? Was God bound to suspend the effect of the natural causes that led to my death at the very time when I had become stained with sin? And that, when God would by no means suspend the effect of the same causes with regard to other innocent persons? Is not the malice of mortal sin so great that God could justly rather have stayed the laws of nature at the very moment of sin, and hurled me into hell by a striking act of His justice?

4. Reflect, in the last place, that so severe a punishment is inflicted justly, not only for a single mortal sin but also in the *case of any one* who dies with the guilt of a mortal sin. Look about in heaven, and look about in purgatory: neither in one nor the other will you find any one who died with the guilt of even one mortal sin. You may dwell also on the number of those who have been cast into hell for a single mortal sin.

III. *A practical conclusion.*

1. If this terrible punishment is justly imposed for one mortal sin, how very great must be the malice of mortal sin! Therefore the very same punishment is due to every mortal sin of mine; in each there is the same malice and filth.

2. What punishment, pray, is due to, and what filth and

malice must be found in, my many and repeated sins? Would it not be that punishment multiplied by the number of my mortal sins? But even this would not seem to be enough, for the malice of the same person committing sin over again is greater than that of so many different persons who sin but once.

SECOND POINT: "Countless Others . . . Have Been Lost for Fewer Sins Than I Have Committed." (Sec. 52)

N.B. It is certain that very many have been damned for more than one sin. Nor can it be doubted that countless others have been damned for fewer sins than mine, supposing, of course, that I have actually been guilty of many sins.

I. *Reviewing the fact.*

See now all those wretched people in the infernal Babylon raising their heads above that sea of fire!

1. *Their condition before sinning:* Ask everyone of them: " Who are you? " and you will learn that all had the same fallen nature that is yours, and the grace of God which you have. In other respects you notice a well-nigh infinite variety of talent, age, state of life, origin, language, customs, etc.

2. *The sins:* Ask everyone: " How did you come hither? " You will find an almost infinite variety of sins as to kind, circumstances, combination, number: sins by thought, word, and deed; sins of commission and omission: this, however, is common to all, that they are sins, and that they are less numerous than mine.

3. *The punishment of the sins:* Ask everyone yet again: " What do you suffer here? " And all will cry out with one voice: " I am tormented in this flame." (Luke 16:24)

II. *Examine the case more closely.*

Reflect that all this concerns—

1. *Human beings,* created in the image of God, destined for eternal union with Him, men and women who had become so weak owing to the sin of Adam. It happened to so many, even though some had previously performed good works, even though Christ had shed His blood for them upon the cross, even though His sacrifice for them is renewed daily on altars throughout the world.

2. Their punishment has been *imposed by God* who is infinitely just, and infinitely merciful.

3. *It is all due to mortal sins,* so various in number and kind. Therefore that which deserves so dreadful a punishment is not the number and kind of sins, nor the condition of the sinner, but the very nature of mortal sin.

4. The *justice of the sentence.* Each and every mortal sin is a deliberate, full, and complete rebellion of the creature against the Creator, his greatest and most faithful patron and Lord. It is a rebellion against the infinite goodness, worthy of love and obedience above all things, and that, too, without ceasing. Consider that the prison of hell is the work of God, inspired by His holiness, designed by His justice, built by His omnipotence, eternal as the decrees of God, an everlasting monument of His holiness and justice.

III. *A practical conclusion.*

1. How great, then, is the deformity and malice of *my* mortal sins, which are the same in kind as the sins of those men, but which surpass them in number, and therefore also in malice!

2. Seeing, then, the great number of the damned, how idle is the excuse that it is easy to escape hell after mortal sin!

3. How mad, then, was my folly to persevere without concern in the state of mortal sin, or even to remain in danger of mortal sin!

COLLOQUY

I. " *Imagine Christ our Lord present before you upon the cross.*" (Sec. 53) I will ask Him:

1. " *Who art Thou?* " He will answer: " I am the Son of God, equal in all to the Father and Creator of the whole world."

2. " *What do You suffer here?* " Reflect on the outward tortures of the body, the inward torture of thirst, the desolation that oppresses His soul, and the insults that surround Him on all sides.

3. " *How did You come to such a state?* " He will answer: " It is due not only to the sin of Adam, or the sins of other men, but also to your sins. Your sins, too, made me come down to earth; they, too, have nailed me to the cross, etc."

II. " *I shall also reflect upon myself and ask: ' What have I done for Christ? What am I doing for Christ? What ought I to do for Christ?' '*" (Sec. 53)

1. *What have I done for Christ?* Is this the first time that I hear of the great love of Christ for me? Certainly not; that was one of the first things I learned as a little child. Yet, what have I, in return, done for Christ from my early years till now? Did I try to return love for love? I have offended Him by my mortal sins.

2. *What am I doing for Christ?* What am I doing now? I am now meditating on the malice of sin. But what am I doing during this meditation? Am I now at least deeply moved with

sincere hatred for my sins, and a serious determination to avoid them in future? Alas! how cold I find myself!

3. *What will I do for Christ?* I will renounce sins, by a firm purpose of amendment; I will set myself free from the occasions of sin, and apply the suitable means: general and particular examinations of conscience, confession, penance. Taking advice from a prudent confessor, I will set my whole life in order.

III. After these preliminary considerations make the colloquy itself, with such reflections as present themselves.

St. Ignatius adds a general hint: " The colloquy is made by speaking exactly as one friend speaks to another, or as a servant speaks to a master, now asking him for a favor, now blaming himself for some misdeed, now making known his affairs to him, and seeking advice in them." (Sec. 54)

CHAPTER V

My Personal Sins

★

THIS MEDITATION is about the personal sins of the retreatant. Although the personal sins of the retreatant have been considered in the previous meditation numerically and as compared with the single sin of others, here the very nature of sin is examined, in order to produce not only shame and confusion but " intense sorrow and tears." (Sec. 55)

The first point consists of an indictment or list of personal sins in succession as they were committed, and as they perhaps increased in number and gravity, year after year. For persons whose lives have been uniform and their sins rarer, it is enough to divide their lives into various periods: childhood, youth, maturity and old age, and the period preceding the adoption of a state of life. In each year or period we are asked " to consider the place where I lived; . . . my dealings with others; . . . the office I have held." (Sec. 56) By recalling these to memory, it will not be difficult to make a fairly complete survey of the more outstanding sins of our whole life.

After drawing up this list of sins we are led, by the second, third and fourth points, to examine more closely the meaning of the words: I have sinned; I have offended God. The second point dwells on the idea of sin in itself, the third on the person sinning, and the fourth on the One offended by sin.

Ample matter for meditation is offered in the second point if we take into account not only the general malice of sin but also the particular malice of those sins to which we are inclined. There is some obscurity in the words " even though it were not forbidden " (Sec. 57), and the explanation can be found by comparing this with the previous meditation. Evidently the prohibition referred to is that of the positive law of God, for if the author was speaking only of prohibition by the natural law, then any malice contained in the sin would bring it under the prohibition of the natural law. In the previous meditation we were not considering the particular malice of sin, only its general opposition to the service of God and His command. In the present meditation the nature of sin is examined, first in general, as opposed not so much to God's prohibition as to His Wisdom, Holiness, etc., then in particular, weighing the particular malice of those sins which are, so to speak, our favorites. This part of the meditation corresponds to those sermons which are given in missions on certain types of sins.

The consideration of the person who has sinned (point 3) follows very much the same lines as have been followed throughout these exercises on sin. E.g., we are told to compare our many sins with the fewer sins of others, to ponder over the intrinsic and special malice of our sins. In this meditation we are also asked to consider our own smallness, both numerically and morally, in comparison with all men now living, with all the angels and saints in heaven, with all God's creatures, and with God Himself. Whether the phrase " all creation " (Sec. 58) includes also the devils, the damned, and the souls in Purgatory is not clear. Perhaps it signifies all God's creatures, even inanimate ones, but indeterminately. We are then told to consider " all the corruption and loathsomeness " of our own being. (Sec. 58)

Notice that the first four points of this exercise tend primarily to increase the sense of shame conceived in the preceding meditation. The last consideration in the fourth point (" His goodness with my wickedness " [Sec. 59]) also directly tends to produce a sense of sorrow. This sense has been prepared for by all that precedes and it is directly induced in the fifth point by the " cry of wonder " at the Divine Mercy, which does not crush the sinner, but pursues him " down the labyrinthine ways " (" The Hound of Heaven ") to heap upon him blessings at the very moment when he is sinning. The fifth point refers directly only to God's mercy to one in the state of sin. However His mercy may also be considered as pre-ordained in the eternal decree of God. Compare the words of the second prelude to the meditation on hell: " if . . . I forget the love of the eternal Lord." (Sec. 65) Therefore we may also consider in this meditation the benefits of the Redemption, planned by the all-merciful and omnipotent Father.

The second exercise concludes with a colloquy of mercy. Since mercy is the manifestation of love to those in need, it moves us not only to shame at our condition but also to an act of perfect contrition whereby we turn from sin to God. It also gives us the sentiment of hope which will be further developed in the third exercise. Without hope, sorrow would neither be salutary nor a useful preparation for making a good choice in life. This colloquy undoubtedly expresses the hope of obtaining both pardon and grace.

First Point: This Is the Record of My Sins.

" I will call to mind all the sins of my life, reviewing year by year, and period by period. Three things will help me in this: First, to consider the place where I lived; secondly, my dealings with others; thirdly, the office I have held." (Sec. 56)

Afterwards I will consider what sin is: " An offense committed by man against God " (for now only the sin of man is considered). I will ask for light carefully to reflect on this definition, and properly to understand the malice of mortal sin.

Second Point: (Cf. Sec. 57) The Malice of Sin

I. *Sin, taken generally,* is:

1. A *disorder,* a violation of the mortal order established by God who is perfect *order*; sin is the worst of all disorders.

2. An *offense* against God, who is Lord and Master of all. Any other offense violates only the right of creatures, but sin violates the right of the Creator; this offense is the highest of its kind.

3. A *rebellion* against God; it is worse than any against a created authority: God is the *Sovereign Majesty;* rebellion against Him is therefore the worst rebellion possible.

4. An *ingratitude* towards God who is the *greatest benefactor* and infinite goodness; it is worse than any ingratitude towards man; it is the very worst possible.

II. *Sin, viewed in particular.*

Here are enumerated only some of the more common kinds of sin.

1. *Indifference.* In a general sense this extends to religious

truths, which are far superior to any other truth, to religious graces, which are of such high excellence, to religious duties, which are far holier than any duties towards our neighbor. Indifference betrays a mentality that is exclusively taken up with worldly things.

2. *Blasphemy*. This is an insult aimed at God and His saints, and this, too, from a mind that once learned things divine, from lips consecrated to God's praise, from a heart destined for God's service and love!

3. *Sacrilege*. This is a wilful profanation of holy things: things instituted for man's salvation are turned into instruments of damnation.

4. *Intemperance*. This is the sway of gluttony over reason. This sin lowers man below the very brutes, clouding the mind, weakening the will, bringing many a time pitiable ruin to individuals and whole families.

5. *Lust*. This is more or less directly a crime destroying the human race.

Reflect how the various sins of your life form, as it were, a texture of wickedness, a great variety of sins supplying the threads, and how this texture is utterly hateful to God.

THIRD POINT: (Cf. Sec. 58) The Offender's Insignificance

A. *Comparison of the offender with others.*

I. *With all men now living on earth.* How very small I am!

1. In number: Europe alone has over 500 million inhabitants, and the world over 2,000 millions.

2. In importance: Very many do not even know of my ex-

istence, very few know my name, still fewer know about my occupation, my position, etc.

3. And this insignificance of mine is well deserved: for what is my knowledge, my skill, my strength and my virtue compared to the knowledge, skill, strength and virtue of all the rest taken together? Suppose I were to declare war on all these? What is my knowledge but ignorance, my strength but weakness, my effort but madness!

II. *With all the angels and saints in heaven.* Compare these with all men now living on earth.

1. In number: So great is the number of the angels, so great that of the saints who in so many past centuries throughout the world have saved their souls!

2. And even if their number was not so very much greater, yet how far superior are the angels and saints in knowledge, skill, experience, virtue.

3. What would be the result if all men were to unite against the angels and saints? They would not even be able to reach the holy citadel of heaven; one ray of heavenly light would be enough to blind all of them; one blow would make the limbs of all stark and stiff. (Cf. Gen. 19:11, 32:35, 4 Kings 19:35)

4. Suppose then I alone were to declare war on the heavenly hosts!

III. *Compare the offender with God Himself.* Suppose that all the angels and saints and all men on earth were to unite and declare war on God:

1. What is their number compared with *God's immensity!*

2. Contrast *God's self-existence* and infinite perfection with their contingency and deficiency.

3. Surely they would be as if they were not; one breath from the mouth of God would consume them and hurl them into the abyss of nothingness.

4. Suppose then that I all alone were to venture to fight against Him!

B. *A view of the offender in himself.*

I will further consider myself as going forth to single combat against God; then I will ask: " Who am I? "

I. *Physically.*

My body is corruptible; then I must be quick lest, while I am engaged in the combat, this wretched armor of my body rot and fall to pieces. It grows old; then I must be all the more quick with the combat, lest the stiffness of old age make me quite unfit.

I will therefore take up the fight in the full vigor of youth. But yet God may send forth any one of His creatures against me, and it will destroy me; He will send forth His angels, and they will crush me; He will send forth animals, and they will devour me; He will send forth plants, and they will poison me; He will send forth water, and it will drown me; He will send forth diseases, and fever will consume me; He will send forth fire, and it will destroy me. No creature is so mean, but by God's will it is strong enough to kill man. Review the list of sicknesses which attack the head, eyes, ears, lungs, and other parts of the body, bringing death with them. Reflect on the uselessness of medicines against these evils. What are these save God's servants and instruments? How very insignificant I am!

II. *Spiritually.*

But I have more than a body. I have also a soul, spiritual like God Himself. But what works come from me, a being animated by a spiritual soul? All I see is sin. How does this happen, since I have been created, body and soul, by the all good God? What blindness of the mind, what weakness of the will! There is in me the germ of sin, producing a plague of all kinds of sin. This very rottenness of sin can only exist by God's mercy. By sin I cry: " I will not serve." I seek to make myself His equal. If I war against God, I have before me the Most High, and behind me the abyss of nothingness opens its jaws.

FOURTH POINT: (Cf. Sec. 59) The Greatness of the One Offended by Sin

I will therefore ask Him who is my opponent: " Who art Thou? " and He will answer me:

1. My name is *the Eternal,* having neither beginning nor end. I, on the contrary, was created in time. I shall die. At death I must appear before God as my Judge, to enjoy Him forever if my life has been good, to be separated from Him eternally if my life has been bad.

2. My name is *the Unchangeable,* having continually the fulness of perfection, being equally incapable of increase and decrease.—I, on the contrary, am wholly changeable, and I do not always change for the better. I am changeable in my very substance, " A King is today, and tomorrow he shall die." (Eccli. 10:12) I am changeable as to the development of body and soul, their growth, progress, and decrease; also as to external goods . . .

3. My name is the *All-knowing One,* knowing all things past, present, and future, learning nothing and forgetting nothing.

I, on the contrary, have such a limited knowledge; I know but a very few things that are at present, and less of the past and the future; and even these things I know very imperfectly; my knowledge is mixed up with any number of errors, uncertainities, and obscurities; I learn those things laboriously, and forget them very easily.

4. My name is *the Almighty One,* having the power to accomplish anything I like, making it out of nothing, by a mere act of the will, without any weariness. " He spoke and they were made: He commanded and they were created." (Ps. 143:5) God's wisdom "reacheth . . . from end to end mightily, and ordereth all things sweetly." (Wis. 8:1) I, on the contrary, am able to make but a very few things; I can create nothing. I only transform the things created by God: " But which of you by being anxious about it can add to his stature a single cubit? " (Matt. 6:27) I set noisily about my work. I am soon overcome by weariness, and I must be refreshed with food and sleep.

5. My name is *the Just One,* providing with the most perfect equity for each and every one, the lowest as well as the highest, in punishing and rewarding, in forming a judgment. I, on the contrary, am full of evil, carried away at one time by anger, at another time by partiality, not caring for small things, rash in judging, and unwary in believing.

By these considerations I will stir up in myself ever increasing feelings of shame, confusion, and fear, as I ponder how great an opponent I have provoked against me.

6. Then I will proceed to consider how this same God is moreover *infinite Goodness,* both in Himself, and in regard to others. While I recall to memory the number and malice of my sins, dispelling the mists of shame and fear, I will let my heart be lit up with the pure rays of sorrow springing from perfect contrition.

FIFTH POINT: (Cf. Sec. 60) The Mercy of Him
Who Was Offended by Sin

I will consider what God did at the very time when I
offended Him by my sins. A man who is offended may return wrong for wrong, insult for insult, and thus the
offender has sometimes some kind of excuse; with God it
it not so.

1. *The angels* are " the sword of God's justice." (Sec. 60)
God's hand is of itself strong enough alone to crush all adversaries; He nevertheless created the angels to be the instruments,
" the swords of His justice," not lifeless swords, but such as
breathe the most ardent love of justice and holiness, and a relentless hatred of sin, well tried swords and forever confirmed in this
love and hatred at the time of Lucifer's defection, when they
were at once drawn against Satan. Consider how these swords,
the angels, " have borne with me," *i.e.*, have not been raised
against me, " and guarded me," *i.e.*, they were raised against my
enemies, to defend me from them; " and they prayed for me,"
doing so not reluctantly, but keeping down, for the time being,
their hatred and wrath, they breathed only mercy. Reflect that
God achieved all this in the angels by His grace and inspiration.
(Cf. Sec. 60)

2. *The saints* " have interceded for me and asked favors for
me! " (Sec. 60), *i.e.*, they were wholly, constantly, and urgently
intent on this task of intercession. And when their intercession
became more insistent, as the number and gravity of my sins increased, God by no means rejected their intercession; nay, He
invited them by His grace and inspiration, and showed that He
would be pleased with it, so that I might at long last be taken up
once more into the company of the saints.

3. Range in thought through (other) creatures . . . . *the
heavens, sun, moon, stars, and the elements; fruits, birds, fishes,*

and other animals—why have they been at my service! (Sec. 60)

Consider how the sky and the air did not crush or choke me in a storm; how the heavenly bodies did not change their light into darkness; the elements, water and fire, did not engulf or consume me; the animals did not tear me to pieces, etc.

These creatures, on many other occasions, combined for the ruin of the wicked. By God's kind providence, they were compelled to serve me, to provide me with shelter, food, even enjoyment. All this at the very time when I was God's enemy, when one could anticipate that I would even use them for committing sin. All this was arranged by God with the view that I might at last be brought back to the knowledge and love of Him and that I should be restored to my eternal salvation.

4. *The earth.* "How is it that the earth did not open to swallow me up, and create new hells in which I should be tormented forever." (Sec. 60) In the case of the rebellious Core, Dathan and Abiron " the earth broke asunder under their feet: and opening her mouth, devoured them with their tents and all their substance." (Num. 16:31) But in my case, according to God's will, it bore me patiently.

5. *God Himself* kept showering benefits on me by means of all these creatures at the very moment when I was offending Him by my sins; nay, He kept heaping on me these and other natural benefits. Moreover, God gave me His own Son as a Redeemer. In the fulness of time the Word was made flesh for me; from the first all His feelings, words, and actions were ordered to my salvation. For me did He found His Church and institute the lasting ministry of absolution so that, after a sinful life, I could still turn myself to God by repentance and the absolution of His priest. For me did He institute the sacrament of the Eucharist, to give me strength for my daily life.

COLLOQUY (Cf. Sec. 61)

I. I shall " cast a reckoning," trying to realize the *greatness of God's mercy* for me:

1. from the vileness of my misery and wickedness;

2. from the persistence of God's mercy, in spite of my ingratitude;

3. from the manifold mercies given me already, and to be given me in the future;

4. from the circumstance that the most merciful God has not the least need for me.

II. Then I shall consider that these numerous and great mercies of God *impose on me the obligation* to give thanks for the past, and to resolve on amendment for the future.

1. These acts are, as it were, the discharge of that "most offensive poison " (Sec. 58) mentioned in the third point: they come from lips so careless about the praise of God, so frequently offending in words; from a memory so forgetful of the divine benefits and the holiest obligations, but brim full with the recollection of vain and wicked things; from a will that has often turned away ungratefully from the Creator, and surrendered itself wickedly to creatures; from a nature wholly dependent, and yet at the same time rebellious, which, but for God's help, cannot even make this act of thanksgiving and this purpose of amendment.

2. Reflect how up to now there has constantly followed ingratitude upon thanks, and fickleness upon good resolutions.

3. Nevertheless, as these acts are due to God, I must by all means make them; and I will do so with the greatest possible humility and sincerity, and at the same time with confidence.

CHAPTER VI

The Vanity
of Worldly Things

★

THIS IS described as "a repetition of the first and second exercises" (Sec. 62), but it contains items not previously expressed. These should be considered before making the colloquies of this exercise. We are invited not only to detest our past sins but also to conceive a horror of at the disorder of our actions and a realization of the vanity of the world.

What St. Ignatius means by the "disorder" of our lives is clear from a consideration of what he means by putting our lives in order. To order our lives requires both the reform of past sins and the choice of a way of life. These two points, reformation and choice, are emphasized throughout the *Exercises* and were explicitly mentioned in the title of the book and instructions on its use. The disorder of life lies in instability, aimlessness, or loose adherence to a state of life already chosen. The actions of such a life are now good, now evil; now they tend in one direction, now in another. There is no definite end in view or fixed principles of conduct. To such disorder is opposed reformation and an intelligent choice of life according to the principles of the Foundation. St. Ignatius, in this exercise, prepares for and suggests the Choice, but at first negatively, by arousing hatred for disorderly life. Whence comes the disorder in the actions of a person not yet bound to a particular state of life? It must be attributed chiefly to the allurements of the world, which flatter the heart's disorderly tendencies not yet subdued by detachment. A man will rid himself of these allurements the more easily in proportion as he puts away the vanity of the world. (Cf. Sec. 63) In this exercise we beg God the Father, His only-begotten Son, and our Blessed Lady to give us a " knowledge of the world." (Sec. 63)

Notice that St. Ignatius proceeds here exactly as he will do in the Two Standards. There he will urge us to overcome our natural repugnance for poverty by exciting in us a general distaste for riches, so close to the heart of Lucifer, and an esteem for poverty, consecrated by association with Christ. In exactly the same manner he here excites a general distaste for the things of this world. These things, though in themselves neither good nor evil, keep us from giving ourselves wholeheartedly to God. He shows us their folly and the vanity of seeking them, thereby leading us somewhat beyond the disposition of mind to which he had raised us in the Foundation.

This is not the only purpose of the present exercise. In addition to a distaste for worldly things it teaches us the use of the colloquy of intercession, a form of prayer of which litanies are an example, a form dear to St. Ignatius.

First Point: *Who Am I Who Ask?*

Repeat the first and second exercises, paying attention to and dwelling upon those points in which you have experienced greater consolation or desolation or greater spiritual appreciation. (Cf. Sec. 62) See what your past sins have made of your life. Compare your sins with those of others. Consider how unworthy you are of pardon.

SECOND POINT: *Whom Am I to Ask?*

I. *God.*

Consider the reasons you have for trust in God, the infinite goodness of God in Himself, the countless proofs of this goodness: He has given us the world; He has given us His Son.

On the other hand you see your *almost infinite unworthiness* and your distance from God. You may gather this from the punishments inflicted on the angels, Adam, and other men, and from the sufferings of the Son of God: I have killed that Son! In God there is infinite holiness; in me there is only the manifold depravity of sin. Indeed I lie prostrate in the depths of sin; how shall I, out of those depths, raise my voice and cry to the Lord " *Kyrie eleison;* Lord have mercy! "

II. *Christ.*

Behold the Son at the right hand of the Father, and ponder the reasons you have for trust in the *God-Man:* His very incarnation is a gift of divine reconciliation; His heart and wounds cry aloud the infinite mercy of God.

On the other hand turn once again to your *infinite unworthiness.* I have inflicted those wounds! I have pierced that heart! How shall I raise my voice to Him whom I have crucified? Christ hear me, Christ graciously hear me!

III. *The Blessed Virgin.*

Behold Mary at the right hand of her Son, and consider what reasons you have for trust in the *Virgin Mother:* she conceived the Savior, and bore Him nine months in her womb; she nursed Him at her breasts; she shared His joys and sorrows; she stood bravely by the cross, when, with dying lips, the Son spoke to her, " Woman, behold, thy son! " Full of confidence you must therefore cry out: O Virgin, it is I, I who crucified your Son; show that you are the Mother of Him who prayed for those who crucified Him! I have insulted Him: show that you are my Mother, being mindful of the words, "Behold, thy son." I am your son, pray for me to your Son Christ, Holy Mary, pray for me! Mother of Christ, Mother of divine grace, Refuge of sinners, pray for me.

THIRD POINT: *What Am I to Ask?*

I shall ask for many, and great, things, for everything, trusting in such intercession, inspired with confidence in the Mother, in the Son, in God the Father.

I. In particular I ask first for the grace suggested by all these meditations, that I may have " a deep knowledge of my sins and a feeling of abhorrence for them." (Sec. 63) I ask for a clearer, and above all for a more inward knowledge; such as does not lie merely on the surface of the mind, but strikes deep root in it; not a sham-abhorrence, but a genuine one.

II. In the second place I ask for " an understanding of the disorder of my actions, that filled with horror of them,

I may amend my life and put it in order." (Sec. 63) I mean the disorder which springs from the aimlessness of my whole life, a life without fixed principles, in which so much is left to chance and whim. I mean, moreover, the disorder which is constantly encouraged by my inordinate attachments which lead me first to so many imperfections, secondly to venial sins, and ultimately to mortal sins. I ask for grace to correct this disorder, to regulate myself, to arrange my whole life by definite principles, and to subject my inordinate attachments by the virtue of detachment.

III. Lastly I ask for " a knowledge of the world, that filled with horror, I may put away from me all that is worldly and vain." (Sec. 63) How empty is the world, since its goods, wealth, honor and pomp are so base in themselves, so fleeting, so deceitful in the pleasure they afford, defiled and desecrated by the constant touch of Lucifer. Accordingly, though there may be sometimes a praiseworthy use of those vanities, yet as a general rule I must not set my heart on them; rather I must on the whole despise them, and keep them from me as much as God's service allows.

CHAPTER VII

Hell

★

WE ARE expressly told that the meditation on hell is the fifth exercise of the day when the meditations on sin are made, and that it is to be made " an hour before supper." (Sec. 72) From this it is clear that, according to St. Ignatius, this exercise cannot be given in any other form except that adopted by him, namely, as an application of the senses. For St. Ignatius was convinced that it would be too tiring for the exercitant to make an exercise " with the three powers " five times in one day.

Hence, in reply to the objections raised by some that this exercise, as proposed by St. Ignatius, is little suited to our age, and that we should dwell in this exercise on the pain of loss rather than on the pains of sense, I should say that the pain of loss should be considered in another part of the *Exercises*. In the Foundation, when we were considering the salvation of one's soul, we were naturally led to think also of the pain of loss. Again, when meditating on the third sin, we thought of the pains of hell, pains both of loss and of sense. As the pain of loss occurs for consideration in the Foundation and as the next exercise stresses both the pains of sense and pain of loss it seems just that this fifth exercise should be wholly on the pains of sense. Although there may sometimes be reasons for omitting this exercise altogether, there should never be any question of altering it by substituting the pain of loss for the pains of sense. Such an alteration would be contrary to the plan of Loyola.

If an application of senses is to be made at all on the subject of sin, clearly such application is impossible when the matter at hand is primarily of a spiritual nature, e.g., a consideration of the nature of sin as such, the pain of loss, and the sin of the angels. It is likewise futile to apply the senses to the temporal punishments of sin in this life, as these pains are not without their remedies, and they also concern persons not guilty of the sins. There remains only the pains of sense which we shall suffer in hell. Here alone can an application of the senses be made. According to the colloquy, the necessary fruit of this meditation is fear lest I should incur these pains, and an act of gratitude because I have not yet done so.

As regards the pains of sense, St. Ignatius holds as certain that the fire of hell is real material fire, even though it may differ from our earthly fire. Consequently the other instruments of torment described in Holy Scripture, such as smoke and sulphur, are to be understood as real material objects, though perhaps more fearful than their earthly counterparts. Since the pain of touch is certain, and the pains of hearing and sight cannot reasonably be denied, we may also assume that the other senses, smell and taste, suffer also. We may legitimately speak of and meditate on the stench, the bitterness, etc. of hell.

The phrase in the first point, " the souls enclosed, as it were, in bodies of fire," (Sec. 66) recalls the first prelude of the first exercise, which speaks of " my soul as a prisoner in this corruptible body." (Sec. 47) Far worse is the state of captivity to which the souls in incorruptible bodies of fire are condemned. Notice too, in the second point, the words: "blasphemies against Christ our Lord and against His saints." (Sec. 67) The soul that has been led by venial sins to forget Divine Love, although no longer moved by the attraction of that Love, may yet shrink from things absolutely opposed to it, such as blasphemy, hatred of God, and the like. It has not yet sunk to the lowest depths; it falls gradually but steadily.

The chief sentiment in the colloquy is akin to that expressed in the colloquy of the second exercise (our fifth chapter), namely, gratitude to God. Indeed it is gratitude for the same benefit given by Him: in the former exercise it was: "giving thanks to Him that up to this very moment He has granted me life" (Sec. 61); here it is to "give thanks to God our Lord that He has not . . . . [brought] my life to an end." (Sec. 71) The greatness of the benefit is enhanced by the considerations just made: "He has not permitted me to fall" into hell. Two categories of the damned are described: "some . . . because they did not believe in the coming of Christ; others, though they believed, because they did not keep the commandments." (Sec. 71) These two categories are further divided into three classes: the first, "before the coming"; the second, "during His lifetime"; the third, "after His life here on earth." (Sec. 71) The retreatant is invited "to give Him thanks" for not having allowed him to fall into any of these classes. What shows us how great is the danger of damnation and how great is the benefit of having avoided that danger is the vast number of men damned: men damned for lack of faith or works; men damned when fewer graces were available; men damned when the fullness of grace was restricted to a single country; men damned even though saving grace was spread throughout the world by Christ's Church. The retreatant has good reason to thank God, so rich have been God's graces to him, especially the grace of forgiveness for past sins and the grace that prompted him to make the present retreat.

If gratitude to God, which had already been expressed in the colloquy of the second exercise, were the only fruit of the present meditation on hell, the sentiments aroused in the retreatant would not surpass those already aroused. But such is not the nature of Ignatian meditations. The meditation on hell, consequently, is linked up with the preceding meditation by its second prelude and raised to a higher level. " If because of my faults I forget the love of the eternal Lord, at least the fear of these punishments will keep me from falling into sin." (Sec. 65)

In the preceding meditation the retreatant, by considering the eternal love in its many effects, had made an act of contrition perfected by charity. He needs no other remedy now. He already has the most efficacious one, charity. Will he not need one later? He will not, unless he forgets the Eternal Love. How could he forget that! He might, for his deliberate venial faults lead to lukewarmness, which leads to forgetfulness of the love of God or robs such love of its efficacy. On the other hand fear of punishment does not lose its force. With this second prelude is connected a statement in the colloquy: " I shall thank Him . . . that up to this very moment He has shown Himself so loving and merciful to me." (Sec. 71) This thought does not come from the mere consideration of punishments; it is more akin to charity than to fear; it begets trust. The meditation on hell—in fact, the entire consideration of sin—leads finally to fear joined with trust, a combination forming a most sure anchor of salvation.

FIRST POINT: The Pain of Sight

Imagine that your Guardian Angel leads you slowly down to that pool of fire, the infernal Babylon.

1. *The place:* " Who hath measured the height of heaven, and the breadth of the earth, and the depth of the abyss? " (Eccli. 1:2) View that place, its " length and breadth "—immense in itself, yet narrow in comparison with the multitude of the damned—its " depth "—separated by an infinite distance from purgatory, earth and heaven.

The damned would so gladly go to purgatory and do long penance there, but they are told: " between us and you a great gulf is fixed, so that they who wish to pass over from this side to you cannot, and they cannot cross from your side to us." (Luke 16:26)—The damned would so gladly go back to earth to do penance and acquire merits, but the answer remains the same.—As for going to heaven, their home, that is impossible.

2. *The atmosphere of hell:* St. Ignatius says " vast fires." (Sec. 66) Their extent is such that there is no place free from fire in the whole length, breadth, and depth of hell; their intensity is extreme from their great extent, whether those fires are of the same as, or of a different kind from, our fire on earth.

3. *The inmates of hell:* they are men whose immortal souls were created for the eternal enjoyment of God in their heavenly home. Now their distorted eyes and faces reveal their desperation. They are exiles and captives in the prison of fiery bodies which the fire cannot consume. They dwell among wild beasts of the worst sort, the devils and the other damned.

SECOND POINT: The Pain of Hearing

Notice, as you descend into that abyss of fire, how you hear:

1. *The crackling of the flames,* like the roaring of the waves of an endless ocean, like the hissing blaze of an immense furnace.

2. Presently you hear, mingled with this, ceaseless *lamentations* resounding from all sides, thus expressing a continual and universal *sadness.*

3. As you go deeper down you can distinguish repeated *howlings* which re-echo from the endless spaces: these express a continual and universal torment.

4. And going yet deeper down you can distinguish cries, not merely expressing sadness and torment in general, but things that are evil of their very nature, *rage* and *despair.*

5. And now, at length, you can hear them speak.

There is no word of divine praise and prayer; yet all there were created for praising God.—There is no word of friendship; yet all there are brothers, descended from the same First Parents.

There are only words of cursing themselves, of hatred for others, of "blasphemies against Christ our Lord and against His saints." Consider that these words of blasphemy extend to everything holy, and that they do not refrain from what is most holy, Christ our Lord. These blasphemies manifest the whole corruption and degradation of the souls that have been changed from love to hatred, from piety to cursing, and from grace to reprobation; the mouths of the reprobate confirm the words: " out of the abundance of the heart the mouth speaks." (Matt. 12:34)

Reflect that those words do not move the bystanders to horror, but to similar expressions of blasphemy. Hence it is evident that all those reprobate souls are led by the same spirit of wickedness, that they form one kingdom, one assembly of evil, in which so many men, so diverse in origin, language, condition and occupation, now combine in the same wickedness, pouring out blasphemy against the Almighty.

THIRD POINT: The Pain of Smell

From the pains of the other senses it follows that hell is a place of torment; therefore smell, too, must have its torments. These pains must torture the smell in every way in which this sense may be tortured: by *irritation,* which is rightly compared to that caused by smoke and brimstone; by *stench,* which is rightly compared to that from a sewer.

These fumes proceed primarily from the bodies of the damned, and then from the surrounding atmosphere; accordingly they are not only most pungent but also continual, uninterrupted and everlasting.

As is the case with very repulsive smells, these torments will pervade the whole sensitive nature, producing nausea, infecting the taste, and unbalancing the mind.

These torments of the bodily smell are but a pale shadow of the spiritual stench of those souls: it issues forth from every thought, word, and deed, causing loathing to God.

FOURTH POINT: The Pain of Taste

1. Consider once more that from the torture of the other senses it follows quite clearly that taste will not be free from its own torment. St. Ignatius conveniently expresses this pain by the words " to taste the bitterness of tears, sadness, and remorse of conscience." (Sec. 70)

2. *Sadness* may indeed infect the taste and make all sweet things bitter; it arises from the consciousness of such great per-

sonal misery, the loss of an infinite good, the eternal fixity of man's greatest misfortune.

3. The stings of the worm of conscience may pervert the taste, owing to the fact that one is getting one's deserts, and that these are just and irreversable.

4. Consider how, in this torture, the body torments the soul, and the soul the body, as both will be united for eternity.— Think of the true nature of this torment, which will never be tempered by any, even the least, sweetness or consolation!

FIFTH POINT: The Pain of Touch

1. Consider how the fire of hell tortures the *bodies*.

It " touches and burns " the entire surface, not in one place only, but everywhere at the same time; it does so inwardly, penetrating them endlessly, and this continually, yet without destroying the bodies.

2. The fire tortures also the *souls*.

It touches them indirectly through the sense of bodily pain; it also " touches and burns " them directly, " in marvellous but true ways," as St. Augustine says. It produces a spiritual blaze of madness and despair. The flames of torment mingle with those of an ardent longing to possess the greatest good, a longing never to be satisfied.

3. Notice that everything which would soothe this torment is excluded.

Instead of love there is hatred of God; instead of hope, despair; instead of grace, cursing. In these flames the damned are terrified by a lively remembrance of the Judge who kindles that fire, whose words ring constantly in their ears: " Depart from me, accursed ones, into the everlasting fire." (Matt. 25:41)

In each of the above points, the sufferings of hell may be compared:

I. With the *corresponding joys of heaven.*

Consider that blissful place of immense extent and lofty height. Its atmosphere is the light of glory, filling soul, body, everything; by nature it is most bright, pleasant and never-fading.

In heaven live God, goodness itself, the angels, and the saints. All is peace, all is happiness, all is love.

By way of sounds you hear the singing of the angels, the conversation of the blessed, and the voice of the Father. Sweet joy pervades body and soul, and there is the embrace of the Father in beatific vision and love.

Compare in all this torture with pleasure, shame with glory, and eternity with eternity.

II. With the *allurements to sin or tepidity* leading to hell.

How meager those pleasures appear if you think of the awful torments; how empty they are! Alluring when you have not got them, and loathsome when obtained. Set this against the awful reality of hell!

Think also of the brief time those pleasures last, and the unchangeable eternity of the torments; the relative ease to do without the former, and the absolute impossibility of getting rid of the latter.

III. With the *self-denial required to avoid hell.*

How trifling is penance—it can even become a source of delight to the soul—in comparison with the awful torments of hell! Contrast the shortness of the one with the eternity of the other; the relative ease to practice mortification with the absolute impossibility of getting away from those torments.

COLLOQUY

I. Gaze upon those souls, and divide them into those who were damned for lack of faith and those who were damned for lack of good works, into those who received fewer and those who received more abundant graces. Give thanks to God that at the present time you are in none of these classes.

None of these souls lacked the light and grace necessary for salvation. There may be among them some who had had greater graces than you; some, with fervor greater than yours, had made more generous resolutions. For them the corruption of nature, bad habits, the allurements of the world, and the snares of the devil had been too strong. Forgetting the love of the eternal Lord they perished. *Ask for the grace of holy fear,* lest you too may be lost!

II. Lift up your eyes and gaze at the proofs of divine mercy: heaven and the cross. God created heaven and earth, all the good things of nature, the supernatural life and sanctifying grace, to help you save your soul. From this God's earnest and unwearied desire for your salvation is evident. Ask for a holy fear and confident trust. Dwell on the sentiments that come to mind. *Our Father.* (Cf. Sec. 71)

Second Week

CHAPTER VIII

The Kingdom of Christ

(Cf. Secs. 91 sqq.)

★

The meditation that gives the spirit of the second week is that on the " Kingdom of Christ." The second week then goes on to put before us the mysteries of our Lord's life from the time of the Incarnation until the Preaching in the Temple.

Part I
The Temporal King

First Point: The Person of the Temporal King

I. I put before my eyes *a human king,* who has lawful authority to provide for the temporal well-being of the community, suitable power as to the choice of means for securing this end, and appropriate majesty, combined with kindliness, to win the goodwill of his subjects.

II. This king has been *chosen by God our Lord Himself.*

He did not obtain the throne by right of succession, but is only one man among others, his equals. He was nevertheless chosen by God, like Saul or David, and so he has the most lawful and sacred authority possible.

III. *All Christian princes and people pay him reverence and obedience.*

Thus his kingship is of the greatest extent among men, though it does not extend to past times nor to eternity. All citizens of this kingdom render the king such service, as praise, reverence, and obedience, as is due to his majesty.

SECOND POINT: The Address of the Temporal King

I. Note how this king speaks to all his subjects, saying: " It is my will to conquer all the lands of the infidel." (Sec. 93)

Consider how just is this purpose, since the land of the infidel is supposed to belong by right to this king; how lofty and liberal, since the king is not satisfied with enjoying the goods already acquired, but desires to give to the rebellious infidel nations the happiness of his rule and the Christian religion; how holy, both on account of its object and its origin from divine inspiration.

II. The king goes on to say: " Therefore, whoever wishes to join with me in this enterprise must be content with the same food, drink, clothing, etc. as mine. So, too, he must work with me by day, and watch with me by night." (Sec. 93)

Consider this condition: It is just, since they that go to war must needs put up with hardships, watching, and privations;—it is generous and kind, since the king might reserve for himself the leadership, and leave all the labors to his followers;—it is honorable, putting the subjects on a level with the monarch.

III. The king concludes his address, saying: " that as he has had a share in the toil with me, afterwards, he may share in the victory with me." (Sec. 93)

Consider this reward: It is glorious, for it means honor, spoils, and rest (goods won by honest labor, yet all temporal, and so, in a sense, vain).—It is also to some extent uncertain, for they who fall in battle will never enjoy the reward; at any rate it is passing, not going beyond the limits of a man's life.

THIRD POINT: The Answer of the Subjects

I. Consider what " the answer of good subjects ought to be to a king so generous and noble-minded." (Sec. 94)

1. Owing to the king's authority, obedience is due him not only when he commands but also when he invites to service; owing to the divine choice and inspiration, whoever resists the king resists God. The king's kindness and generosity are clear from such a just, holy, and noble plan; from his way of acting, making a friendly request where he might rightly give an order; from the condition which cuts short every excuse not to labor; from the reward offered so generously.

2. The subjects must accept the whole request as it stands, *i.e.*, the proposed expedition, and the condition added, whereby they acquire the right to the promised reward, and, what is more, the favor of so gracious a king.

II. Consider that " if anyone would refuse the invitation of such a king, how justly he would deserve to be condemned by the whole world, and looked upon as an ignoble knight." (Sec. 94)

If any one were not to accept this useful, glorious, and

holy request, when the king only invites where he might command—and, mind, so excellent a king, with lawful authority, distinguished for valor and kindness, a king who offers such a generous condition and reward—that subject would be worthy of blame, for he would clearly be ruled by sloth and cowardice; and very much so indeed, since neither the brilliant gain and glory offered, nor the gracious invitation of so great and good a king, nor the generous condition of service can move him to action. Such a one would incur blame from the whole world, from the companions summoned with him to the royal meeting, from his contemporaries and even from posterity, nay from the very enemies. This blame might conveniently find expression by publicly depriving that knight of the badges of his rank: his sword, his spurs, and his mount!

Part II
The Kingship of Christ

FIRST POINT: The Person and Address of Christ the King

I. I see " *Christ our Lord, the eternal King.*" (Sec. 95)

Christ as man was anointed with the Holy Spirit, and destined to be the Savior of the world. He is *our Lord*, God, the Son of God, the Sovereign Lord, possessing every divine perfection. He is the eternal *King*, a descendant of David to whom kingship had been promised by God, a King by His divine nature, eternally generated from the Father, " The King of kings and Lord of lords." He is the eternal King whose rule begins on earth, and ends in heaven; here it may be unknown and despised, but there it is glorious and everlasting. He is surrounded by the heavenly Court, His glorious Mother and all the saints.

II. I behold Christ " *before whom is assembled the whole world. To all His summons goes forth . . . to each one in particular.*" (Sec. 95)

1. The *whole world:* this means that the Kingdom of Christ includes *all men,* Jew and Gentile, superiors and inferiors, the wise and the simple, the good and the bad, all men, even me. It includes all according to their whole being. It is above all a spiritual Kingdom which demands acknowledgment of the understanding, the submission of the will, and free service in the outward execution.

2. Christ is *calling:* As Creator He calls the world out of nothing; as Redeemer He summons it from the universal infection of sin; to be created and redeemed is to be called to grace. Christ, by particular invitations of grace, urges us to leave our disorderly lives. From this call arises in us a strict *obligation* derived from the very fact of creation; it is an inviolable obligation that is paramount over every other right.

III. Christ says: " *It is my will to conquer the whole world and all my enemies, and thus to enter into the glory of my Father.*" (Sec. 95)

1. The Kingdom of Christ is in a state of rebellion which began with Adam's sin, and is increased by each one's own sins; the Kingdom is held by the enemies: the concupiscence of the flesh, and the concupiscence of the eyes, and the pride of life.

2. Consider Christ's will to save; this is put into effect already by the fact of calling, yet it requires man's free co-operation.

3. The manner of re-conquest laid down by Christ is the following: His will is to fight and labor, to descend into the arena,

to undergo the fight of our wretched human nature; accordingly He puts on the armor of human nature, liable to death and suffering, so that, by the example of His human life, by the preaching of His human lips, He may teach us how to fight and conquer our enemies, and impart to us life and strength through the merits of His life and passion, and through the ministry of His sacred flesh.

It is His will in His own human nature to throw heaven open to us, to be in heaven our Mediator of all graces, and finally to make us share in His own and the Father's eternal glory in heaven.

IV. *"Therefore, whoever wishes to join me in this enterprise must be willing to labor with me, that by following me in suffering, he may follow me in glory."* (Sec. 95)

1. He must labor to resist soul-killing sin and worldly attachments leading to sin by making himself detached: such is the *end*.

2. He must labor *with me*, Christ, as leader, companion, helper, and model: such is the *condition*.

3. He must *follow me*, first in hardship, then in glory: such is the *reward*.

SECOND POINT: The Answer of Christians

I. *" All persons who have judgment and reason will offer themselves entirely for this work."* (Sec. 96)

1. They will do so with a view to the *end*.
That end demands labor taken on freely. That end ultimately finds its fulfilment in the salvation of their souls, the supreme task of life. The opponents of that end are stronger than the Christians seeking it. To attain it Christ is needed, both to battle the opponents and to give the help positively required.

2. Christians do so with a view to the *condition* offered.

It is most honorable to labor with the Son of God as our leader and associate; it is most easy to work with the help of the Almighty; it is most profitable to labor when God gives the reward; it is absolutely necessary, since he who does not labor with Christ cannot follow Him in glory, and since every one will be a companion in glory to the extent to which he has been so in labor.

3. Christians do so with a view to the *reward* which is so excellent and so lasting.

4. They do so with a view to the Person of Christ, so noble and amiable, our Brother, King, and God.

II. *He who would not accept the request of such a King, would lack true judgment and reason.*

1. He would have no sense of utility, for he rejects a fair, honorable, and profitable condition; he renounces the Savior's co-operation to be had only on this condition; and he yields himself freely to his inner and outer foes; he renounces in this way his eternal glory and salvation which cannot be made secure when the Savior is set aside, and he irrevocably incurs eternal damnation. Compare then the labor required by Christ with the torments of the damned; and the comforts of present slothfulness with the delights of eternal happiness.

2. That man would have no sense of honor, for he declines the most generous, fair, and honorable invitation of his King; he separates himself from the whole heavenly court to which he was invited by a fondness for passing idleness, and dislike of brief labor.

3. That man would have no sense of love, for he opposes the call of the most gracious King, the most loving Brother, and the infinitely amiable God.

THIRD POINT: A More Excellent Offer

I. There is good reason why we should be more desirous *to show affection towards Christ, the eternal King and universal Lord.*

Indeed, Christ has in Himself infinite goodness, and He is therefore worthy of all love. His Kingdom is universal in extent and duration, and He does not need us; what prompts Him to call us is the infinite love of His heart, which made Him become man, that He might give to us His glory in heaven. This loving kindness of His heart is manifested in all His feelings, words, and deeds, and above all in His five glorious wounds. I was the cause of these wounds which He received for my sins; looking at these wounds, I asked myself, (in the meditation on sins), " What ought I to do for Christ? " Is it not, therefore, meet and just that I, a sinner, nevertheless kindly invited by Christ, should desire to have greater attachment to Him, and to distinguish myself in following Him?

II. From this disposition it follows that *we should wish to distinguish ourselves in entire service of our King.* (Cf. Sec. 97)

1. Love of our King urges us to seek not so much our own gain, but His good pleasure, and that by serving Him. As our whole nature was made for serving Him, there is no other way for us to please Him; and we are to seek His good pleasure in entire service, seeing that every straying from His service displeases Him.

2. Love of our King also urges us to seek to distinguish ourselves in His service not only by accepting Christ's call, but

by making " offerings of greater value and of more importance." (Sec. 97)

This refers (a) to the object of our offer: volunteering to undertake the labor required to make our salvation safe and to act against our own love of comforts, and against carnal and worldly love. We must imitate Christ not only because it is necessary to salvation, but, in order to please Him more, by absolute imitation " in bearing all wrongs and all abuse and all poverty, both actual and spiritual " (Sec. 98), and we must do so as a perpetual state of life.

It also refers (b) to the disposition with which I make this offering after mature consideration, " in the presence of [His] infinite goodness, and of [His] glorious mother, and of all the saints of [His] heavenly court." (Sec. 98) It springs from an ardent desire, a serious will, and a deliberate determination. The only condition provided is that of God's holy will: " should Thy most holy majesty deign to choose and admit me to such a state and way of life." (Sec. 98)

" This exercise should be gone through twice during the day, that is, in the morning on rising, and an hour before dinner, or before supper." (Sec. 99)

CHAPTER IX

The Annunciation to Our Lady and the Incarnation*

Cf. Luke 1:26-38; *The Exercises*, Secs. 262 and 101 sqq.

★

WE SHALL here make some remarks preliminary to the contemplation of the mystery before us, points that will aid us penetrate, to some extent, the meaning of this great mystery.

Holy Scripture presents the Incarnation under a two-fold aspect: (1) that of the love of the Father who gave us His only-begotten Son; (2) that of the humiliation, renunciation, and obedience of the Son.

In this mystery St. Ignatius wishes to emphasize both these aspects. He gives us a picture of the world without Christ, the world which had proudly boasted that it needed not the almighty God. We see the sorry state of such a world and the men and women in it, men and women fallen from a supernatural life, unable, by themselves, to remedy their ill. We are led to consider the Three Persons of the Trinity, " seated on the royal dais or throne of the Divine Majesty. They look down upon the whole surface

---

* For all the mysteries of our Lord's life we have taken the points directly from the text of the *Exercises* as translated by Puhl. However all scriptural quotations from the New Testament are taken from the Confraternity Edition, even though Puhl used a different translation.

of the earth, and behold all nations in great blindness, going down to death and descending into hell." (Sec. 106) Moved by mercy the Blessed Trinity states " Let us work the redemption of the human race." (Sec. 107) Here we can see an imitation of the words of man's creation, " Let us make man etc." All these considerations are designed to move us to the love of the Father who gave us His Son, so that we might be redeemed from sin and enabled to enter paradise.

St. Ignatius emphasizes the humility and humiliations of Christ by telling us " to ask for an intimate knowledge of our Lord, who has become man for me, that I may love Him more and follow Him more closely." (Sec. 104) By such an intimate knowledge we are to see how willingly the Second Person of the Blessed Trinity embraced humiliations, and all for our sake. He had nothing to gain. If such is the generosity of God to sinful men, what should be our attitude when He calls us to follow Him?

First Point. *The angel, St. Gabriel, salutes our Lady, and announces to her the conception of Christ our Lord: " And when the angel had come to her, he said, ' Hail, full of grace, the Lord is with thee . . . thou shalt conceive in thy womb and shalt bring forth a son.' "* (Luke 1:28-31)

Second Point. *The angel confirms what he had said to her by announcing to her the conception of St. John the Baptist: " And behold, Elizabeth thy kinswoman also has conceived a son in her old age."* (Luke 1:36)

Third Point. *Our Lady replied to the angel: " Behold the handmaid of the Lord; be it done to me according to thy word."* (Luke 1:38)

First Point: The Incarnation Is Prepared and Announced.

I. *The preparation: The angel was sent.*

1. Whither? *To this earth.*

Take a survey of the earth: its greatness shows God's omnipotence and His liberality towards mankind; the desolation on earth brings out our First Parents' sin by which earth was changed from a paradise to a desert.

Look at the *human race.*

It began from a common origin, and it was directed to a common end; its infinite diversity is the result of God's blessing: " Increase and multiply, and fill the earth," (Gen. 1:28); " and from one man he has created the whole human race and made them live all over the face of the earth, determining their appointed times and the boundaries of their lands." (Acts 17:26)

At the same time mankind displays another unity besides the one intended by God, *viz.,* the unity in sin and its consequences, both in souls and in bodies, in death and in damnation; hence mankind is subject to the curse of vanity whereby all its worldly pomp, progress, knowledge, etc. does not secure peace and merit; nay, it suffers from a complete inability to escape death and damnation, and to reach its last end. Hear every creatures groaning, as it were (Cf. Rom. 8:22), with the longing for redemption, which nevertheless it cannot procure for itself.

2. Whence? The angel was sent from on high.

Look at *heaven:* its greatness, brightness, and eternity proclaim the glory of God; its relative desolation is the effect of sin, first that of the angels, and then that of our First Parents. True, the choirs of angels are singing the " Thrice Holy," but very many seats are empty; the consequences of sin reach up to heaven, and the glory due to God remains impaired.

Worship *God* " on the royal dais or throne of the Divine Majesty." (Sec. 106)

God's Trinity in Unity is the prototype of every created unity and variety; His whole unity and variety bears the moral character of holiness, which is peace within (in opposition to the strife among creatures), and glory without (in opposition to the depravity of creatures).

Hence the *divine decree of Redemption.*

It bears the same character of holiness, both to the end, which is the sanctification of fallen man, and to the means, all of which are most holy, and also to the reward to be gained, namely, glory and peace.

Reflect that God had at His disposal all the means for effecting the Redemption: the angels are obeying humbly, and ready to accept a mission; men, too, are ready; above all there is available the ineffable power of the Holy Spirit. Now God chooses, in order to obtain the most noble effect and to show more clearly His glory, the most abject human instruments: the *time,* " the fulness of time," when the whole human race had been corrupted, and the chosen people Israel was on the verge of civil and moral ruin; the *place,* a despised province, an unknown small town, and in this a lowly little cottage; the *persons,* a young virgin and a just man, poor and lowly.

II. *The Annunciation of the Incarnation.*

God now proceeds to raise on the foundation of humility the lofty structure of the Redemption.

This humility appears first in the angel who says: " Ave, Hail! " The angel is a heavenly being, higher and nearer to God than was Lucifer before his fall. As for the angel's ministry, he is serving, obeying, accepting a commission, acting as a messenger; he is sent not to another angel in heaven, but to a maiden on earth; not to a palace, but to a poor house; he carries out his mission swiftly, accurately, and joyfully. Ministering to God is the angel's end, happiness, and glory; this mission in particular brings joy and glory to himself, peace to mankind, and glory to God.

This humility appears secondly in Mary.

Admire the previous working of God in the Blessed Virgin. The words " full of grace " express the abundance of sanctifying grace and of every virtue; " the Lord is with thee " affirms her intimate union with God and His special protection; " blessed art thou among women " declares a very special blessing for the end of her sublime calling; finally, the words " she was troubled " reveal what is the foundation of all other graces, namely, the deepest humility, characterized by a promptness to do God's will not for one's own glory, but for His.

With the foundation thus laid bare, there is revealed also God's saving plan concerning the Blessed Virgin. Mary, gifted with these graces, is to become the Mother of the Savior: " Behold, thou shalt conceive in thy womb and shalt bring forth a son; and thou shalt call his name Jesus." (Luke 1:31) Mary is to become the Mother of God, the eternal Messianic King: " He shall be great, and shall be called the Son of the Most High; and the Lord God will give him the throne of David his father, and he shall be king over the house of Jacob forever; and of his kingdom there shall be no end." (Luke 1:32-33) Lastly, when the humble Virgin does not take pride in the promised exaltation, but sees only the difficulties of the offer: " How shall this happen, since I do not know man? " (Luke 1:34)—then the divine choice is declared most magnificently by the promise of the virginal conception by the Holy Spirit: " The Holy Spirit shall come upon thee and the power of the Most High shall overshadow thee; and therefore the Holy One to be born shall be called the Son of God." (Luke 1:35-36)

SECOND POINT: The Message of the Incarnation Is Confirmed.

I. The fact confirming this message is marked by humility, like everything else relating to this mystery.

There are two persons, both of them just, advanced in age, Zachary and Elizabeth, from whom one can hardly expect anything glorious. The husband is a priest of the Old Law, but because of loss of speech he is incapacitated, if not according to the letter, at least according to the spirit of the Mosaic law, and by its interpretation then in force. The wife is known to be barren, and therefore naturally disabled in the case. The sign referred to is indeed miraculous, but it is so little striking that after six months from its beginning it has not even become known among the relatives.

The fact is nevertheless perfectly suited to confirm the truth in question.

As a miracle it shows God's omnipotence, and more particularly omnipotence as regards the very laws of generation; if joined to the angel's words affirming this to be a sign, it is a certain sign of the God-Man's virginal conception.

II. The object of the confirmation is to show that " nothing shall be impossible with God " (Luke 1:37); therefore even the Incarnation of God is not impossible; this expression marks the Incarnation as being of all possibilities the one nearest to impossibility, in other words, as the very greatest of miracles. This mystery is referred to in Holy Scripture and the liturgy of the Church with words that express an altogether astounding miracle.

In the Incarnation the Son of God came down from heaven, leaving His court and throne; laying aside His royal dignity, He took the form of a servant. He, God, came to lead man back to God from whom he had fled. "The Word was made flesh" (John 1:14), uniting in Himself two limits farthest removed from each other. He "emptied himself" (Phil. 2:7), an expression denoting the incomprehensibility of the mystery of the Incarnation.

THIRD POINT: The Accomplishment of the Incarnation

I. "Behold the handmaid of the Lord." (Luke 1:38)

The highest motive to which the humble Virgin subordinates everything, and even the divine Motherhood, is God's service; this is really the immediate purpose of the whole creation, of Redemption, of the Incarnation of the Son of God, and of the choice of the Virgin. Neglect of this divine plan, initiated by Lucifer's rebellion, has brought all evil into the world; adherence to this plan restores glory to God and peace to men.

II. "Be it done to me according to thy word." (Luke 1:38)

When man serves God with perfect faithfulness, a divine light is communicated to his understanding, so that his thoughts coincide with those of God, and there is one "fiat," common to God and man. Divine power is imparted to the will, which is, in a sense, identified with the power of the Most High. Divine holiness is given to the soul by the indwelling of the Holy Spirit; there is brought about an intimate, personal union of God with man. There is formed in the Virgin's womb, through the overshadowing of the Holy Spirit, Christ, the Son of God.

III. " And the Word was made flesh." (John 1:14)

The " be it done " of the humble virgin is effective. The Holy Spirit, as high priest, anoints the Savior's humanity with the chrism of the divinity, and clothes it with the stole of grace and the crown of charity. Thus is achieved what had been said: " And behold, the house was filled with the glory of the Lord." (Ezechiel 43:5) Glory fills the humanity of Christ, anointed as the King of glory and Prince of peace; glory fills the Holy Spirit in the accomplishment of such a great mystery; the Eternal Father says: " This is my beloved Son," (Matt. 3:17) and the angels, with Gabriel at the head, are adoring and rejoicing.

Consider the first affections of the Sacred Heart of Jesus. " I am Thy servant, and the son of Thy handmaid." (Ps. 115) " Therefore in coming into the world, he says ' Sacrifice and oblations thou wouldst not, but a body thou hast fitted to me: In holocausts and sin-offerings thou hast had no pleasure. Then I said, Behold, I come—(in the head of the book it is written of me)—to do thy will, O God.' " (Hebr. 10:5-7)

Consider lastly how Christ begins to " dwell among us." He begins a life of lowliness in exile from heaven, shut up in the Virgin's womb; He will dwell with us during the whole of His mortal life, and dwell with us to the end of time in the Blessed Sacrament.

CHAPTER X

The Visitation of Our Lady to Elizabeth

Cf. Luke 1:39-56; *The Exercises*, Sec. 263

★

First Point. *When our Lady visited Elizabeth, St. John the Baptist in his mother's womb knew the visit of our Lady. " And it came to pass, when Elizabeth heard the greeting of Mary, that the babe in her womb leapt. And Elizabeth was filled with the Holy Spirit, and cried out with a loud voice, saying, ' Blessed art thou among women and blessed is the fruit of thy womb.' "* (Luke 1:41-42)

Second Point. *Our Lady chants the Magnificat, saying, " My soul magnifies the Lord."* (Luke 1:46)

Third Point. *Mary stayed with her about three months, and returned to her own home.*

First Point: Mary Comes to Elizabeth.

I. *Our Lady visits and salutes Elizabeth.*

1. Who is visiting?

Our Lady, the Mother of God, exalted above all in dignity, exceptional graces, and glory; in particular she is exalted above St. John and his mother: she who is higher visits those who are lower; in and through her, Jesus, the Incarnate Son of God, also visits them.

2. From what motive does Mary visit?

She is prompted by humility: it is the mark of humility to comply with the very least inspirations of God; a hint is given in the angel's words: " And behold, Elizabeth thy kinswoman also has conceived a son in her old age." (Luke 1:36) Humility readily acknowledges the effects of grace in others, and gladly renders service to others.

3. Under what circumstances does Mary visit?

" Now in those days Mary arose and went with haste into the hill country " (Luke 1:39): at once, on foot, like the poor, with only a small bundle.

II. St. John feels the visitation. There is remarkable efficacy in the humble Virgin's salutation:

It produces forthwith St. John's sanctification in the womb; it renders him conscious of the sanctification he received; it makes him miraculously leap up in the womb; it makes his mother share in the fulness of the Holy Spirit. Notice that all these many graces are occasioned by the single visit and greeting of the most humble Virgin; ultimately they proceed from the Word dwelling in her womb, in a state of deepest humility.

SECOND POINT: Mary Sings the Magnificat.

I. The humble Virgin does not glorify herself at so many graces shown; nay, she declares herself to be a humble handmaid; she refers all the glory to God, the fountainhead of all graces: " My soul magnifies the Lord; and my spirit rejoices in God, my Savior." (Luke 1:46)

II. In particular Mary extols the greatness of the grace received:

1. As to the persons to whom it extends.

The Virgin herself, (He hath done great things to me); the Chosen People, (He hath received Israel, His servant); the whole human race, (All generations).

2. As to the times to which it extends.

The present, (He hath done great things); the past, (as He spoke to our fathers); the future, (for behold from henceforth all generations shall call me blessed).

3. As to the nature of this grace; for it strikingly manifests:

a. God's Omnipotence: "He who is mighty has done great things to me."—Consider in this the distance to which God's power penetrates: from heaven to the lowest abyss of sin; see the enemies who are overthrown: sin, hell, death, and all the consequences of sin; reflect on the very work which is the close union between God and man: first the hypostatic union, implying the communication of the divine perfections; secondly, God's union with men. In duration this work has no end.

b. God's Holiness: "And holy is his name." Notice here the holiness bestowed, in view of the Savior, on the Virgin and St. John the Baptist. Here also is the source for all the holiness to come from Christ, from Christ as a child, from Christ as teacher, from Christ on the altar of the cross, from Christ as present in His Mystical Body, the Church. The sole purpose of this central event in human history is to enable all men to become holy, holy as the Holy One of Israel.

c. God's Mercy: "His mercy is from generation to generation on those who fear him." Reflect on the greatness of the misery that needed relief, the numbers of wretched people, the nobility of the restoration brought about, the purity of the motive.

III. Reflect that while all this eulogy of the benefits of the Incarnation proceeds directly from the pure and truthful lips of the Blessed Virgin, it comes ultimately from the Holy Spirit who inspires her and from the Word who rejoices with her.

THIRD POINT: After Staying with Elizabeth, Mary Returns.

Observe the conduct of genuine humility.

I. " Mary remained with her . . ."

She would constantly review in her mind the mysteries thus far disclosed to her and foster feelings of humility and gratitude. She perseveres in serving her cousin and performing low and humble services. Jesus remained there with her, inspiring these feelings and continually rewarding her with greater graces.

II. ". . . about three months."

It seems that shortly before the birth of the forerunner, when other women were at hand to help Elizabeth, Mary, in her humility, withdrew from the festive meetings and crowded conversations.

III. " She returned."

Without hurrying and without loitering; without greeting and gossiping on her way; she continues her contemplation of the same mysteries and makes acts of humility and gratitude; Jesus is journeying with her, and continually encouraging these dispositions of hers.

IV. " To her own house."

Not to other people's houses to tell what has happened, but to her own lonely, quiet modest house. Notice how carefully the Blessed Virgin avails herself of every help that modesty can offer, in order to preserve humility. Consider how Jesus takes the utmost delight in this modesty, calmness, and humility.

CHAPTER XI

The Birth of Christ Our Lord

Cf. Luke 2:1-14; *The Exercises*, Secs. 264 and 110 sqq.

★

WRITERS ON the *Exercises* not infrequently interpret the contemplation of the Nativity as intended solely to bring out the poverty of Christ. Poverty does indeed stand out in the gospel narrative, and St. Ignatius indicates it when he says: " to see and consider what they are doing . . . . that our Lord might be born in extreme poverty." (Sec. 116) Yet why does St. Ignatius insert the words: " They [Mary and Joseph] are going to Bethlehem to pay the tribute that Caesar imposed "? (Sec. 111) Those words are not part of the gospel account quoted. They must be taken along with matter added in the contemplation: " That our Lord might be born in extreme poverty, and that after many labors, after hunger, thirst, heat and cold, after insults and outrages, He might die on the cross " (Sec. 116) —in all this poverty alone is not indicated; there is much else. I should say, therefore, that in this exercise we are to meditate on the poverty of Christ at His birth, and also on His hardships and humiliations, and in particular on His subjection to men. Thus we find again an idea dear to St. Ignatius, the idea of poverty with its humiliations, among which St. Ignatius gives first place to obedience. For St. Ignatius this idea of poverty and obedience shows us the very food, livery and clothing of Christ, or, to leave meta-phors aside, Christ's inner humility is manifested by out-ward poverty and obedience. We have seen this Ignatian idea previously in the meditation on the Kingdom of Christ and we shall meet it again, particularly in The Two Standards. By our interpretation the present medita-tion is easily joined to the two preceding ones.

It may seem strange that in the third point of the cor-responding mystery (Cf. Sec. 264) St. Ignatius introduces the song of the angels, which really belongs to the mys-tery of the shepherds and not that of the Nativity. Apart from the consideration that the angels were doubtless pres-ent at the birth of our Savior and realized that this birth promised glory to God and peace to men, these words of the angels are an incomparable summary of the whole mystery of the Nativity, and bring into light the fact of the Incarnation now manifested by the Nativity. For this reason, it was fitting that the angels be introduced in this mystery, lest they be omitted altogether, since the mystery of the shepherds is not assigned to the first or second day of the second week, and is only mentioned after the twelfth day, where it is included among the mysteries which may be added for those who wish to prolong their retreat.

First Point. *Our Lady and her spouse Joseph go from Nazareth to Bethlehem. " Joseph also went from Galilee out of the town of Nazareth into Judea into the town of David, which is called Bethlehem . . . to register, together with Mary his espoused wife, who was with child."* (Luke 2:4-6)

Second Point. "*And she brought forth her firstborn son, and wrapped him in swaddling clothes, and laid him in a manger, because there was no room for them in the inn.*" (Luke 2:7)

Third Point. "*And suddenly there was with the angel a multitude of the heavenly host praising God and saying, 'Glory to God in the highest, and on earth peace among men of good will.'*" (Luke 2:13-14)

FIRST POINT: Events Before the Nativity

I. *They go to Bethlehem.*

1. Who are making the journey?

Our Lady, the Mother of God, exalted above all in dignity, graces, humility, and destined to be the highest of all creatures in glory. Her Spouse Joseph, the just man, whom God assigned as her guardian, who was honored by the angel's visit. "With Mary . . . who was with child." (Luke 2:5) Hence there is present also, in the Mother's womb, Jesus, the Word made Flesh.

2. How are they making the journey?

Jesus is a child in the Mother's womb, hidden in the state of deepest humility; He did not change the poor condition of His parents at the moment of His Incarnation, nor does He change it now with a view to His coming birth; He makes the journey to His birthplace attended by His poor parents, content with the circumstances of poor people, to make His entry into this world as the member of a poor family.

3. *Why* are they making the journey?

a. Joseph the son of David, chosen as the foster father of the Messiah, makes the journey to own subjection to Caesar; the noblest of David's descendants presents himself as one of the lowest of Caesar's subjects.

b. Christ also went to own subject to Caesar; He would be born not only as the son of Joseph but also as the subject of

Caesar; He begins His life with an act of obedience in keeping with the lowly condition He had assumed. Notice here that the authority of the one who gives the order is usurped, that the ordinance itself was extremely burdensome because of the long and tiring journey, and that it was very humiliating, since Joseph was of the house and family of David.

c. They make the journey in order that the Lord, as a result of this subjection to a man's rule, may be born in the greatest *poverty*, deprived even of the modest comforts of their own home at Nazareth.

II. *They arrive at Bethlehem,* and " there was no room for them in the inn." (Luke 2:7)

There was no home of their own; no room in the houses of the clansmen of David's family, no room in the travellers' inn.

There was no room *for them*: for the Son of God in any town in the world, for the Messiah in any town of Judea; no room could be found for the Son of David at Bethlehem, David's city! Neither for Him, nor for Mary and Joseph, the foremost in His Kingdom! The reason was their poor outward appearance.

But why was this poor exterior chosen? Because poverty, want, hardship, rejection, and obedience are the natural consequences and suitable outward display of the state of humility which the Redeemer had assumed in the Incarnation. As a result the Lord was to be born in the greatest poverty, and destitution of every kind.

SECOND POINT: Events at the Nativity.

I. *When* is Christ born? " It came to pass while they

were there, that the days for her to be delivered were fulfilled." (Luke 2:6)

The natural time for birth was completed. That this happened at a moment when they were in such wretched want was not due to chance; it was due to the loving providence of God.

The time is completed for the Coming for which the angels had been longing since the beginning of creation in order that the ruin in heaven might be repaired. The time is now come to realization, the time prayed for by the just on earth and in limbo, the time for which even irrational creation had been groaning (Rom. 8: 22), the time of which hell was mightily afraid.

II. *Who* is born?

The world lies in darkness of error, and there is born the *Light of the World*. The world lies in the death of sin, and there is born the *Life of the World*. The world lies overpowered in the captivity of the devil, and there is born the *King of the World*. He is also *King* of the *glory* to be given to God and to us; the *Prince* of the *peace* to be restored in the universe.

III. *How* is Christ born?

His dwelling: Our King's palace is a stable; His court consists of His Mother and Foster-father.

His food: Our King sees the light in the shape of a man, a servant, a babe; He is nourished first by the blood and then with the milk of His Mother, being altogether dependent on her.

His clothing: Mary wrapped Him up in swaddling

clothes; a few poor bands, yet withal most dear to the Redeemer, because they are His poor Mother's first gift. This is the King's apparel; with these ornaments does humility deck her followers.

His bed: Mary laid Him in a manger; it was a hard, uncomfortable couch, and one that was borrowed. This is the throne of the humble King.

IV. *Why* is Christ born like this?

" Because there was no room for them in the inn." (Luke 2:7) The inn would have provided better comfort. "That after many labors, after hunger, after thirst, heat, and cold, after insults and outrages, He might die on the cross, and all this for me." (Sec. 116)—"Being rich, He became poor for your sakes, that by his poverty you might become rich." (2 Cor. 8:9)—His poverty leads us on to spiritual poverty, His rejection to love of reproaches, and finally to humility: and if we possess this, we are rich indeed.

THIRD POINT: Events after the Nativity

Behold the heavenly witnesses, and reflect:

1. On their *number:* " a multitude."

2. On their *nobility:* " of the heavenly army."

By nature they are angels, angels too in glory; their knowledge embraces the divine plan of the Redemption; their experience is that of lookers-on, witnessing the world's history from its beginning; their kindness makes them men's friends; they obtained a lasting abode in heaven; their condition is that of soldiers, the army of the King of kings, of highest fame; they are most valiant, and able to overthrow the gates of hell; they will fight till the day of judgment, when they will appear along with the Judge, and demand an account of us, how much we have progressed in the teaching which the Redeemer imparts in this mystery.

3. Reflect on their *proclamation:*

a. " Glory to God in the highest." (Luke 2:14) The humility, poverty and obedience of God Incarnate restore God's glory, which had been violated by the pride of angels and of men. This glory includes also our glorification which is to be merited by a like humility: humility achieves glory; the lowering of oneself has its reward " in the highest "; poverty opens out the riches of heaven.

b. " And on earth peace among men of good will." (Luke 2: 14) The humility of God Incarnate is substantial peace between God and man. Consider the close union of both natures in Christ's person; the inward peace of the Sacred Heart of Jesus with God and with His own Self; and the peaceful disposition of this Sacred Heart towards men. He who has been constituted by God the Prince of peace, offers men His peace; the only condition laid down is good will, the will of following Him with His grace in His humility, which leads to peace.

CHAPTER XII

The Shepherds

Cf. Luke 2:8-21; *The Exercises*, Sec. 265

★

IN THIS mystery, as in the mystery of the Magi which is to follow, we can see a close relation to the meditation on the Kingdom of Christ. As Christ is King, the Magi seek the new-born King of the Jews, and the shepherds are sent to the Savior born in the city of David, the awaited King who would restore the Kingdom of Israel. St. Ignatius shows Christ the King " before whom is assembled the whole world." (Sec. 95, The Kingdom of Christ) The gospel shows Christ before whom are kings and shepherds, superiors and inferiors, Gentiles and Jews, rich and poor. The entire world is, in a manner, represented; indeed rightly so, for it is here a question of " good news of great joy which shall be to all the people." (Luke 2:10) ·Christ the King calls the world to Him. Through the appearance of a star the infant Christ calls the Magi; through the message of an angel He summons the shepherds. He calls each of us. These words can be compared to the matter stressed at the end of every point in the meditation on the Incarnation and the Nativity, and with the words: " I will reflect and draw some spiritual fruit from what I have seen." (Sec. 116) This reflection, made with the grace of God, and the resulting spiritual fruit may justly be regarded as a particular call to the retreatant. The shepherds are summoned to go and see; the Magi to adore; all are summoned to follow.

The words of the Kingdom of Christ: " that by following me in suffering, he may follow me in glory " (Sec. 95)
have no parallel clause in the mystery of the Magi, but
there is one in that of the shepherds, where the poverty of
the King is indicated by the sign of the swaddling clothes
and the manger; while glory is suggested by the brightness of the angelic messenger. Corresponding to the words:
" all persons who have judgment and reason will offer
themselves entirely for this work " (Sec. 96) is the adoration of the shepherds and the Magi. The same point is made
negatively by the different behavior of Herod, who lacks
judgment and reason. Again the " offerings of greater
value and of more importance " (Sec. 97) imitate the royal
presents of the Magi.

First Point. *The birth of Christ our Lord was made known to
the shepherds by the angel: " I bring you good news of great
joy . . . for today in the town of David a Savior has been born
to you, who is Christ the Lord."* (Luke 2:10-11)

Second Point. *The shepherds go to Bethlehem. "They went
with haste, and they found Mary and Joseph, and babe lying in
the manger."* (Luke 2:16)

Third Point. *" The shepherds returned, glorifying and praising God."* (Luke 2:20)

First Point: The Calling of the Shepherds

I. *The shepherds.*

They had been called to grace and redemption in Adam,
their First Parent; they had been called and chosen in
Abraham, the father of the chosen people; they had been
called by all the graces whereby God had so strongly and

gently instructed and drawn to Himself all their ancestors; they had been called by all the graces previously bestowed on them personally, among which are their poverty and lowly condition which helped to make them humble in spirit, and to give them the virtues based on humility: faith, hope, and charity; they were called, lastly, by the Incarnation and the Nativity, mysteries performed also on their behalf. This calling of theirs, begun so very long before, is about to be completed by the coming of the angel.

II. *The angel.*

1. *His person:* " The glory of God shone round about them." (Luke 2:9)

This brightness is an expression of the uncreated light of God who sends the heavenly messenger; it is an expression of the spiritual glory enjoyed by the angels, since the time when they faithfully followed the call of the Creator to His service; it is an expression of the glory that will some time be ours, if we follow the call of Christ; it is an expression of the spiritual light which enlightened the minds of the shepherds, so that they could easily understand and gladly follow God's call, conveyed through the angel.

This brightness " shone round about them," dispelling the darkness of night, and clearly showing to the mind the mysteries of God.

2. *His words:*

" Do not be afraid." (Luke 2:10) Fear and confusion must be removed before the divine call can be heard with fruit. Do not fear, I come as a brother, not as an adversary; as a messenger of the merciful Father, not as a servant of the avenging Judge.

" Behold, I bring you good news of great joy." (Luke 2:10) The angel introduces himself as a messenger of joy, of a great and universal joy.

" Today in the town of David a Savior has been born to you."
(Luke 2:11) The Savior of all from evil shall save us from sin and
its consequences; He shall lead to grace and glory, to eternal
salvation.

" Who is Christ the Lord." (Luke 2:11) He is therefore God,
the anointed one of the Holy Spirit, and He shall anoint us with
the same Spirit; the Messiah in whom all the prophecies are fulfilled; the King of eternal glory, yet humble and poor.

" Today in the town of David." (Luke 2:11) The shepherds
have not, then, to wait long, like the Patriarchs, nor to set out
on a long journey, like the Magi.

" And this shall be a sign to you: you will find an infant
wrapped in swaddling clothes and lying in a manger." (Luke 2:12)
They will find no powerful monarch, but a weak little Babe, yet
lovely and yearning to receive them. He is clothed in no garments of state, but in poor clothes. He is cast out, poor, without
the comforts of life; this sign expresses the nature of His Kingdom; all that are to follow Him must accept its humility, poverty, and self-denial.

All these words give to the shepherds the *call to go and see*.

SECOND POINT: The Coming of the Shepherds

I. *Jesus.*

His *person:* He is the Lord, the Christ, the King.

His *heart:* He is calling all that labor and are burdened,
distributing all interior and exterior graces, rewarding co-
operation with each grace by yet another greater grace;
aiming at this alone, to bring us into His Kingdom, and
make us partakers of life eternal.

His *court:* It consists of Mary and Joseph, adoring the
infant King, and praying that His Kingdom may come.

II. *The shepherds.*

1. Consider their *co-operation* with the divine call.

They go to Bethlehem. They consent at once to the call by a resolution of their will, without any wavering, setting aside everything else: " Let us go over," say they, " and let us see! " (Cf. Luke 2:15) They are faithfully carrying out their good resolution: " They went with haste." (Luke 2:16) The further they advance in obedience to the divine will the more grace is working in their hearts, increasing their faith, hope, and charity.

2. Consider *the fruit* of their co-operation with the divine call.

" And they found Mary and Joseph, and the babe ": the holy persons themselves; " the babe lying in the manger " (Luke 2: 16): they recognize Him by the sign of lowliness and poverty. Enlightened by inner grace, they understood more fully who this Child was, King and Savior, God and Man, Light and Life; who Mary and Joseph were, the first members of His Kingdom; what were their own (the shepherds') place, duty, and expectation. Hence their hearts were kindled with ardent love for the Babe, so as to embrace with all their heart Him and His humility, offering themselves wholly for His service.

THIRD POINT: The Shepherds' Return

I. The *shepherds* returned.

In joy and peace they relish a foretaste of the eternal happiness of Christ's Kingdom, and they go back with a new spirit to their former way of life. Consider how their life was not changed materially, but now, being inspired by a higher motive, its excellence was increased in the eyes of God.

" Glorifying and praising God for all that they had heard and seen." (Luke 2:20)

Sincere love cannot be restrained within, it manifests itself without. Having faithfully co-operated with the first grace, they receive forthwith another grace: from the fulness of the affection of their hearts, from love for the infant King, and from the desire to spread His love, from eagerness to make their neighbors share in their own joy, they become the first heralds of the infant King: thus they foreshadow the *state of the apostolic life*.

II. " But *Mary* kept in mind all these things, pondering them in her heart." (Luke 2:20)

1. The Virgin Mother, in view of her womanhood, and in order to forestall honor, observes silence.

2. In affectionate meditation she pondered what had taken place. Her example may have prompted Ignatius to pen the words: " As soon as I awake, I . . . will . . . call to mind frequently the mysteries of the life of Christ our Lord from the Incarnation to the place or mystery I am now contemplating." (Sec. 130)

3. Consider the heart of the Blessed Virgin as a treasury of divine love, where all God's favors, gathered from the consideration of the life of Christ, are stored up, guarded, and reviewed; thus they wonderfully dispose the soul further to receive other graces of the divine calling; thereby the Blessed Virgin becomes the model for the soul that is preparing, by diligent consideration of Christ's life, for a solid and firm choice of a state in life.

III. *Jesus* by His divine grace initiates, fosters and directs all this process of the divine calling in the souls both of the Blessed Virgin and of the shepherds.

CHAPTER XIII

The Circumcision

Cf. Luke 2:21; *The Exercises*, Sec. 266

★

In the third point St. Ignatius lays stress on the shedding of Christ's blood. We may contemplate in the first point also how the Child suffers by the shedding of His blood, and in the second point how He is for us *Jesus*, the Savior by blood. Here is already intimated the goal at which our Lord intends to aim, namely the practice of humility, poverty and obedience, ending finally in the shedding of His blood.

First Point. *They circumcised the Child Jesus.*

Second Point. "*His name was called Jesus, the name given him by the angel before he was conceived in the womb.*" (Luke 2:21)

Third Point. *They returned the Child to His Mother, who felt compassion for Him because of the blood He shed.*

First Point: The Child Is Circumcised.

I. *Circumcision is the sign of the Covenant.* Through circumcision a man shared in the election and graces of the Covenant; but at the same time he became subject to the Law of the Covenant.

1. By the Incarnation the Son of God became God's servant, and the son of His parents; by His birth He became the subject of Caesar, and by His circumcision He becomes a subject of the

Law. He takes on Himself all the *obedience* which the Father decreed that He should take. He faithfully kept, throughout His life, the obedience to the Law taken on Himself in the circumcision.

2. To be subject to the Law is not only a duty, it is also a favor, for which it is fair that man should pay a price. *Blood* is the price of circumcision. Learn the excellence of every obedience which God demands of you either by precept or by counsel; if necessary, pay for it cheerfully, at the cost of riches, honors, comforts, and even blood.

3. Christ was circumcised *on the eighth day* of His life: do not, then, put off becoming subject to the law of God.

II. *Jesus is circumcised.* He is a new-born child, and therefore delicate, lovely, and innocent; He is our King, whom we have sworn to follow; He is our God.

1. Consider in this Christ's human nature united with the divine nature: hence His *humanity* as a whole and in all its parts has been elevated, made holy, adorable, and capable of infinite merit; it is the paradise in the whole of God's creation.

2. In this human nature consider the *Sacred Heart,* as a spring which distributes the streams of life all over this paradise, and imparts infinite fertility to each and every action.

3. Consider lastly in the Sacred Heart the *Sacred Blood:* it is infinitely precious because of its dignity, and its various and excellent powers:—to wash (Apoc. 1:5) and cleanse (Hebr. 9:14; 1 John 1:7) the spiritual stains of the soul;—to make peace (Col. 1:20) between God and man, if that Blood is offered to God as a sacrifice; to bring peace to man, distraught by sin, if drunk in the Holy Eucharist: and, with individual persons at peace, to make peace among all, " whether on the

earth or in the heaven " (Col. 1:20)—to sanctify (Hebr. 13:12) and give life (John 6) to others.

III. *The first-fruits of the Blood of Jesus.* The promises are the greatest of the graces of the Law. Jesus was to fulfil the promises of the Law; He was to pay as price all His Blood; the Blood of the circumcision is the first-fruits of the Savior's Blood, which will be shed for the salvation of all men. Why so?

1. Because it is a law laid down by the Father: " Without the shedding of blood there is no forgiveness." (Hebr. 9:22) The Father had decreed from eternity to accept the most precious Blood of His Son as the price for the ransom of the world.

2. Because the Son, on coming into the world, had written this law into His Heart; in obedience to this law He resolved to humble Himself, to become obedient, to undergo suffering even unto blood and death; to empty Himself even to the shedding of His Blood and the giving up of His Life.

3. By thus submitting to the law of mortification, which is shown in the circumcision, He sanctions and promulgates the same law forever as the fundamental law of salvation, to be kept by all who would follow Him, and be clothed in the same garment as His.

SECOND POINT: Giving the Name Jesus

I. *His name was called Jesus.*

Previously He had already the name " the Son of God " (Luke 1:35), fully expressing His divine nature and person. Now He takes a new name, corresponding to the call which the Father gave Him to fulfil in His human nature, the name Jesus: He shall be the Savior of *all*; the Savior from *all evil,* from sin and all its consequences; He shall be *wholly* Savior, giving His very lifeblood for the salvation of His brethren. He receives this name on the score of His cross: " he humbled himself, becoming obedient to death, even to death on a cross. Therefore God also has exalted him and has bestowed upon him the name that is above every name, so that at the name of Jesus every knee should bend of those in heaven, on earth and under the earth." (Phil. 2:8-10) He takes possession of it in the circumcision, giving as it were the earnest-money of His Blood.

II. " The name given him by the angel." (Luke 2:21) Consider the qualities of that name.

1. *Holiness.*—It comes from God to whom the angels sing " Holy, Holy, Holy "; it comes to earth through the holy angel; it is given to the most holy person, and it is destined for the holiness of the world.

2. *Sweetness.*—It sums up in itself the Blessed Trinity's saving decree and all its execution.

3. *Power.*—It is the watchword of angels and of fallen man in putting to flight the wicked spirits, and there is attached to it the promise of divine help.

III. *Before He was conceived in the womb.*

This name, then, had been decreed *from eternity,* since God has loved us with everlasting love (cf. Jerem. 31:3); it is *for eternity,* since all salvation will for ever come from this Jesus; it is a *unique* name, " Neither is there salvation in any other. For there is no other name under heaven given to men by which we must be saved." (Acts, 4:12) —He who bears this name had to be conceived in the womb, to be born and circumcised as a child, and to die on the cross; for so it had been laid down by the Law, before He was conceived in the womb. The same Law also awaits us.

THIRD POINT: The Child Is Restored to His Mother.

I. *They gave back the Child to His Mother.*

" They gave back "; for the Child, His heart and blood, belongs truly to His Mother, to His brethren, to ourselves: " For a child is born to us, and a son is given to us." (Is. 9:6)—They give Him back, after He has been marked by the wound and the name, to be nursed and reared for the cross.

They give Him back " to His Mother." The Child carries the cross with Him to the parents' house; at the same time He becomes for them Jesus, their Savior, by the cross. While He Himself is living with Mary and Joseph, preparing Himself for the cross, they and His brethren must share the same life: there is no relationship with Jesus and Mary, there is no salvation, unless we profess with them the cross; indeed, to all extends and in the hearts of all must be written the Father's Law: " Without the shedding of blood there is no forgiveness." (Hebr. 9:22)

II. *Who had compassion for the blood which came from her Son.*

1. Reflect here on the Virgin's sorrow: for the suffering of her Son in the circumcision; for His future sufferings of which the

present one is a foretaste. This sorrow of Mary is also a sign that more sorrow will come to her.

2. Reflect on the Virgin's *solace:* Mary receives consolation from the name given to her Son; she was the first to experience its power, its sweetness, and its holiness.

3. In the cross of Jesus linked with the consolation of Jesus consists our whole and only happiness on earth.

CHAPTER XIV

The Three Magi

Cf. Matthew 2:1-12; *The Exercises*, Sec. 267

★

First Point. *The Three Kings, Magi, guided by the star came to adore Jesus saying, " we have seen his star in the East and have come to worship him."* (Matt. 2:2)

Second Point. *They adore Him and offer Him gifts, " and falling down they worshipped him . . . and offered him gifts of gold, frankincense and myrrh."* (Matt. 2:11)

Third Point. *" And being warned in a dream not to return to Herod, they went back to their own country by another way."* (Matt. 2:12)

First Point: The Magi Are Called and Come.

I. *The Magi.*

1. Consider their calling. It began with our First Parents, was continued by primitive revelation, in particular by the promise of the Messiah and His future star. This calling was promoted by the knowledge of astronomy which had been cultivated for so many years in the country of the Magi; it was completed by the appearance of the star, joined to an inner inspiration of the Holy Spirit.

2. The object of the calling. It was *difficult* because of the journey's length, because of the high state in life of those called, distinguished as they were among their countrymen by learning and rank, because of its very nature, since they were ordered to come to the King of another nation, and to adore

Him as a mark of subjection. At the same time the calling was *honorable*, since it meant finding God the Savior, and adoring the King of all, pointed out by God Himself.

3. See the Magi's *co-operation* with the calling: They come from their country in the East, through the inhospitable desert, to Judea, a foreign land, to Jerusalem, a city full of curious crowds, right into the court of Herod, an ambitious, suspicious, and cruel king, and finally to the lowly stable near Bethlehem. Their good will is constantly helped by God who leads them at first by the knowledge they had of the way, then by the information of the inhabitants, by the solemn and unanimous answer of the priests, by the very wiles of Herod, and again by the new appearance of the star. All the while God inspired them with perseverance, trust, peace and great joy.

II. *Herod and the Jews.*

1. The progress of their calling. It had been prepared by all the previous revelations, both primitive and Mosaic, by accurate knowledge of the Scripture telling them how to recognize the Messiah and esteem the benefits of His Kingdom. Their calling was being completed by the ministry of the star and the Magi.

Nevertheless their hearts were caught in the nets and captured by the chains of pride, Herod's heart burning with ambition to command, and the hearts of the Jews slavishly adhering to a false interpretation of the Law.

2. The object of their calling. It was the King of the Jews who called them; their lawful King, both by His descent from David, and by the indication of God, when the Romans were already threatening to overthrow their nation; the King of the whole world, and for this reason He would be the glory of His people Israel; the King of all ages, the Life and Resurrection of His own; the Savior King, who would deliver from

every evil, and give every good thing. It was their duty to come to Him, and their duty to adore Him.

3. See, lastly, the *neglect of this calling.*—On perceiving the divine call, all the Jews are troubled, especially their priests; but they do nothing and welcome not God's call. Thus they sin by great ingratitude against God, who gives them His only-begotten Son; by their neglect they grievously offend the Messiah, their King and their God; they expose themselves to the danger of losing all the promises, and of losing even their salvation; they give grievous scandal to the Magi who are not Jews; and the priests are, moreover, giving scandal to the Jewish people. Contrast their neglect with the obedience of the irrational star and of the non-Jewish Wise Men.

As for *Herod*, he opposes the divine call; he resolves to destroy the King Messiah: thereby he renounces for himself all the benefits of the Redemption; he tries to make void the whole plan formed by God for the salvation of the world! Herod imagines that by cunning and deceit he can delude God Himself.

SECOND POINT: The Magi Adore and Offer Gifts.

I. *Jesus.*

The Child in the manger is the new-born King of the Jews; all the divine promises and the very choice of the Jewish people pointed to Him; therefore He is their sovereign good and greatest benefactor; He is Emmanuel, God-with-us, the Wonderful, the Prince of peace, the Light, Life, and Savior of the world. Although He lies in the manger, He is guiding the star and directing every creature for the salvation of the elect; through His inspirations He appeals to the hearts of the Magi, Herod and the Jews. Yet, at the same time, the Child is poor, humble and subject to many discomforts.

II. *The Magi.*

1. " Falling down, they worshipped him." (Matt. 2:11)

—They *find* in a poor house a poor Child, with Mary and Joseph who are poor; but by the witness of the star they believe that this is the King of the Jews. They *are enlightened* so that they know the eternity and universality of His Kingdom, the divinity of His person with His infinite loveliness, and the dignity of His Mother and Foster-father.

With their body the Wise Men *fall down* before the Child; with their mind they *acknowledge* His superiority over them; the King of kings is above their kingship, God above man; with their heart they break forth into most ardent acts of adoration, love, and self-oblation.

2. " Opening their treasures they offered him gifts." (Matt. 2:11)

They offer *gifts* in recognition of His Lordship, as a proof of their love, and as a pledge of their perfect submission. Theirs are *precious* gifts, taken from their treasures to show the intensity of their faith, love, and submission by the very price and nature of the offerings: *love* is the purest *gold,* consecrating to God all the affections of the heart, and the whole life; love is the choicest *frankincense,* whereby man's whole life is made a whole burnt-offering, offered in honor of God; love is the strongest *myrrh,* keeping away all corruption of sin.

THIRD POINT: The Return of the Magi

I. *Herod.*

The crafty king plans a snare that is all but impenetrable to human shrewdness: he asks to be informed by those whom he had given accurate information; he pretends to have the intention of adoring the Child, whereas he is scheming the ruin of the Magi; he sends them unguarded to Bethlehem to have them the more surely come back to him; on their bringing the wanted information, death is ready for them, because they professed such sincere devotion for the new-born King. Herod has all human means at his disposal: cunning, dissimulation, cruelty, power, wealth, and experience in schemes of this kind.

II. *The Magi.*

The Wise Men neither suspect nor fear anything; even if they had a suspicion, they were nevertheless helpless. They experience the greatest joy as they visit the Child day after day, and converse intimately with Mary and Joseph. Mary, who had kept all words, pondering them in her heart, now communicates all to the Wise Men, pouring it out from her heart into theirs, and so increasing their love and devotion.

III. *Jesus.*

The Divine Child knows Herod's deceits and snares, and permits them to have their day; the Child also knows the devotion of the Magi, and is determined to free them in due time from all danger. He finally avoids the shrewd plans of Herod by a supernatural intervention, a dream; Herod had never thought of that! However, the intervention is not sensational, and expresses better the Savior's humility; in this manner, too, the shrewd devices of Herod are the more utterly put to shame. Jesus protects the Wise Men on their whole journey; He prevents their being found out; He fills them with joy, and draws them ever closer to Himself.

CHAPTER XV

The Purification of Our Lady and the Presentation of the Child Jesus

Cf. Luke 2:22-39; *The Exercises*, Sec. 268

★

First Point. *They take the Child Jesus to the temple to be offered as the first-born to the Lord, and they offer for Him " a pair of turtledoves or two young pigeons."* (Luke 2:24)

Second Point. *Coming into the temple, Simeon received Him into his arms saying, " Now thou dost dismiss thy servant, O Lord, according to thy word, in peace."* (Luke 2:29)

Third Point. *Anna came " up at that very hour, . . . and began to give praise to the Lord, and spoke of him to all who were awaiting the redemption of Jerusalem."* (Luke 2:38)

FIRST POINT: The Presentation of the Child

I. *They take the Child Jesus to the temple.*

1. They bring Jesus.

Jesus is the true *gold*. His humanity is gilt with the gold of the divinity; in particular He is gold as regards His Sacred Heart which is purest gold through its holy affections and actions, also as regards the most precious blood which exceeds the value of every created good.

Jesus is true *frankincense* of the sweetest odor before God, suited in the highest degree to be presented as an offering to God.

Jesus is the true *myrrh;* for He is the Savior, the antidote against all corruption of sin through His grace, through the example of His humility, poverty, and cross: by these alone is sin overcome through the sacramental reception of His body and blood.

2. *To the temple.*

It is the temple spoken of by Malachias (3:1): " Presently the Lord whom you seek, and the angel of the testament whom you desire, shall come to His temple."—The temple really belongs to this Child, as the son and heir of David and Solomon who first erected the temple; as the true high priest, and as God.

3. They bring the *Child.*

They carry their treasure in an earthern vessel, since He is a weak helpless Child, who must be brought, who cannot present Himself, but needs to be presented, who cannot offer Himself, but needs others to offer Him.

II. *To be offered as the first-born to the Lord.*

Consider the priests and levites in the temple, solemnly performing the ceremonies and sacrifices: they were chosen instead of the first-born to serve the Lord for them. They ignore the Child and the poor parents standing there with the modest offering of two young pigeons, keeping them waiting a long time while they attend to the rich.

Consider, moreover, the invisible majesty of God, filling the temple; consider the Holy Spirit and the choirs of angels who sing: " Lift up your gates, O ye princes and be ye lifted up, O eternal gates: and the King of glory shall enter in." (Ps. 23) This is the spiritual ornament of the temple, and the levites and priests are blind to it.

The Father declares that He will no longer accept the victims substituted by the levites: " To what purpose do you offer me the multitude of your goods, saith the Lord. I am full . . ." (Is. 1:11) "I have no pleasure in you, saith the Lord of hosts: and I will not receive a gift of your hand." (Mal. 1:10)

The Savior offers Himself ready to take the place of these victims: "Therefore in coming into the world he says, 'Sacrifice and oblation thou wouldst not, but a body thou has fitted to me.'" (Hebr. 10:5) "And the Lord smelled a sweet odour." (Gen. 8:2) The Father accepts the Son's offer, and embraces Him in the Holy Spirit, who is the mutual love of the Father and the Son. "Come, O Sanctifier, Almighty, Eternal God, and bless the sacrifice prepared for Thy holy Name!" (*Missale Romanum*) In this embrace of the Father and of the Son and of the Holy Spirit there is included the Son's humanity, and in this the whole human race, we also.

III. *And they offer for Him "a pair of turtledoves or two young pigeons."* (Luke 2:24)

They who offer are Mary and Joseph, poor people, of no account in the opinion of men; they do not offer directly with their own hands, but through the hands of the priests, legalistically more holy and exalted above them by a special calling from God.

They offer "*according to the custom of the Law.*" The sacred text stresses this altogether five times: (Luke 2:22, 23, 24, 27, 39) He submits to the Law of God who is the servant of God, and the Son of God's handmaid; He submits to God in particular in the sacrifices which prefigure that of the cross; He submits to God not merely in general, but in every detail: all things are accomplished according to the Law of the Lord, all is done, so to say, according to the rubrics of the Old Testament.

" *A pair of turtledoves or two young pigeons.*" This was the usual offering of the poor. Hear the bleating of the lambs offered there for other, richer children, who are, in men's opinion, of greater importance.

They offer " *for Him* "—not to Him who has one nature with God—for His divinity is in under His humanity; " *for Him,*" on account of Him and of His birth. One pigeon is offered for sin, as if His birth had defiled the Mother, whereas " He bears our iniquities " (Is. 53:11); the other pigeon is offered as a holocaust, in acknowledgement of God's *complete lordship* over Him, in particular as far as He is destined to be a victim; " *for Him,*" in His place: thus all the sacrifices of the Old Testament were for Him, they prefigured His sacrifice, and derived their worth from His sacrifice; in the end He will be sacrificed Himself as a holocaust for sin.

Second Point: Simeon Prophesies.

I. *Simeon's person.*

This man was just and devout; these words express above all the outward appearance of sanctity.

". . . *looking for the consolation of Israel* " (Luke 2: 25); this denotes the inward cause of the justice observed for such a length of years; it was the root and motive of the outward sanctity. With most ardent prayers he kept imploring God for the consolation of Israel, the coming of the Savior; and he kept practicing justice, that he might one day enjoy this consolation. (Luke 2:25)

" *And the Holy Spirit was upon him.*" (Luke 2:25)
The Holy Spirit was the first and chief cause of such holy
conduct, and withal its fruit and reward. Consider how the
Holy Spirit seeks to lead the elect to Jesus, by exciting in
their hearts a longing after Him, and by cherishing it with
His promise; then, at the time decreed by the Father, He
brings them to Jesus.

II. *Simeon's actions.*

1. " *And he came by inspiration of the Spirit* " (Luke 2:27)
It is the place of prayer where God's servants pay the tribute of
adoration to the Sovereign Lord; it is the place for making sacrifice; it is the place for being heard by God: as such it is described
at length by Solomon at the solemnity of the first consecration:
" That Thou mayest hearken to the prayer which Thy servant
prayeth in this place to Thee." (3 Kings 8:19)

2. " *He also received him into his arms.*" (Luke 2:28) Guided
by the Holy Spirit Simeon beheld the Child; by the light and
inspirations of the Spirit he also recognized, amid so great poverty,
lowliness, and destitution, the *King*, the ' Salvation ' of the world,
' the light to the revelation of the Gentiles,' ' the glory of Israel,'
God's people; and the same will also be our only consolation and
peace. With all his heart Simeon is lavishing on the Child the
gold of glory, the incense of adoration, and the myrrh of self-
oblation; he embraced the Child: we cannot embrace Christ unless we embrace at the same time His poverty, humiliation, im-
molation, and cross.

III. *Simeon's words.*

1. " *Now thou dost dismiss thy servant, O Lord, according to
thy word in peace; because my eyes have seen thy salvation.*"
(Luke 2:29)

Simeon receives the Savior and Victim only to fold Him in his arms; yet he enjoys the most complete granting of his desire; he no longer wishes for any earthly thing; he dreads nothing, not even the terrors of death; he partakes of the consolation and peace promised at the Savior's Nativity.—We must likewise embrace Christ's poverty and humility not in order to pass on to other things, but to find in this all our consolation.

2. *And he said to Mary*, Christ's Mother: " Behold, this child is destined for the fall and for the rise of many in Israel, and for a sign that shall be contradicted. And thy own soul a sword shall pierce, that the thoughts of many hearts may be revealed." (Luke 2:34-35)

Simeon foresees the mystery of Christ's Passion, and he foretells Mary's co-passion; she will live and see the time of the Passion. Inspired by the Holy Spirit Simeon addresses the Mother in the Temple so that she may be less oppressed by grief when seeing her Son on the cross. The Passion is declared to be quite certain: The Child is set for a sign. Simeon stresses, not the exterior tortures of the Passion foreshown in the blood of the circumcision, but the sorrow of the heart which does not so much strike the imagination. This sorrow will be great, he declares, through Passion in the Son, and through co-passion in the Mother. The cause of the sorrow is declared to be the contradiction or enmity of many; and this will also bring about their fall.

THIRD POINT: Anna Confesses.

I. *Her person.*

Anna had prepared herself " *with fasting and prayers, worshipping night and day* "; and " *she never left the temple.*" (Luke 2:37) Her prayer was continuous, and it had lasted now over half a century: she first set about this work in the fervor of youth, then she continued it in the vigor of ripe age, and she did not leave off in the weakness of old age; all this time she was waiting and praying for the redemption and the consolation of Israel; nor did she think she was doing too much to obtain so great a boon.

II. *Her actions.*

"*Coming up at that very hour.*" (Luke 2:38)

Anna, who always remained in the Temple, does not seem to have been specially brought there now, by the Holy Spirit; but while Simeon prophesied amid the admiration of the crowd, Anna also joined them. It seems she did not take Jesus into her arms, but only saw Him: enlightened by the Holy Spirit, she recognized Him, and the sight alone filled her with consolation.

III. *Her words.*

1. "*She began to give praise to the Lord.*" (Luke 2:38) Anna began to magnify the Lord because He had granted her the sight of the Redeemer, because He had shown to her the mystery of His humiliation, because He had led her to the Redeemer by the ever so rough road of penance and prayer, because He had shown such mercy to her and the human race, giving eternal rewards for temporal crosses, an immense weight of glory for slight tribulation, and for assigning His only-begotten Son as a companion in every trial.

2. "*And she spoke of him to all who were awaiting the redemption of Jerusalem.*" (Luke 2:38)

True love of God and Christ inspires apostolic feelings. Not all are led directly by the Holy Spirit to Jesus like Simeon; the majority are guided by the ministry of other men, and the practical judgment of reason. This apostleship, too, is marked with the seal of the cross, since its instruments are means in the eyes of the world, and its chief object is the humility of Christ's cross. In the hearers there must be some sort of disposition, some good will, a sincere expectation of the blessings of the Redemption.

CHAPTER XVI

The Flight into Egypt

Cf. Matthew 2:13-38; *The Exercises*, Sec. 269

★

WHEN PRESCRIBING this contemplation for the second day of the second week, St. Ignatius calls it " the Flight into Exile in Egypt." (Sec. 132) These words indicate one reason why, as viewed by St. Ignatius, the angel's order must have been very hard for St. Joseph. The mysteries of the Flight and the Return both give us a striking example of obedience. As previously stated the mysteries from the Incarnation to the Return from Egypt are a preparation for the choice. The practical teaching of these mysteries, from this point of view, is this: the basis of all salvation and holiness is humility and obedience. True interior humility prefers the exterior apparel of poverty. Humility and obedience must be embraced, not halfheartedly, but completely, and the test of such a complete embrace is obedience. Here we have the core of solid perfection, demanded by St. Ignatius and expressed by him in the Constitutions.

First Point. *Herod wished to kill the Child Jesus and so killed the Innocents, but before their death the angel warned Joseph that he should flee: " Arise, and take the child and his mother, and flee into Egypt."* (Matt. 2:13)

Second Point. *He withdrew into Egypt: " So he arose . . . by night, and withdrew into Egypt."* (Matt. 2:14)

Third Point. He "*remained there until the death of Herod.*"
(Matt. 2:14)

FIRST POINT: St. Joseph Is Told to Flee.

I. *Herod shows the disorder of a will opposed to the will of God.*

1. Herod's *character*.

He was a man of quite unusual natural gifts: shrewd, brave, wealthy, raised to the highest position, excelling among contemporary princes in state-craft. By very many graces (reviewed already in the mystery of the Magi) he has been prepared to follow the call of Christ, the eternal King. Nevertheless he is completely the slave of *pride;* he is unwilling to humble himself and obey the law of God; he does not want to have the Messiah as King, and he is not waiting for the " consolation of Israel."

2. Herod's *actions*.

a. From pride follows disorder in the pursuit of a definite goal. Herod wanted to kill the Child Jesus—Herod, a king whose duty it was to defend right and innocence and to hinder others from murder, now planned murder himself. He was not carried away by sudden rage, but deliberately drew up his plan of action. It is a question of destroying a child, an innocent one who cannot come to his own defense, who cannot possibly give any offence by action. This Child is Jesus, the Redeemer of Herod and of all men.

b. From pride follows further disorder in the choice of *means:* Herod decides to kill all children under two years of age. The destruction of Jesus is intended as a means to add strength to Herod's temporal rule; yet the slaughter is superfluous, since the temporal rule of Herod is not at all in danger. The murder of the Innocents, in Herod's eyes, is an infallible means of destroying Jesus; yet it fails in achieving this. However much Herod excels in cunning and talent, ambition blinds him in every plan. He heeds not God who is, of course, able to evade all the plans of the tyrant.

c. By pride Herod is led to all other *vices*: to direct rebellion against the divine decree of Redemption, the greatest crime against religion, the worst wrong against the neighbor through the attempt to kill the Redeemer of all, the greatest injustice, cruelty, neglect of a King's duties in slaying so many innocent children, falsehood and hypocrisy as regards the Magi etc. . . .

II. *The holy Innocents show us the example of a will resigned to divine Providence without its free choice.*

God allows persecutions, even hard ones, also that of the Innocents, who are not in a position to foresee or avoid them. God uses those persecutions for sanctifying and glorifying the Innocents. For nearly two thousand years these infants have been enjoying the vision of God, and they are honored with special devotion by the Church.

III. *The Holy Family show us the example of a will conforming freely and fully to the divine Will.*

1. God allows persecutions, also those of His own Son, and those, too, of a most serious kind; therefore we as well must expect adversity. God knows how to save His Son from persecution; therefore He will save us as well. God rescues His Son for the time being, only to give Him up, later on, to the cross, therefore we too must not, here on earth, look for complete immunity from persecution, but we must know that we are reserved for the cross.

2. God saves His Son by using the means suited for the weak, namely by *obedience*.

a. The *object of obedience*: " Flee! " This is the way to safety apparently unworthy of God, and much opposed to human vanity. " Into Egypt ": a far distant country, and a hard journey, a foreign land, as it were an exile; it was always to be an exile, never a home, and therefore a hard order.—" Take the child and his mother ": both are delicate, and so it is apparently a cruel order.—" Arise ": at once, no time being allowed to procure the necessaries for the journey. " Remain there until I tell thee ": for an indefinite time, and so apparently an order contrary to human prudence.

b. The *price of obedience*: Through obedience man submits to God the most noble part of himself, his will, and with it all other things: man makes himself truly and fully God's servant; he also makes himself a victim, keeping nothing at all for himself; his intellect is conformed to the highest truth, his will is subordinated to the highest goodness, his efforts are assisted by the power of God, and a very special Providence. By obedience God is glorified more than by miracles, and most of all the obedience of the most holy of all persons, Jesus, Mary, and Joseph.

Second Point: Joseph's Flight to Egypt

I. *Who obeys?*

Joseph, the " just man ": there is no true holiness without obedience; Mary, the Mother of God: no dignity exempts from obedience; Jesus, the God-Man: it is the part of created nature to obey.

II. *Whom do they obey?*

St. Joseph obeys the angel as the interpreter of the divine will; Jesus and Mary obey Joseph as the natural head of the family: in both instances the Holy Family obey God.

III. *How do they obey?*

" He arose, and took the child and his mother by night, and withdrew into Egypt." (Matt. 2:14)—St. Joseph " arose," giving up his own rest; " by night," not waiting for daylight, and not staying to think the matter over. " Into Egypt ": besides the goal of the journey, hardly anything else is indicated, neither the dangers, nor the requisites: human prudence and precautions are given up. " He took the child and his mother ": St. Joseph sacrifices his sensitive affection for the holy Persons. " He withdrew ": sacrificing his love for the Holy Land.—St. Joseph is doing all this without complaining exteriorly or interiorly; he is doing so, according to the words, as the order was given; and he complies at once, without any delay.

In every point Mary was submitting herself with equal perfection to the divine Will, which came to her no longer through the angel, but through St. Joseph.

Jesus inspires with His grace the obedience of Mary and Joseph, and He confirms it by the selfsame obedience of His Heart.

IV. *The fruit of their obedience.*

1. The first fruit of their obedience is *glory for God.*

God is glorified by the fact that He all alone, without the help of man's wisdom, and by the unseemly means of the flight, sets at naught Herod's snares, provides for the Redemption of the world, and upholds the order laid down by Himself; by the fact that in obeying this command these three most perfect wills are sacrificed to God in such a perfect manner.—Notice here the glory and inward good pleasure of the Blessed Trinity: " And the Lord smelled a sweet savour." (Gen. 8:21) Notice the external glory from all the angels who witnessed that surrender, and the glory from all the elect who would, at some future time, consider it. This glory is far more excellent than that which was then derived, or could ever be derived, from all the victims of the Jewish temple; it made reparation to God for the glory which had been violated by the sin of the angels, and by the offenses of Adam and his descendants.

2. The second fruit of their obedience is *peace for men*.

The Holy Family enjoy, during this flight, the deepest peace. They trust that they will be defended from the dangers of the journey by God; they know that their action agrees perfectly with the will of God. Their obedience brings peace to the rest of men: on account of the striking example they give of obedience, the imitation of which brings abundant peace, and on account of the merit of Christ's obedience, through which we receive the grace to imitate His obedience and to win peace for ourselves.

THIRD POINT: St. Joseph's Stay in Egypt

I. *On the way to Egypt* the obedience of the holy persons continued to be the same.

Hour after hour, day after day, by day and by night, in fine and in rough weather, through all privations and all dangers, they persevered in their obedience. As they went further and further on their way, the appearance of the landscape changed more and more: first in the region of the Philistines, and then in Egypt; the manners and language of the inhabitants was so different from what they were used to in Judea; as days went on St. Joseph, the delicate Virgin, and the weak Child felt the weariness of the journey more and more. And as the distance from home increased, the more vividly stood before their minds the image of the Holy City, the surroundings of Bethlehem, and their humble house at Nazareth, while there loomed before them, ever equally dark, the uncertain future and the prolonged exile. In spite of that there remained continually an even resignation, cheerfulness and peace, and they gave glory to God in all these happenings.

II. *At the arrival in Egypt,* a place of exile as it were, their obedience continued quite as perfect.

Now they were experiencing a climate altogether different from what they had been used to; it was the same with the landscape, the vegetation, and the food; the people were different in dress and in manners, and most of all in language, " He heard a tongue which he knew not." (Ps. 80:6) The religion, too, was different; in fact, is was pagan.

On the other hand there was the lively recollection of the Holy Land, and the temple, of the manner and language of the Jews. The prospect of having to live in this country among these people must have seemed worse than ever, and there was moreover the uncertain duration of the exile. Nevertheless their obedience was always the same, and so was their own peace and the glory of God.

III. *The beginning of their stay in Egypt.*

At first all the inhabitants, it seems, were unknown to Joseph and Mary; then they made one or the other acquaintance, and later on many more. The first days were probably spent in a corner of some stranger's house, until Joseph was able to build a simple hut; little by little he provided some furniture. At first he may have in vain offered his services to many; next he found one or the other slender chance to do some odd job as a carpenter; at length he must have managed to have always work on hand, and to provide for his own and his family's needs. All this time Mary was taking care of the Child, and looking after the many household wants. And all the while their obedience was perfect; they enjoyed true peace of mind, and they gave glory to God.

IV. *The prolonged stay in Egypt.*

At length the Holy Family became acquainted with the country and its customs; they understood the language, some neighbors had befriended them, and their house was now fairly comfortable; Joseph has always work waiting for him, and the Child and His Mother have picked up strength: thus exile almost became a home. All that time Jesus, Mary, and Joseph were ever giving thanks to God for all those benefits that they received; nevertheless they never set their hearts on them: they were mindful of the fact that they had not in Egypt a " lasting city "; they always cherished the memory of, and longing for, the Holy Land and the temple, whither God's voice would at length call them. In their Egyptian home was begun the hidden life of obedience that was to be continued for so many years in the house of Nazareth.

As Jesus advanced in age, He began to practice outwardly the obedience which He had undertaken at the Incarnation, and which He was to practice until death, even to the death on the cross.

Reflect on the glory continually given to God by all these actions, and the peace which filled the hearts of Jesus, Mary, and Joseph.

CHAPTER XVII

The Return from Egypt

Cf. Matthew 2:19-23; *The Exercises*, Sec. 270

★

First Point. *The angel admonished Joseph to return to Israel:* " *Arise, and take the child and his mother, and go into the land of Israel.*" (Matt. 2:20)

Second Point. " *So he arose and . . . went into the land of Israel.*" (Matt. 2:21)

Third Point. " *But hearing that Archelaus was reigning in Judea in place of his father Herod . . . he withdrew into the region of Galilee.*" (Matt. 2:22)

FIRST POINT: St. Joseph Is Called back from Egypt.

I. *Before the order to go back.*

See in the hearts of Jesus, Mary, and Joseph the peaceful *desire* to return to Judea; it is constantly and religiously tempered with cheerful *resignation* to stay on in Egypt: " Not my will, but thine be done." The continued perfect offering of the three most noble wills transforms the house of exile into a temple; God and the angels look down on it, smelling the savor of sacrifice, and the Father says, " This is my beloved Son in whom I am well pleased." (Matt. 3:17) At last God fixes the time for the recall, not according to mere natural likings of the human heart, but according to the measure of glory and peace pre-ordained by Himself.

II. *The recall from exile.*

1. Note the *order* given: " Arise " from exile; " take the child and his mother," both of them being stronger now; " and go "; He does not say " flee ": they may now take the easier route; " to the land of Israel," their home-country, the Land of Promise; " for those who sought the child's life are dead " (Matt. 2:20); the cause of the former danger has disappeared.

2. Consider the *joy* and happiness of the Holy Family at each and every word of the angel. Their joy is the deeper and purer owing to their previous resignation; it is some foretaste of the joy which the saints will experience one day, in due time, when they are called out of this world's exile to the heavenly home.

SECOND POINT: The Return of St. Joseph from Egypt

I. *The resolution to go back.*

St. Joseph obeys accurately to the letter; as the words, however, allow a certain margin, he uses his own discretion. To the word " arise " is not now added " by night ": and so Joseph does not arouse Jesus and Mary in the middle of the night, but, waiting till daylight, when they had been refreshed by sleep and food, he invites them to make the journey.

" Go," not " flee ": hence St. Joseph makes suitable preparation; he makes provision for the comfort of the journey, and duly bids farewell to all acquaintances; he sets out without hurry; he marks a set time for rest and other needs of the journey, occasionally he prefers a comfortable road to a shorter, but rougher way.

" To the land of Israel ": the destination is given quite vaguely. Hence St. Joseph, keeping before his eyes only the service of God, ponders with himself, whither he should go: to Jerusalem, Bethlehem, or Nazareth? He takes counsel with the Blessed Virgin, and weighs before God the advantages and disadvantages of going to one place or to the other, and recommends the whole matter in prayer to God; finally, moved by the sole wish not to shirk God's order, but to carry it out accurately, in the manner best suited to the circumstances, he chooses to go on to Judea, rather than to Nazareth.

II. *The execution of the plan.*

Notice how quietly St. Joseph sets to work, without haste, even when he now draws near the borders of the Promised Land. He is recollected, and so far from joy interfering with his prayers, it gives them a further incentive and ardor.—Reflect on the glory given to God by such perfect obedience, and on the peace it brought to the Holy Family.

THIRD POINT: St. Joseph Retires to Nazareth.

I. *" But hearing that Archelaus was reigning in Judea in place of his father Herod."* (Matt. 2:22)

Quite as well God might have pointed this out through an angel, in order to keep Joseph from adopting the less suitable plan to go to Judea, and to lead Jesus and Mary thither on a useless journey; yet God allowed Joseph to make a miscalculation, and consequently to take Jesus for some time on an unnecessary journey towards Judea. Thereby God would teach us that superiors may in fact fall short of prudence in their actions, and we must not obey for the reason that superiors are supposed to enjoin always the most prudent course, but because they hold the place of God, and wield His authority.

II. " *He was afraid to go there.*" (Matt. 2:22)

Man must not rely too much on his own counsels, even if they have been formed with the best intention and the greatest circumspection. When a prudent doubt arises one must, with St. Joseph, have recourse to prayer; that he did so may be gathered from the words " being warned in sleep," of course by God.

III. " *He withdrew into the region of Galilee . . . and settled in a town called Nazareth.*" (Matt. 2:23)

1. On God's warning him St. Joseph gives up his cherished plan. The leisurely travelling gives way again to a more cautious and quick progress: but in all things St. Joseph is ruled by the same spirit of obedience, he enjoys the same peace, he aims only at the glory of God.

2. Consider the nobility of his obedience. In a manner that could not have been foreseen by men, God's will, long since expressed by the prophets, is now fulfilled through Joseph's obedience.

Consider the fruit of the same obedience: from the readiness with which St. Joseph turns away from Judea to Galilee dates the beginning of the sojourn of the Holy Family at Nazareth: " And he . . . settled in a town called Nazareth; that there might be fulfilled what was spoken through the prophets, ' He shall be called a Nazarene.' " (Matt. 2:23) With that sojourn are connected all the graces derived from the hidden life of Christ which were bestowed on the Holy Family, and on the whole human race.

CHAPTER XVIII

The Life of Christ Our Lord from the Age of Twelve to the Age of Thirty

Cf. Luke 2:51-52; *The Exercises*, Sec. 271

*

WE NOW come to the mysteries which illustrate the different states of life available for choice. St. Ignatius wants us to see in the present mystery, in which Jesus was obedient to His parents, an example of the first state which consists in the observance of the commandments. Elsewhere Ignatius stresses this point of Jesus' obedience to His parents. In the mysteries of the Flight and Return it was primarily and directly the obedience of Joseph that was proposed for contemplation; here it is that of Jesus Himself. More important still, the former consisted in acts of obedience, the latter in embracing a state which consists in the obedience of the commandments. Only the fourth commandment is mentioned, the Son of God observed the other commandments while living in obedience to His parents. E.g., He fulfilled a religious duty by going up to the temple when He was twelve.

First Point. *He was obedient to His parents.*

Second Point. " *Jesus advanced in wisdom and age and grace.*" (Luke 2:52)

Third Point. *He appears to have practiced the trade of a carpenter, as St. Mark seems to show in chapter six: " Is not this the carpenter.*" (Mark 6:3)

FIRST POINT: The Example of the State of Obedience to the Commandments

I. *Jesus " was subject to them.*" (Luke 2:51)

Jesus, the Son of God, the Word of the Father, and His equal in intellect, power, and goodness, was subject to creatures: to Mary, the mother who had given birth to Him as man; and to Joseph, His foster-father.

The subjection extended to all His faculties: His was the most noble intellect, enlightened by the constant vision of God; and He subjects it, considering as right and just whatever He is told to do by His parents. Jesus subjects His most noble human will which was constantly in conformity with the divine Will, and by a special help of grace necessarily to be kept from any disorder whatever; also His exterior activity, of infinite nobility, perfection and merit.

These faculties are subjected *in all things* to whatever Mary and Joseph would order, and in general in the whole regulation of His life; also *at all times,* from childhood to His thirtieth year.

The Lord professed such obedience as a *permanent state of life,* not merely in certain actions. The *motive* was God, the author of the Fourth Commandment. The *object* was this and all the other Commandments that were explained and inculcated by His parents, as, for instance, the obligation to go up to the temple.

II. *Mary and Joseph* practiced obedience as a married couple, and as parents.

Reflect on the excellent *graces* bestowed on both, even before their marriage. Then, in wedlock, consider their mutual *fidelity* and *chastity;* see their *union:* they were " two in one flesh "; they were united in an absolutely indissoluble bond, directly effected by God. This mutual union of theirs derived its origin and efficacy from their close union with God, and it manifested itself in a common faith, religion, resignation and holiness.—In the last place consider the holy parents' *authority,* exercised so gently, evenly, and humbly over the Son of God.—Mary and Joseph professed all these obligations as a *permanent* state.

Second Point: The Fruit and Value of the State of Obedience to the Commandments

1. *Jesus advanced in age.*

The parents determined the quality and quantity of food for nourishing the sacred body of Jesus, the manner of dress, the amount and order of bodily exercise, the place, time, and way of sleep and rest. Thus were brought to perfection, under the influence of obedience, the whole growth of the body that was to be sacrificed for us, the formation of His temperament, the composition of the precious Blood that was to be shed for us. Christ was growing from childhood to boyhood, from boyhood to youth, from youth to manhood, preparing Himself for the Sacrifice of Calvary.

2. *Jesus advanced in wisdom.*

Whereas Jesus was full of all wisdom and virtue, yet that wisdom was revealed outwardly only by degrees: He chose to be instructed like other children. Hence, under the guidance of holy obedience, He was taught how to walk, speak, read, work, and in particular how to exercise the trade of a carpenter. Under the same guidance His outward behavior was moulded: modesty, exterior devotion after the model of Mary and Joseph; aye, the outward look of His virtue so copied that of Mary and Joseph that people who saw Him would tell Him as their Son by this likeness of behavior.

There was visible in all these traits a progress that was indeed striking, yet it did not go beyond the natural proportion; from wisdom such as is becoming for boyhood (cf. Jesus in the temple, when twelve years old), it advanced to the appearance of youthful, and then of manly wisdom, not by leaps and bounds, but step by step.

3. *Jesus advanced in grace with God and men.*

The Son of God, living in the state of obedience, showed Himself as the most accomplished Servant of God; He made Himself a most perfect whole-burnt-offering, and He was progressing most efficiently in the development of His human nature. Accordingly the Father was well pleased with such obedience of His Son; His merit was increasing in proportion to His virtue; the Holy Spirit used Him as the choicest instrument for the redemption of the world, living in Him as in the holiest of temples, decking out this sanctuary from day to day with ever more exquisite graces.

The effects were continually revealed more clearly and openly, and thus Jesus was advancing in grace with men; they would, day after day, venerate and love Him more and more. " They marvelled at the words of grace that came from his mouth." (Luke 4:22); " And all who were listening to him were amazed at his understanding and his answers." (Luke 2:47)

II. Similarly *Mary and Joseph advanced in age.*

1. Women age more quickly than men, and more so among eastern people than among western. Joseph grew old, became sick, and died. Yet while the vigor of the body was diminishing, the virtue of the soul was ever increasing.

2. Mary and Joseph *advanced in wisdom.*

Their progress was due to their constant union with God, with each other, and with Jesus: through prosperity and adversity, in health and in sickness, in life and in death.

3. Mary and Joseph *advanced in grace.*

In their case, too, their faithful union according to the law of God was a state of obedience, a most worthy whole-burnt-offering, most fruitful in merit, and most pleasing to God.

THIRD POINT: The Outward Condition of the State of Obedience to the Commandments

I. As regards *Mary and Joseph* the Gospel says: " he [Joseph] went and settled in a town called Nazareth." (Matt. 2:23)

The holy parents had their constant residence in the same insignificant township, in the same house with its poor furniture; theirs was constant intercourse with the same persons of lowly condition, constant humble occupation either in the household duties or in the carpenter's trade. In the worldly sense, time brought no advancement, although they were advancing so wonderfully in wisdom and grace. They did not advance in wealth or honor or fame; but in their lowly obscurity their souls were always content.

II. As regards *Jesus,* it appears that He " practiced the trade of a carpenter, as St. Mark seems to show." (Sec. 271)

1. Consider that the Evangelists have not informed us explicitly about the outward occupation professed by the Savior in the state of obedience; St. Mark seems to hint at it only in passing. The reason is that it does matter greatly.

Whatever the material object of obedience, the good pleasure of the Father remains the same, because He takes into consideration not the material object, but the motive. The important thing is that we yield ourselves to God. He uses the " foolish things of the world . . . to shame the ' wise,' and the weak things . . . to put to shame the strong." (1 Cor. 1:27) The perfection is the same, the merit the same, since these are proportioned to the nobility and purity of the motive. The whole-burnt-offering is equally excellent, since it consists in the sacrifice, not of the material object, but of our own self.

2. Jesus practiced the *trade of a carpenter.*

The Lord did not profess a dignity by which He would be above others, nor a knowledge that would show forth His talent, nor some liberal art. He chose a manual craft of the lower kind that did not require over-much talent, that served the material purposes of life and did not bring wealth to the artisan, but only the necessities of life. Jesus lived in lowly and needy circumstances till the thirtieth year of His life. His intention was to teach us the more evidently that it does not matter what is the material object of obedience; nay, everything else being equal, that there is a more complete submission to God, and a more pleasing holocaust, in a humble state of life, because God chose poverty and humility Himself in order to save the world, and because we are thereby the more conformed to Christ, who was poor and humble.

3. Consider Christ's constant *serenity of mind* in that humble condition.

Jesus does not regard such a state as unjust and unworthy of His dignity; He knows that the Father is well pleased. He has the constant testimony of the Holy Spirit that He is the Son of God, and that He is doing a work worthy of the Son of God; He knows what value that kind of life has for the glory of God, for His own merit, for our instruction and for the redemption of the world. Jesus enjoys purest peace in the company of Mary and Joseph, since that peace does not depend on the outward condition of persons, but on the unanimous devotion of their wills to God's service, and on the love they have for each other. Accordingly He takes the greatest pleasure in this lowly house, this company, and this occupation all the time from His childhood to His thirtieth year.

CHAPTER XIX

Jesus Goes up to the Temple at the Age of Twelve

Cf. Luke 2:41-50; *The Exercises,* Sec. 272

★

THE SCOPE of this contemplation is stated in the Introduction to the Consideration of Different States of Life. It should give us a picture of " the second state, which is that of evangelical perfection." (Sec. 135) Christ gave us an example of this state when He " remained in the temple and left His foster father and His Mother to devote Himself exclusively to the service of His eternal Father." (*Ibid.*) An example of the second state can be given in two ways: first by showing how that state, once chosen, is to be lived; secondly by showing how it is to be embraced and the preceding state, that of observing the commandments, abandoned. In this mystery Christ gives us the example in the second way, and that example does not precisely show us how to embrace the second state, but indicates how we can make such an act. The main point of the contemplation is to be found in the words: " He remained . . . and left His foster father etc."

In other places St. Ignatius speaks of the Finding in the Temple and the Coming to the Temple. In those places he speaks reservedly, wishing to avoid the error of forcing retreatants to choose evangelical perfection. This reservation was specifically stated by him in the fifteenth of his introductory remarks, " The director of the Exercises ought not to urge the exercitant . . . to one state of life . . . more than to another." (Sec. 15) He had also pointed out that the retreatant derives greater spiritual profit from what he has found out for himself than by what he has been told. (Cf. Sec. 2) One need not be afraid that the idea of embracing a more perfect state will escape the notice of those who are fit for it, since, besides the movement of the Holy Spirit, the mystery itself cannot fail to suggest it.

First Point. *Christ our Lord at the age of twelve years goes up from Nazareth to Jerusalem.*

Second Point. *Christ our Lord remained in Jerusalem, and His parents did not know it.*

Third Point. *After three days they found Him disputing in the temple, and seated in the midst of the doctors, and when they asked Him where He had been, He answered, " Did you not know that I must be about my Father's business? "* (Luke 2:49)

FIRST POINT: Christ Goes up to the Temple.

I. *He goes up to Jerusalem.*

It was the *City of God*, consecrated in a very special manner to God's worship; here God's glory was to be revealed in a very special way to all men; from here, as from the Capital, peace was to flow into all the cities of the Holy Land. Jerusalem is described as the center of the Messianic Kingdom: " I am appointed King by him over Sion his holy mountain, preaching his commandment." (Ps.

2:6) "And in the last days the mountain of the house of the Lord shall be prepared on the top of the mountains, and it shall be exalted above the hills, and all nations shall flow to it." (Is. 2:2) (Cf. Is. 2:9.)

Its ministries are: to teach, sacrifice, sanctify, and pray; its citizens are a sacerdotal race. "God loves the gates of Sion above all the tabernacles of Jacob." (Ps. 86:2)

II. *He goes up from Nazareth.*

1. Review the *circumstances of the place:* the dwelling, company, occupation, and graces of so many years in that place; there was in it no sin, no earthly attachment; all was breathing virtue, holiness, merit, and everything was full of consolation; this life, however, was so far concerned with a less perfect degree and state.

2. Reflect on the entirely *orderly affection* of the heart of Jesus for that place. Indeed, the Savior led for so many years a hidden life, not from carnal love for the place, work, and company, but solely from a desire to serve God; therefore He abstained at appointed times from the usual occupation on the sabbaths and feasts; He sacrificed the company of Mary and Joseph during the hours set down for private prayers, and He left the house at Nazareth at least once every year in order to go to the temple. Mary and Joseph shared these dispositions with Jesus.

SECOND POINT: Christ Remains in the Temple.

I. *He remained and His parents did not know it.*

If His parents had known it, they too would have remained, and the temple would have been another Nazareth for them. He remained, allowing their sorrow, thus con-

secrating the sorrow of other parents who give up their
children to the service of God. He remained, allowing His
own sorrow, caused by theirs, and consecrating the sorrow
of the children who leave their parents in order to comply
with the divine call.

II. *They did not know it.*

1. His parents did not know where was the Child who had
been specially entrusted to them, a Child quite dear to them.

They did not know why He was absent, nor did they know
whether He would be restored to them at all.

2. *Accordingly they sought Him sorrowing.*

They looked everywhere " among their relatives and acquaintances " (Luke 2:44), and when these did not know where He
was, " they returned to Jerusalem in search of him." (Luke 2:
45) There they looked for Him among strangers in the twisted
streets and finally they returned to the temple.

They sought Him with perseverance: the evening of the
first day and the following night, the second day and the second night, and still at the beginning of the third day. Although
the search had so far proved fruitless, they did not abandon it.
Their sorrow continued to increase as the time of their separation from Jesus became longer, as their inquiries failed to receive
the wished-for answer, as the vain search increased their bodily
fatigue and mental anguish.

3. Consider that the sorrow of parents who give up their children is *far less* than that of Mary and Joseph.

They know for certain that their children are enrolled in the
heavenly Jerusalem, and follow the Savior more closely; they
know for certain the reason of the sacrifice, namely, the counsel
of God who calls their children to fulfil His work; they know
for certain how long the sacrifice will last, for they will be
united to their children in heaven; they know for certain the dig-

nity and merit of this sacrifice. Wherefore parents and children have reason not to sorrow, but to rejoice: the child once called by God must not be sought by the parents, nor must the parents be sought by the child.

III. *He remained.*

1. *Why?*—Christ had been called by the Father's counsel, and not by His command, for a foretaste of the future public life, and consequent separation from Mary, Joseph, and Nazareth. Accordingly Mary, and Joseph too, would keep all these words in their hearts; they would understand that the happy condition of the intercourse at Nazareth was not the final intention of God for them on earth, but that it would only last as long as it was God's will. They must always be ready, at the Father's will, to let Jesus leave their house, their company, and the exercise of His trade; it was in this spirit that they were to spend their whole life in the house of Nazareth.

Notice that Christ inspired both the parents with this disposition, though He knew that the Blessed Virgin alone would actually make this sacrifice, while St. Joseph would, before that, depart this life.

2. *When?*—" When he was twelve years old." (Luke 2:41) Already at twelve the Heart of Jesus had conceived and cherished these sentiments; He had been entertaining them ever since His childhood; He had conceived them at the Incarnation, and He kept them all the remaining years until His death. He did so for my sake, that I might be redeemed and instructed by these sentiments of His Heart. I will therefore ask myself: What have I done in this matter for Christ? What am I doing? What ought I to do?

I shall consider that in this disposition consists the perfection of obedience; in the person of the parents it obeys God alone, and therefore it obeys only in so far as their will agrees with the good pleasure of God. In this consists perfect self-sacrifice; it extends not only to the precepts but also to the counsels. This is the perfection of humility and poverty, which renounces not only the attachment to worldly things but also, if God so pleases, the things themselves.

3. *How?*—When Jesus remained, He foresaw the sorrow of His parents, and anticipated their grief beforehand; in His omniscience He accompanied them through all the circuits of their inquiry, to the continual increase of His own sorrow; He remained the first day and the following night, the second day and the night that followed, and still at the beginning of the third day; indeed He remained when they at length came near the temple, and set foot into it. All this time He controlled Himself, not asking the Father—who would certainly have heard Him for His reverence—to deliver them from the painful uncertainty, not leading them to Himself by an inner light, not sending angels to guide them: angels ready at hand for any service He might wish.

Let us learn from Jesus that we must not only go up, but that we must also remain; even if parents should afterwards seek us sorrowing, we must remain, because God's counsel and call remains, and there also remains in God the power to console parents, provided they be willing; believing parents are consoled better by the perseverance of their child, than worldly parents by an untimely return.

THIRD POINT: Christ Is Found in the Temple.

I. *" They found him in the temple, sitting in the midst of the teachers."* (Luke 2:47) Notice how different everything is from the house at Nazareth.

1. *The place:* Jerusalem is a teeming City; the temple is a spacious building; both places are far removed from the loneli-

ness, humility, and simplicity of which Jesus had been so fond in the house at Nazareth.

2. *The company:* the doctors were naturally far less friendly to Him than Mary and Joseph: they had not been prepared by such great graces of God to converse intimately with Him; assuredly not all were men of remarkable holiness, though all possessed learning—partly genuine and partly fictitious—and possibly they were to some extent puffed up by it. Jesus not only approaches them, but He is " in their midst," surrounded by them; and He " was seated " there as if that was His proper place.

3. *His occupation:* " *asking them questions.*" (Luke 2:46) They did not unanimously think the same with Him, like Mary and Joseph, nor did they let themselves so willingly be brought round to His opinion; He was " listening to them, and asking them questions," of them who were by far His inferiors in knowledge, and who were not led by the desire of learning from His knowledge. The immediate result of the discussion was not so much to kindle docile minds, like those of Mary and Joseph, but to rouse the barren astonishment of the bystanders. All this was hard in itself, but the Father's will made it sublime and meritorious.

II. When Mary and Joseph asked Him where He had been, He answered: " *Did you not know that I must be about my Father's business?* " (Luke 2:49)

1. Parents have properly the right to demand that a child not yet of age remain with themselves in the same place, that he cheer them with his company, and help them with his labors; this right belongs both to the natural mother, on the score of generation, and to the adoptive father on the score of adoption. Mary and Joseph had this right all the more for having cherished Jesus with a love that far exceeds the love of all other parents;

and they could properly demand of Jesus not to give them cause for so great sorrow. Hence the parents' sorrow, complaint, and question " where He had been " were quite lawful.

2. Nevertheless there was room for an answer to that question and to those complaints; such an answer must be sincere, as was the case with the Savior: He *must* obey the divine counsel of such authority owing to the Father's dignity, of so great usefulness, and so dangerous to neglect. He *must* do so as soon as the Father calls, and likewise ever afterwards. The truth is that the heavenly Father is more a father than the parents; He has a right higher than that of the parents; and therefore He can even call a child away to live in His holy house and to be occupied in directly procuring His honor.

3. Jesus *knew* this right of the Father, and He had it ever written in His Heart; induced by reverence for this right, He had remained in the temple without His parents' knowledge. The parents *should have known it also*. They did, in fact, stop questioning Jesus as soon as they understood that God the Father wished to exercise His right.

Grant me, O Lord, to know Thy good pleasure, and—after I have found it out—to do what I ought to do.

4. Consider Jesus going down to Nazareth with His parents; thus He foreshadows the joy with which Christian parents will receive in heaven the children whom they have allowed to go away on earth at the call of God.

CHAPTER XX

The Two Standards

Cf. *The Exercises*, Secs. 136-148

★

St. Ignatius gives three preludes. These are:

First Prelude. *This is the history. Here it will be that Christ calls and wants all beneath His standard, and Lucifer, on the other hand, wants all under his.* (Sec. 137)

Second Prelude. *This is a mental representation of the place. It will be here to see a great plain, comprising the whole region, about Jerusalem, where the sovereign Commander-in-Chief of all the good is Christ our Lord; and another plain about the region of Babylon, where the chief of the enemy is Lucifer.* (Sec. 138)

Third Prelude. *This is to ask for what I desire. Here it will be to ask for a knowledge of the deceits of the rebel chief and help to guard myself against them; and also to ask for a knowledge of the true life exemplified in the sovereign and true Commander, and the grace to imitate Him.* (Sec. 139)

According to the directions of St. Ignatius " this exercise will be made at midnight and again in the morning. There will be two repetitions of the same exercise about the time of Mass and the time of Vespers. The same three colloquies, with our Lady, with her Son, and with the Father, will close all these exercises." (Sec. 148)

Part I and Part II may conveniently form each a separate meditation.

Part I
The Standard of Lucifer

FIRST POINT: Lucifer's Person and Surrounding.

I. Lucifer's person.

He is an angel who received this name from God, a being created to serve God. Now he is the deadly enemy of all men. Through the sin of pride he became an enemy of God, and consequently of God's creatures; he has a special hatred for men, who were created to fill in heaven the seats of the reprobate angels. Lucifer hates me, not on account of some secondary things that might change or disappear, but on account of my human nature.

Lucifer is " the chief of the enemy," not by means of creation, by which all men are subject to God, nor by means of his sin, which could never give him any rightful claim, but solely by means of his violence and cunning. The submission of his followers is due to the degeneracy of their own nature that led to the slavery of sin.

II. Lucifer's surrounding.

The vast plain of Babylon, extensive enough to contain all men. See how many are already gathered there, deceived by the snares of Lucifer. Babylon means confusion, which is in opposition to the peace of Christ; there you see discord between creature and Creator, between creature and creature, and between the flesh and the spirit.

Lucifer is " seated on a great throne of fire and smoke." (Sec. 140) His being seated is a sign of his eminence which is not grounded on any lawful title. The followers are meanwhile busily moving about, but the unrest and rage that agitate the chief do not allow him to enjoy his place of repose.

That throne is the one mentioned by Isaias (14:13). It was to be exalted above the stars of God, but it is now set in the Babylonian plain; its height is in proportion, not to true excellence, but to an imaginary greatness; that very throne marks Lucifer as a fallen angel.

The seat is " of fire and smoke " (Sec. 140), lacking firmness, for fire and smoke do not yield a support, lacking reality, for the fire shows vain splendor and the smoke vain conceit. Contrast that fire and smoke with the glory Lucifer enjoyed when an angel, the " light-bearer " of God.

His is an appearance " inspiring horror and terror." (Sec. 140) His outward ugliness expresses his inward depravity that sin caused, especially the sin of pride. By sin Lucifer became an object of horror even to God, who is infinitely good, beautiful, and holy. Lucifer is a relentless enemy, bent upon the worst evil, the ruin of my very nature; hence I must dread and abhor him above everything.

From this consideration I learn that I have a relentless, cunning, invisible enemy: this is true in general, and it applies in particular to the most serious business of choosing a state of life. I must therefore be wary, and not proceed rashly.

Second Point:

I. Lucifer " summons innumerable demons." (Sec. 141)

Consider in each of *the devils* the wickedness, cunning, strength, and the hatred against God and God's creatures, against me, too! *The number* of those enemies is countless, and it will never become less, since they are hardened in evil. At the convocation that is called, consider that all those many enemies are gathered under *one chieftain* to secure unity of action, whence Christ calls them a kingdom. (Matt. 12:26)

All obey that chieftain, whence Christ says that Satan is not divided against himself. Examine in detail: Who obey?—Angels.

Whom do they obey?—Their equal, devoid of any lawful authority.

What is their motive?—Hatred of God's legitimate authority and desire to harm.

What is their reward?—Shame and eternal torment.

How do they obey?—Without grumbling, slackness, hesitation, like a well ordered army.

In what business do they obey?—Though they are so many in number, and so great in strength, they have no other business except to draw souls away from God, and then drag them to eternal ruin.

From this consideration I learn that I have many enemies, who are as much to be dreaded as Lucifer himself; they are united among themselves, lying of set purpose in wait for me, both on other occasions, and especially in the business of the choice.

II. Lucifer scatters the demons throughout the world,

" some to one city and some to another, throughout the whole world, so that no province, no place, no state of life, no individual is overlooked." (Sec. 141)

1. Reflect on the *universality* of this assault:

As regards place: survey the vast extent of the whole world, and consider that no province and no place is left out, whether near by or far off, whether populous or solitary.—*As regards persons:* consider their well-nigh endless variety in outward qualities, character, passions, etc., and note that among such a variety no state, no individual is left out.—*As regards time:* this universal assault has been going on from the very beginning of the world's history, and will be kept up to the end of time.

2. Reflect on the *unity* of the assault, since so many devils under a single chieftain are all the time in every place so united in working for a common purpose.

From this consideration I learn that in no place and at no moment of time can I consider myself secure.

THIRD POINT: Lucifer's Address

I. Proposing the plan.

" Consider the address that he makes to them, and how he goads them . . ." (Sec. 142) The insistence with which Lucifer speaks betrays a relentless hatred, and the violence shows the pride with which he exalts himself unbearably above his own helpmates. They are " to lay snares for men, to seek to chain them. First they are to tempt them to covet riches (as Satan himself is accustomed to do in most cases) that they may the more easily attain the empty honors of the world, and then come to overweening pride. The first step, then, will be riches, the second honor, the third pride. From these three steps the evil one leads to all other vices." (Sec. 142)

II. A study of the plan.

1. Pride leads on to all the other vices.
This is clear from the example of the devils and our First

Parents; from their pride all evil came into the world. This is further clear from the fact that pride is most opposed to God, and therefore most withdraws God's grace, opening the way to corruption. Pride, moreover, infects self-esteem, and so paves the way to every deceit. Pride also produces presumption, and so leads to neglect of the means to repel temptations. Lastly pride conceals the greatness of the first fall, and so renders conversion more difficult.

2. The vain honor of the world leads on to pride.

Honor is vain in as much as it mostly follows those gifts of man on which true greatness does not depend, and it exaggerates those inferior gifts. Honor is even paid to things which are not at all respectable. Furthermore, it overlooks interior defects, and eagerly lessens or sets aside exterior faults. Now such honor leads on to *pride,* because it produces an attachment to worldly honor, ignoring its hollowness and seeing only its attractiveness. Attachment to worldly honor, in turn, leads one to judge oneself as the world does, to exaggerate one's own worth, to minimize one's own defects, and consequently not to acknowledge that all our worth is from God: a disposition that is pride.

3. Riches lead on to vain worldly honor.

Wealth provides a favorable chance to obtain honor, and stimulates the desire for it. Again the desire of reaping profit from other people's riches prompts men to show honor to the rich.

4. Consider how Lucifer is actually ruining very many people in the aforesaid manner; he begins with the first stage, that of riches, such is his wont in most cases; then he goes on to the second stage, honors; then to the third stage, pride.

Ponder by what long experience, *viz.,* since the beginning of the world, this method is recommended. " As fishes are taken with the hook, and as birds are caught with the snare, so men are taken in the evil time." (Eccles. 9:12)

From this consideration I learn that I have very many cunning enemies, gathered under one chieftain, lying in wait for me in every place and at any time, and that they follow, moreover, a most efficient plan, which has been tested by the experience of all ages.

III. The snares are laid bare.

1. Therefore *riches* and *honors*, though indifferent in themselves, are nevertheless continually defiled by the touch of Lucifer. If in making my election I come to a point where—all else on both sides being equal—I hesitate between what appeals to my cupidity and vanity, and what will bring poverty or humiliation, then I will rather turn away from the former, because therein Lucifer's snares are often lurking.

2. Therefore Lucifer proceeds *by degrees* from the indifferent and harmless to the sinful. I shall, then, not choose or admit anything merely because it is indifferent; nor shall I despise anything because it is a small matter. I will reject the first suggestions of Lucifer.

3. It is easy enough to give way in one step, but very difficult indeed to recover the ground lost, because Lucifer immediately involves in nets and chains him who yields. He does not proceed rashly, but little by little, completing and strengthening each step with countless temptations; he proceeds, not by force, but by enticement; he has at his disposal a thorough knowledge of man's heart, an active command of opportunities and circumstances that enable him to tempt every one more efficiently. By all these means he *ensnares* the unwary, and *burdens* his victims *with chains:* for nature left to itself cannot recover the lost grace, nor free itself from evil habits. Lucifer is continually placing new obstacles in the way of a soul that has been thus ensnared.

Thereby he weakens *liberty* of the will by constantly strengthening evil habits, and by infecting all the powers of the soul; he is above all restricting the liberty of doing good, in which consists properly our likeness with God, and our excellence as men; this is the true life, which brings true peace and merits a happy eternity.

Therefore I must not put off a generous choice lest Lucifer capture and seize my soul.

Conclude with the colloquy to our Lady, her Son and the Father.

" A colloquy should be addressed our Lady, asking her to obtain for me from her Son and Lord to be received under His standard, first in the highest spiritual poverty, and should the Divine Majesty be pleased thereby, even in actual poverty; secondly, in bearing insults and wrongs, thereby to imitate Him better, provided only I can suffer these without sin on the part of another, and without offense of the Divine Majesty. Then I will say the *Hail Mary.*" (Sec. 147)

A second colloquy will be " to ask her Son to obtain the same favors for me from the Father. Then I will say, *Soul of Christ.*" (Sec. 147)

A third colloquy will be " to beg the Father to grant me the same graces. Then I will say the *Our Father.*" (Sec. 147)

Part II
The Standard of Christ

FIRST POINT: Christ's Person and Surrounding (Cf. Secs. 143-146)

I. Christ's person.

Christ our Lord is God and man and through the utmost emptying Himself in the Incarnation, He is humility personified. Christ is *the sovereign and true Captain,* by the most universal and true titles, because He is the Lord of the whole world; He is the King preordained by God through the prophets; He is the highest in dignity and authority, clothed with the power of the Most High, therefore invincible.

II. Christ's surroundings.

"*In a great plain about the region of Jerusalem.*" (Sec. 144) The extent of the plain is sufficient to contain the whole of mankind. See how relatively few are gathered there about Christ. Jerusalem means " The City of peace."

Christ takes His stand in a lowly place. He behaves as if He were among equals, whereas He is greater than all; He will personally engage in battle, and be a companion in all labors; though He is going to war, His Heart enjoys perfect peace and calm. Christ took a *lowly place* from the moment of the Incarnation, throughout all the mysteries of His childhood; such a place suits His most humble Heart, whereas He shall be exalted above all the angels.

The bearing of Christ is "*beautiful and attractive.*" (Sec. 144) The outward appearance mirrors the beauty of His divine person, which is " the brightness of eternal light, and the unspotted mirror of God's majesty, and the image of His goodness." (Wisd. 7:26) He is gracious, as His name Jesus or Savior expresses; He seeks nothing on earth but our salvation; He is ready to give even His life and blood for it. His manners, too, are most gracious.

From this consideration I learn that I have a most powerful and loving friend near by whom I am efficiently protected against the snares of Lucifer; in particular while making the election of a state of life.

SECOND POINT: The Followers of Christ

I. He chooses ministers.

He chooses as ministers human beings, inferior to the angels in wisdom, activity, strength, and experience; through Adam's sin they have been spoiled in their natural gifts, and deprived of the supernatural ones. Christ chooses ever " *so many*," but not " countless numbers "; in comparison with the devilish hosts, those chosen by Christ are few, and each individual may always make a wrong use of his liberty and lose that noble vocation. " *The apostles, disciples, and others* " (*Ibid.*); they are " the weak things of the world," plain men of low condition, scanty knowledge and experience, and but little virtue.

Christ is *choosing* His own: The choice does not proceed from some natural inclination on the part of those chosen, nor from the harmony of their wills—" you have not chosen me "—but it comes from God's grace alone—" I have chosen you." (John 15:16) Grace had preordained this choice from eternity, and put it into effect in due time; it was brought about infallibly and at the same time gently, as inner light and impulse were added to the outer calling.

Christ gives His apostles neither purse nor scrip, that is, He leaves them without human helps. He equips them, however, with all the greater supply of supernatural helps: He teaches them for three years by His holy words, example, and miracles; the saints of the Old Testament had longed in vain to see this; on this preaching, and not on direct perception, was to be built the entire holiness of all the saints of the New Testament. Christ, moreover, gives to His apostles the most wonderful powers: to give a new life, to remit sins, to consecrate bread and wine. Christ promises the perpetual help of Himself and the Holy Spirit.

Equipped with all these gifts the apostles are not only equal to, but far stronger than, the gates of hell.

From this consideration I draw great courage, above all the most difficult business of my election; for, although my spiritual enemies are many and mighty, yet, in the Church of Christ, I can be calm and safe from all their snares.

II. He sends them forth.

Christ " *sends them throughout the whole world to spread His sacred doctrine among all men, no matter what their state or condition.*" (Sec. 145)

1. Reflect on the *nobility* of this mission: it is the same mission that Christ had received from the Father, the same by which He makes the Apostles His royal messengers and heralds.

2. Reflect on the *object* of the mission: it is to scatter His teaching like seed. If received, it will blossom into an abundance of all graces; the teaching is holy in its origin, content, and purpose; it is His own, the teaching of the Son of God, and therefore truth and life.

3. Reflect on the *extent* of the mission: *as regards place,* " throughout the whole world "; *as regards time,* " unto the consummation of the world " (Matt. 28:20); *as regards persons,* " no matter what their state or condition."

From this consideration I learn that no place and no time is inaccessible to the grace of Christ.

THIRD POINT: Christ's Address

I. Proposing the plan.

" *Consider the address which our Lord makes to His servants and friends* " (Sec. 146); it is so gentle, and the kindness of His humble Heart appears clearly. He tells " *them to seek to help all* " (Sec. 146); it is so emphatic and we see clearly the solicitude of His Heart for us. They are to lead all " *first, by attracting them to the highest spiritual poverty, and should He deign to choose them for it, even to actual poverty. Secondly, they should lead them them to a desire for insults and contempt, for from these springs humility . . . . From these three steps, let them lead men to all other virtues.*" (Sec. 146)

II. The plan unfolded.

1. Humility leads on to all the other virtues.

This is clear from the example of Christ; all His virtues sprang from the humble union between the divine and the human, and from the humility of His heart; it is seen from the example of the Blessed Virgin; all her virtues were raised on the foundation of the most profound humility; it is seen in the fact that humility forms the basis of right order between man and God: this right order requires the exercise of the other virtues; lastly, humility draws down grace, which begets the other virtues.

2. Reproaches and affronts, if accepted willingly and eagerly, lead on to humility.

They exclude vain honor which most occasions pride. When pride is thus shut out, humility comes in. They let us more easily perceive in our selves the things that ought to humble us in reality; they make us Christlike, in fact and in feeling. Thus they pave the way for habitual conformity with Him through the habit of humility.

3. Voluntary poverty, in deed or in spirit, opens the way to the willing submission to reproaches.

Poverty destroys ambition for honors: for why should a poor man seeks honors? Poverty makes one more ready for reproaches; since there is a natural affinity between want and contempt. Poverty makes us like Christ who was poor, disposing the soul for further conformity with Him, and it gains grace.

4. Consider how many saints, ever since the time of Christ, have been helped by these three stages—poverty, contempt, humility—in acquiring perfection. This will urge me on to strive to hold in high esteem, to love and to trust, the plan proposed by Christ.

III. Christ's plan explained.

1. Therefore *poverty and reproaches,* though indifferent in themselves, are nevertheless continually consecrated by the touch of Christ. Accordingly, if in making my election I come to a point where—all else on both sides being equal—I hesitate between what appeals to my cupidity, comfort and vanity, and what will bring poverty and humiliation, then I will rather embrace the latter, because these are more akin to Christ.

2. Christ, too, proceeds *by degrees.* He does not expect perfection to be accomplished in one leap; He takes delight in small beginnings: I will not, then, lose courage when progress is slow.

3. With Christ the beginning alone is difficult; progress becomes ever easier with the help of grace. Here there is no deception, no slackness, but perfect human *liberty:* the mind is freed from a false esteem of self and things; the will is freed from the bonds of worldly attachments, supplied with the loftiest motive of love of the God-Man, and of the desire to be like Him; humility provides the foundation of true liberty; in the virtues that follow it consists the most fruitful growth of this liberty. In this true liberty consists the only true *peace,* based on a just subordination to God; the only true *strength,* based on a con-

stant union with God, and the giving up of all unbecoming dependence; the only true *life,* demanding above all the right use of liberty. This, then, shall be the aim of my choice, to draw as near to Christ as I can.

Conclude with the colloquies given at the end of the first part.

CHAPTER XXI

The Three Classes of Men

Cf. *The Exercises*, Secs. 149-157

★

IF IT is asked why St. Ignatius speaks here of " classes,"
the answer is that at this stage of the exercises we are
thinking of Christ as " calling," especially as calling us
to His service. In the Gospel the Apostles are frequently
divided up into pairs or classes. In the Gospel the question
deals with the following of Christ in the apostolic life, by
the profession of actual poverty. The three classes of men
are concerned with the following of Christ in any state of
actual or spiritual poverty. The men in the Gospel stood
before Christ going about on earth in the company of a
few chosen disciples; the retreatant stands " in the presence of God our Lord and of all His saints." (Sec. 151)
He seeks, in the presence of such a court, to discover what
is best for him. In this meditation Ignatius emphasizes that
disorderly attachment to things of this world is a hindrance to our perfection, that at times the only way to tear
from our souls such an attachment is immediate rejection
of its object. The obstacle to perfection is reduced to a
concrete form, " ten thousand ducats." Naturally we must
not apply this meditation in such a way that it pertains
only to the rooting out of greed; it must be adapted to our
needs. Perhaps our greatest obstacle to perfection is some
other inordinate attachment, such as fear of leaving home
to follow Christ.

Why, then, does St. Ignatius choose the example of attachment to money? He does so in accommodation to the Gospel, as well as to the preceding meditation on the Two Standards, where among Lucifer's deceits prominent place is given to his command that the demons are " to tempt [men] to covet riches." (Sec. 142) The meditation on the Two Standards shows how the devil plans to capture souls by inordinate attachments; the meditation on the Three Classes of Men teaches those who are captured how to free themselves from the devil's deceits. We may put it concisely in this way: against the tricks of Lucifer inactivity is of no help; a half-hearted fight is valueless; generosity alone will succeed.

The meditation on the Three Classes is made after making, on the same day, four times the meditation on the Two Standards. Therefore St. Ignatius means it to be an easier exercise, an application of the senses to the matter of the standards. Of course not all five senses are applied; it seems that St. Ignatius wants us to *see and hear* the three classes of men.

FIRST POINT: The First Class of Men

" They would like to rid themselves of the attachment they have to the sum acquired in order to find peace in God our Lord and assure their salvation, but the hour of death comes, and they have not made use of any means." (Sec. 153)

I. Reflect on the condition placed by this class.

1. See the eternal love of God for these men: it is clear from the creation and redemption, and from their present desire to

obtain perfection. See the loving look with which Christ is now waiting for their election: " And Jesus, looking upon him, loved him and said to him, ' One thing is lacking to thee; go, sell whatever thou hast, and give to the poor, and . . . come, follow me! ' " (Mark 10:21)

2. Examine in their hearts the attachment for the money acquired: it is a fertile source of faults; see their feeble desire for salvation and perfection; it is barren, since it cannot resolve on giving up the money or on using any other means.

3. The result is that a change is constantly put off under pretence of making more mature reflection, waiting for clearer light, and first settling other business; if nothing worse befalls, no real effort is made, and this mentality will end only with the natural course of death.

II. Examine this condition more closely.

It is absolutely without any generosity; it foolishly plays with the grace of God, with one's own safety and peace, with precious time; it ruins all these values for the cheap consideration of ten thousand ducats; it is without the least merit, but there is great treasure to be acquired in heaven; like the young man of the Gospel such a person goes away sadly, and he will never find God his Lord in peace; it endangers salvation. The danger arises from the corruption of human nature which cannot remain at the same spot, but as soon as it stops going upwards, begins to go downwards; there is further danger from the continual assaults of the watchful enemy, the devil.

III. Reflect how such a mentality is judged by others.

1. By *Lucifer,* who is always urging on his agents to cherish that disorderly attachment, to multiply snares and chains, to

make such a conscience ever more hardened, to entice to more and worse faults.

2. By the *angels,* who are friendly to men, and who see through Lucifer's frauds.

3. By all the *saints* gathered round Christ: they are themselves poor in spirit, and they pity such unworthy brothers.

4. By *Christ,* who proclaims aloud: " With what difficulty will they who have riches enter the kingdom of God." (Matt. 10:23)

5. By the *Divine Majesty:* God created those men for His service, and their slothful conduct moves Him to loathing; God so loved them as to give His only-begotten Son for them, and now He sees their love to be so weak; He has called them to perfection, and He sees that they are paying no attention to His call.

6. By the *men themselves* at the hour of death: the two of them, the one as well as the other, though living in places or countries apart, and not knowing each other—in fact as many as you like who are infected by such disorderly attachment: wherever it be found, " write this man barren! " (Jer. 22:30)

IV. Are you such a man, especially when deliberating about the choice of a state of life?

SECOND POINT: The Second Class of Men

" They want to rid themselves of the attachment, but they wish to do so in such a way that they retain what they have acquired, so that God is to come to what they desire, and they do not decide to give up the sum of money in order to go to God, though this would be the better way for them." (Sec. 154)

I. Reflect on the condition of this class.

1. Hear Christ calling them: " Follow me."

2. See in such people's mind the wish to save themselves and to find God in peace, and also a general purpose to apply some means, but at the same time an attachment to the ten thousand ducts keeps them from using the only effective means. That attachment is not subordinated to whatever the glory of God may require. Their desire to please God and keep the money determines the means they will choose to give up their attachment to the money. Notice how these two men do not go straight to Christ; they wait for Him to come and meet them; they do not accept His Call absolutely, but make a reservation: " let me first go and bury my father . . . let me first bid farewell to those at home." (Luke 9:59-61) Putting their hand to the plough and looking back at the same time, they are not fit for the Kingdom of God.

3. Hence they choose certain means, but inefficient ones; they reject the only efficient means, which is giving up the money. Hence there is at the most a temporary and apparent progress, but soon the former slothfulness will infect everything.

II. Examine their condition more closely.

Consider its lack of *singlemindedness*: instead of aiming solely at the service of God, they are trying to combine two ends, which in the circumstances cannot possibly be combined; its *barrenness*: they reject from the outset the only efficient remedy against that disorderly attachment; its *meanness*: they are bargaining with Christ; its *deceitfulness*: they are under an illusion about their own intention; they imagine they are earnestly seeking the service of God and the salvation of their souls, when they are doing nothing of the kind; they are deceived in thinking that their salvation is now secure, when it is not so at all. Examine lastly its *danger:* this mentality springs from self-delusion, it rests upon a weak will, it indulges in self-complacency, it is deprived of the more special grace of God which must be merited by generosity: being what it is, it lies open to the assaults of Lucifer.

III. Reflect how such a condition is judged by others.

1. By *Lucifer:* he looks on this class as belonging to him; he knows that he can easily seduce them from this first fraud to further frauds, that he may so weaken their wills that, after repeatedly experiencing the barrenness of their efforts, they will slip back to the idle slothfulness of the first class.

2. By all the *angels* and *saints:* these are the ministers of God's lights and graces, yet their well-meant efforts are frustrated by the wilful illusion of this class.

3. By *Christ:* He gives the warning: "No one, having put his hand to the plow and looking back, is fit for the kingdom of God." (Luke 9:62)

4. By the *Majesty of God:* the infinitely Wise is not deceived; the infinitely Holy permits no fraudulent sacrifice.

5. By the *men themselves* at the hour of death: "They have slept their sleep, and all the men of riches have found nothing in their hands." (Ps. 75:6)

IV. Are you such a man?

THIRD POINT: The Third Class of Men

" They want to rid themselves of the attachment, but they wish to do so in such a way that they desire neither to retain nor to relinquish the sum acquired. They seek only

to will and not will as God our Lord inspires them, and as seems better for the service and praise of the Divine Majesty. Meanwhile, they will strive to conduct themselves as if every attachment to it had been broken. They will make efforts neither to want that, nor anything else, unless the service of God our Lord alone move them to do so. As a result, the desire to be better able to serve God our Lord will be the cause of their accepting anything or relinquishing it." (Sec. 155)

Reflect on the condition of the third couple.

1. Hear Christ calling them: " Follow me."

2. These two men have the will to procure their own welfare and peace; it is sincere; it is bent on attaining one thing, and it does not try to reconcile two things that are irreconcilable; it is earnest: it is ready to embrace any means, none excepted, in so far as it helps to serve God better; it renounces the money in spirit before seeing whether God demands actual renouncement; in earnest prayer it asks God for light, and offers itself of its own accord for that which is most opposed to nature.

3. To such a generous disposition there comes as ready answer the continual increase of divine light and strength.

II. Examine this condition more closely.

Consider its wisdom: it seeks exclusively the only necessary end of God's service; its *generosity:* it resigns itself wholly to God; its *security:* it is proof against human frailty, and against Lucifer's frauds; its *usefulness:* it gains merit; its *happiness:* it finds peace on earth, and a treasure in heaven.

III. Reflect how this condition is judged by others.

1. By *Lucifer:* he gives up all hope, as he sees no access left for his frauds.

2. By the *angels and saints:* they rejoice at the plentiful fruit of all their good inspirations that they were giving.

3. By *Christ:* from His Sacred Heart He pours forth in them a continuous stream of life and truth.

4. By the *Divine Majesty:* God is well pleased in these faithful followers of His Son.

5. By the *very couple:* at the hour of death they are truly rich and truly happy.

IV. Are you such a man?

" *I will make use of the same three colloquies employed in the preceding contemplation on Two Standards.*" (Sec. 156)

" *It should be noted that when we feel an attachment opposed to actual poverty or a repugnance to it, when we are not indifferent to poverty and riches, it will be very helpful in order to overcome the inordinate attachment, even though corrupt nature rebel against it, to beg our Lord in the colloquies to choose us to serve Him in actual poverty. We should insist that we desire it, beg for it, plead for it, provided, of course, that it be for the service and praise of the Divine Goodness.*" (Sec. 157)

CHAPTER XXII

Christ's Baptism

Cf. Matthew 3:13-17; *The Exercises*, Sec. 273

★

As HAS been noted previously, the mysteries of the Public Life are chiefly to help our choice, which is usually made in the course of these contemplations. They have many affinities with the meditation on the Two Standards. Thus, if, with the Church, we think of baptism as a renunciation of Satan and all his works and pomps, the present mystery may be considered as the military initiation of Christ the Leader and His declaration of war against Lucifer, while the Father's witness is heaven's proclamation of His leadership.

First Point. *After Christ our Lord had bidden farewell to His blessed Mother, He went from Nazareth to the River Jordan where St. John the Baptist was.*

Second Point. S*t. John baptized Christ our Lord. When he wished to excuse himself because he thought himself unworthy to baptize Him, our Lord said to him: " Let it be so now, for so it becomes us to fulfill all justice."* (Matt 3:15)

Third Point. *The Holy Spirit descended upon Him, and the voice of the Father from heaven testified, " This is my beloved Son, in whom I am well pleased."* (Matt 3:17)

FIRST POINT: What Took Place Before the Baptism of Christ.

I. See the *whole world,*

oppressed by the slavery of the devil, steeped in sin, the outcome of pride turning away from God to self, ultimately the result of disorderly attachment to creatures.

II. See *heaven,*

where the Blessed Trinity decreed from eternity the liberation of mankind, to be brought about through the humility and abnegation of the Savior: this eternal decree is the consecration of the standard of humility.

III. See the *house of Nazareth.*

1. See there *Jesus.*

He has the law of humility written in His heart. He has actually practiced, during His whole life of thirty years, poverty and obedience, considered by all to be the son of Joseph and Mary, whereas He was the Son of God; for a carpenter, whereas He was the maker of the world; for the " brother " of James, Joseph, Judas, and Simon, and consequently their equal, whereas He surpassed all men in dignity; for a person of ordinary wisdom and virtue, whereas He was greater than any in any kind of perfection, not only human but also divine.

In particular Jesus professed, in the mystery of the visit to the temple, when He was twelve years old, a higher state of renunciation, one that He would later embrace. Now at length He is to take the step which He there foreshadowed. He tears Himself away from the paternal home and slender inheritance with its scanty comforts, from His most holy Mother and His relatives, and from the love and honor He enjoyed in their company. All these things were in themselves indifferent, and they held not the very least danger for Him. Christ tears Himself away with high courage, that would never swerve, because it was pleasing to the Divine Majesty, which had picked Him for this.

2. Observe *Mary*,

blessed indeed among women, yet subject to the same general law of abnegation. During the whole of the past thirty years she had willingly kept that law in her heart, and now at long last she puts it into execution, bidding farewell to such a Son, for whose sake alone she liked her house and all other things. He is never to return, but He will go on from Nazareth to Mount Calvary! And the Mother's heart, pierced with the sword of sorrow, all the same breaks forth once again in the words of her Canticle: " My soul magnifies the Lord! "

IV. See the *country near the Jordan*.

By sin the earth has been changed into a desert, but now it shall be graced by the humility of the Messiah. Behold there the standard-bearer of God's kingdom, St. John, and hear him calling all the combatants to that standard.

" Repent! " Therefore the standard of penance, of separation from sin, and all inclination to sin.—" For the kingdom of heaven is at hand." (Matt. 3:2) The kingdom of Christ, that is, with all the Messianic blessings. There is therefore a necessary connection between humility and the kingdom of Christ, both that one may be enrolled in that kingdom, and that one may enjoy its advantages.

SECOND POINT: What Took Place at the Baptism of Christ.

I. St. John baptized Christ our Lord.

God had decreed that as an immediate preparation for the Messianic kingdom the last of the prophets, St. John, should stir up in men's minds the present desire of redemption, and prepare their hearts for receiving the Messiah. Therefore, John's baptism was a renunciation of Satan, and the profession of a new life under the standard of the cross.

Accordingly Christ's baptism in the Jordan is:

1. *A military oath;* for by this humiliation Christ began His public ministry and pledged His faith to the standard of humility.

2. *The knightly dubbing* conferred on Him by the last leader of the Old Testament, who, by his whole speech and dress, was professing humility and abnegation; through this dubbing Christ is acknowledged as a member of the army of the elect, serving under the standard of humility.

3. *A declaration of war* against Lucifer. Christ is, therefore, with high and generous courage, unfurling His standard, and advancing to the fight against Lucifer. Ask that you too may follow Him with great courage, under the same standard, and to the same fight, especially in the business of your choice of life.

II. *John wanted to excuse himself,* thinking himself unworthy to baptize Him.

1. This baptism of Christ was a striking humiliation, because the Son of God entered on His public life distinguished in nothing from the rest of men, " appearing in the form of man." (Phil. 2:7) The Son of God subjected Himself to St. John. Though the Holy One of God, He was likened to sinners.

2. The baptism was all the greater a humiliation for Christ, because He Himself had His own better baptism " with the Holy Spirit and with fire." (Matt. 3:11)

3. This wrong, if we may so call it, was duly perceived by St. John, and he tried to excuse himself, saying: " It is I who ought to be baptized by thee, and dost thou come to me? " (Matt. 3:14) St. John knew that he had been conceived in sin and that the One before him now was the Almighty, the Incarnate Word, who was indeed the source of all holiness.

4. Christ, however, answers: " Let it be so now, for so it becomes us to fulfill all justice." (Matt. 3:15)—*Justice* is everything God commands or counsels. As the prophets had pointed out the Messiah beforehand, so God would have the last of the prophets join the Messiah to the ranks of those who were longing with all their heart for the Messianic kingdom that was to come shortly.

Jesus had fulfilled *all other justice* when He had been circumcised, presented in the temple, and when He observed the Law; it was becoming that He should fulfill *also this justice,* and be baptized. He stood among those who were receiving the baptism of penance, and confessing their sins. The Heart of Jesus accepts all justice, without any regard for His own advantage and His own honor.

THIRD POINT: What Took Place After the Baptism of Christ.

I. *" And behold, the heavens were opened to him."* (Matt. 3:16)

The heavenly Jerusalem, closed long since by the pride of our First Parents, is unlocked by the humility of our Savior. At the same time is shown the prize of the war we must wage against Lucifer; for, as we shall have shared in Christ's humility, so shall we also share in His heavenly glory.

II. " *He saw the Spirit of God descending as a dove and coming upon him.*" (Matt. 3:16)

The humble Savior is shown as endowed with strength from on high to conquer Lucifer. This strength will redeem the whole world from the flood of sin and will do so by a " baptism " in humility. But this " strength is made perfect in weakness." (II Cor. 12:9) The Holy Spirit came down in the form of a dove, a weak and humble bird. The dove is at the same time the emblem of peace, as once in the Ark of Noe; for the fruit of Christ's humility, and of Christ's fight against Lucifer, is our peace.

III. " *And behold, a voice from the heavens said, ' This is my beloved Son, in whom I am well pleased.' *" (Matt. 3:17)

1. What had been shown by the opening of the heavens, and the coming down of the Spirit of God, is confirmed by the explicit witness of the Father; this is a truth most necessary to know and to keep firmly in mind. It is the foundation of the spiritual life.

2. Jesus is proclaimed Son of God: but if Son, heir also and king. The law of humility is sanctioned by the Father's openly declaring His good pleasure in His humbled Son, who is to be the *Commander-in-Chief* in the warfare against Lucifer: " Hear ye him."

CHAPTER XXIII

The Temptation of Christ

Cf. Luke 4:1-13; Matthew 4:1-11; *The Exercises*, Sec. 274

★

THIS MYSTERY is akin to that on the Two Standards in that both present Christ as doing battle with Lucifer. Yet there is a difference. In the Two Standards Christ and Lucifer pitch camp against camp, army against army. In the temptation they step forward to single combat. As in the Two Standards Lucifer proceeds by three stages; from greed to riches to seeking of honors to pride; so here he tempts Christ first with craving for exterior things, food, then with longing for honor or praise caused by a miracle, and finally consummate pride, which is at the same time consummate self-abjection.

Nevertheless these temptations are not in the same way successive steps as are the deceits in the Two Standards. They are steps only temporally, not substantially: the second temptation merely comes after the first, the third after the second; but the first and second do not act as steps to induce Christ to consent to the second and third temptations. In fact, Christ most perfectly resists every temptation, so that the next derives no efficacy at all from that which preceded. The case is different in the third temptation, where Christ is actually enticed to pride by a promise of all earthly goods and honors. Riches joined to honors are shown as steps to pride, but not riches separately as a step to honors. As noted before, St. Ignatius gathers this lesson, not from any mystery, but from daily experience: " As Satan himself is accustomed to do in most cases." (Sec. 142)

Christ repels every temptation by humility. He constantly has recourse to the words of God in Holy Scripture, and He submits Himself to them. His humility is that of the third kind, since in His words He submits Himself to the law of humiliation and self oblation which the Father has prescribed for Him. By actually doing His Father's will He becomes for us the pattern of the most perfect kind of humility.

First Point. *After He had been baptized, Jesus went to the desert where He fasted for forty days and forty nights.*

Second Point. *He was tempted by the enemy three times: " the tempter came and said to him, ' If thou art the Son of God, command that these stones become loaves of bread . . . throw thyself down . . . All these things will I give thee, if thou wilt fall down and worship me! ' "* (Matt. 4:3, 6, 9)

Third Point. *" Angels came and ministered to him."* (Matt. 4:11)

FIRST POINT: What Took Place Before the Temptation of Christ.

I. *He went to the desert.*

1. *Whither* did Christ withdraw?

He withdrew yet further from Nazareth than when He went for baptism, further from all human company and possession; into a *barren place*, lacking all fertility, property, dwelling, company, comfort, and food. Paradise had been changed into a desert through sin: formerly it yielded fruit, now it is a place of fasting; formerly it was teeming with tame animals, now it is the haunt of wild beasts; " he was with the wild beasts." (Mark 1:13) The desert has a special relation to the devil, as may be seen from Tob. 8:3 and Is. 13:21.

2. *Who* was withdrawing?

Jesus, the new Adam. His body and soul form a single being, but in consequence of sin it is destined to a violent separation by death. The body has degenerated from the abode of the soul to its prison, not as if Christ's soul was, like ours, subject to the bonds of oblivion, error, passion, and sin, but in so far as His body, too, was weighing down His soul with weariness, hunger, sadness, and loathing, and in so far as external ills reach, by means of the body, also the soul.

The *Holy Spirit*, dwelling in Christ—having also dwelt in the first Adam—accompanies Jesus to the desert: He is intent on the destruction of Lucifer's kingdom through the humility and abnegation of the Savior; the Spirit " leads," " urges," nay, " drives " Christ into the desert.

II. *He fasted forty days and forty nights.*

1. This *fasting* was undertaken to acknowledge by a voluntary sacrifice of Himself the sovereign dominion of God, and the utter *need* of grace *inherent* in human nature; this grace must be implored even by personal penance. Christ would offer satisfaction for sins, not His own, but those of the world.

2. Consider in this fasting the greatest *voluntary actual poverty* or lack of all things that are most necessary for life.

3. Consider that this fasting was a *humiliation*, since it shows Christ lowering Himself before the Father, according to the condition of human nature, practicing penance according to the

condition of man's fallen nature; and Christ is doing so, not for His own sins, but for those of others.

4. Consider that this humiliation came from the deepest *humility* of Christ, whereby He acknowledged Himself " the servant of God," and made Himself " the lamb of God," the victim atoning for the sins of the world.

5. Consider the *most excellent effects* of Christ's humility: the long protracted prayer, with the exercise of every virtue; the grace to overcome the devil's temptations, as a pledge of the all-round victory to be won over Satan later by the thirsting Savior; the most useful instruction for us, how by renouncing external goods, and undergoing humiliations, we must prepare ourselves to overcome the devil.

Second Point: What Took Place at the Temptation Itself.

I. *The Person of Him tempted.*

In dignity the Person of Christ is the Son of God, holiness itself, the ruler of the demons. It is Christ's earthly mission to show Himself the servant of God, to restore the kingdom of God, and overthrow Satan's kingdom. Christ, with His whole will, seeks only the good pleasure of God: " In the head of the book it is written of me: that I should do thy will; O my God, I have desired it." (Ps. 39:8)

II. *The person of the tempter.*

Satan is deservedly called in this passage " the enemy," as he is called in the Two Standards " the chief enemy of our human nature "; he is bent on sin, on diminishing God's glory, on destroying men's peace, and on subjecting the Savior to his own power.

III. *The circumstances of the temptation:*

1. The *time:* The tempter comes near: from this we may conclude that the devil is not always actually tempting us, but does so only as far as God allows him. Now, God will not allow His faithful servants to be tempted above their strength; and the devil tempts according as he judges the time suitable for obtaining his end, namely, our ruin. Therefore, because our insight does not penetrate the extent of God's permission nor the time of the devil's assault, we must be always ready.

2. The *occasion:* This was the very consolation granted to Christ at His baptism, when He was declared to be the Son of God; in fact the temptation is based on this.

Consider these words of St. Ignatius: " When consolation is without previous cause . . . there can be no deception in it, since it can proceed from God our Lord only. But a spiritual person who has received such a consolation must consider it very attentively, and must cautiously distinguish the actual time of the consolation from the period which follows it. At such a time the soul is still fervent and favored with the grace and aftereffects of the consolation which has passed. In this second period the soul frequently forms various resolutions and plans which are not granted directly by God our Lord. They may come from our own reasoning on the relations of our concepts and on the consequences of our judgments, or they may come from the good or evil spirit. Hence they must be carefully examined before they are given full approval and put into execution." (Sec. 336. Rule 8 of the Second Week)

IV. *The object of the temptation.*

First, inordinate desire of food, in opposition to abstinence and poverty.—Second, inordinate desire of honor, in opposition to humiliation.—Third the height of pride, in opposition to humility. In the third temptation rebellion is suggested, instead of God's service. Instead of the cross on which the Lamb of God was to be sacrificed for the salvation of the world, that most noble and precious cross, since it comes from heaven and leads to heaven, there is offered worldly pomp, so empty and fatal, since it comes from hell and leads to hell. Instead of the divine Sonship there is proposed complete submission to Lucifer.

V. *The gravity of the temptation:*

How grievous the temptation was for Christ may be seen from the exhaustion of His strength, " afterwards He was hungry "; from the repetition of the temptation three times; from the progressive gravity of the objects; from the ever-increasing power allowed the devil. At first there was only an outward suggestion, then power over the body of Christ, finally an illusion of the senses. The devil was allowed anything that could possibly be allowed concerning the person of the Savior.

VI. *The deceitfulness of the temptation.*

1. The tempter pretends pity, but he is full of hatred; he pretends power, but his powers are limited; he pretends interest in confirming the divine Sonship, but seeks to destroy it; he takes the appearance of an angel of light, but he is in truth darkness itself.

2. What he promises is deceitful, namely passing satisfaction, vain honor, empty pomp. Magnifying the gains, he keeps hidden the losses, which are the renunciation of God's spiritual help, the ministry of the angels, and the glory of the divine Sonship.

3. By proposing things that are indifferent in themselves, but not at all indifferent in the given circumstances, the devil tries to allure Christ to things that are forbidden.

4. Satan uses words full of ambiguity: " All these things ": how vain and fleeting they are! " Will I give thee ": I, to whom none of those things belong, to thee, who art the Lord of everything!—And by what right are they claimed by the devil? " To me they are delivered ": of course, not by rightful transfer, but only by permission.—" And to whom I will, I give them ": he can do no more than what God allows. " All shall be thine ": not by any true title, and with not one moment's safe enjoyment.

VII. *The reason for allowing this temptation of Christ.*

The Lord wished to become in all things like unto us, sin alone excepted; He wished to avenge the first Adam's defeat in the enemy of our nature; He wished to teach us by His own example how to overcome temptation, and to merit for us the grace to do so.

VIII. *The manner of overcoming temptation.*

There stands out the obedience corresponding to the first degree of humility: Christ makes God's word the only rule of His action: " It is written." Add the memory of God's benefits, for there is reference to the manna, to God's readiness to work miracles at the proper time, and to the promised land with all its goods. (Cf. Dt. 8:3; 6:16; 6:13.)

In the outward behavior of Christ there is an imposing calm and firmness. All these perfections are the fruits of the Holy Spirit, who is directing Christ in everything.

THIRD POINT: What Took Place After the Temptation.

I. *See the angels.*

They are the servants of Christ according to His divinity, and His friends according to His humanity; they had gladly witnessed the First Man's creation, by which was to be restored the glory of God violated by the angels' defection; afterwards they had, at God's command, closed the entrance of paradise against our First Parents: nevertheless they had continually, as mediators of salvation, been helping Adam's descendants; and they had been promoting the work of redemption even from the Incarnation and Nativity of the Savior.

II. *" And behold, angels came."* (Matt. 4:11)

The angels are always near every one, especially at the time of temptation, although their presence is not always felt; at their own time their presence is felt, when God so disposes, under the influence of their love towards us, and when our prayers bring them near. The fruit of their coming is light, strength, peace, and joy.

III. *" And they ministered to him."* (Matt. 4:11)

1. The angels strengthen the exhausted nature of Christ, possibly with food which they offered, but still more by words proceeding from the mouth of God; they bear Him up in their hands, and render Him every kind of service; they adore and glorify Him. This ministry of theirs is inspired by the Holy Spirit, who also directly strengthened Christ's soul inwardly. This consolation was a pledge and foretaste of heavenly bliss,

when Christ, the King of the angels, would enjoy everlasting happiness, glory, and adoration.

2. Consider how true is this consolation, having no deceit mixed with it; how excellent it is, both as regards the persons from whom it proceeds, and as regards His own nature which is wholly centered on supernatural and spiritual things; how solid it is, reaching from the present life to life eternal; how closely connected it is with Christ's humility and obedience, as it were its natural outcome!

CHAPTER XXIV

The Call of the Apostles

Cf. *The Exercises*, Sec. 275

★

Part I

IN THIS contemplation, it is the call of Christ rather than the following of Christ which is emphasized. So it was in the meditation on the Two Standards, where the call appeared as part of Christ's plan. The following which we owe to Christ was considered in the meditation on the Three Classes of Men. Nevertheless consideration of the following of Christ is by no means out of place here, and the Apostles' following of Christ should be especially considered by those who may recognize in this part of the *Exercises* that the apostolic vocation is also being addressed by Christ to them. Indeed, this consideration should not be omitted by others to, since it shows with what eagerness they should prepare themselves to embrace the third kind of humility, either in effect or at least in spirit.

When contemplating the (unrecorded) call of the other Apostles, we may reflect that two factors contribute to every genuine vocation. The first is the grace of Christ, either interior alone or also exterior, more or less perceptible, but always gentle in its action. The second are the natural faculties of the soul, mind and will, the operation of which is never excluded, even in the most miraculous calls, such as that of St. Paul. In the case of ordinary vocations, their activity is of the greatest importance.

First Point. *St. Peter and St. Andrew seem to have been called three times. First, to some knowledge of our Lord. This is evident from the first chapter of St. John. Secondly, to a following of Christ in some way, but with the intention of returning to the possessions they had left. St. Luke tells us this in the fifth chapter. Thirdly, to follow Christ our Lord forever, St. Matthew, chapter four, and St. Mark, chapter one.*

Second Point. *He called Philip, as we read in the first chapter of St. John. He called Matthew, as is recorded by St. Matthew himself in the ninth chapter.*

Third Point. *He called the other Apostles, of whom no special call is mentioned in the Gospel.*

FIRST POINT: The Call of Sts. Peter and Andrew

A. THE FIRST CALL: "TO SOME KNOWLEDGE"

I. Christ calls

1. *St. Andrew.*

This call was prepared by the fact of creation, and the whole revelation of the Old Testament; then by all the graces bestowed on Andrew before the preaching of St. John; among these graces must be mentioned the poverty and humility in which St. Andrew had grown up. Christ calls him *by means of the Baptist,* a man who had gained the full confidence of Andrew and his companion; the Baptist had long before admonished his disciples about the impending arrival of the Messiah, and about the necessity to follow Him. When the Messiah had arrived at the Jordan, the Baptist again and again pointed Him out, proclaiming His eternity and divinity: "He was before me"; "This is the Son of God." Also His humility, meekness, and vicarious atonement: "Behold the lamb of God, who takes away the sin of the world." (John 1:29) Thus the Baptist kindled the desire to follow the Messiah, and at the same time trust in Him.

Lastly *Christ Himself is calling* through His friendliness of behavior and speech: He first turned to them, for they would scarcely have dared to join Him first. Jesus looks at them with a loving and winning glance, and invites them very kindly to what they had then alone distinctly in view, namely, " some knowledge " of Him. He calls out to them " Come and see! " (John 1:39) For the rest of that day the Lord most kindly conversed with them.

2. Christ calls *St. Peter*.

This call, too, was prepared by all the earlier graces, and by the teaching of the Baptist, then by the words pointing out the Messiah and related Andrew, and by the latter's information " We have found the Messiah, the Christ " (Cf. John 1:41); also by the report about the gentleness and friendliness of Christ.

Lastly, Peter, too, is called through the condescension of the Savior, His most loving look and the words, " Thou shalt be called Cephas, the rock." (Cf. John 1:42) Thus Christ rewards the faith of Peter who had believed his brother's report; Christ, however, does not yet mention the necessary condition of the following, namely, imitation of His poverty and humility.

II. The two disciples *follow the call*.

1. *St. Andrew*

fully co-operates with the Baptist's words, indicating the Messiah: " the two disciples heard him speak, and they followed Jesus." (John 1:37) St. Andrew fully co-operates with Christ's first invitation; " ' Come and see! ' They came and saw " (John 1:39); and when the Lord keeps them back, St. Andrew is again co-operating: " They stayed with him that day " (John 1:39); and immediately, with apostolic spirit, he relates the grace received to his brother Simon.

2. *St. Peter,*

on hearing his brother's account, at once co-operates with grace; he inquires further, and goes up to Jesus. Peter has faith in the Baptist's witness about Christ, reported by Andrew, and confirmed by the conversation with Jesus. Peter accepts the distinction held out to him, based on his following the Messiah; this is clear from the fact of his following Christ and the proposed change of his name. At the same time Peter, though not yet knowing what it all means, is ready to do whatever else the Messiah will demand.

B. THE SECOND CALL: " TO FOLLOW IN SOME WAY "

I. *Christ is calling.*

1. The second call of the two Apostles had been prepared by the previous call, and confirmed by many miracles of Christ, by constant experience of His friendship and holy teaching, also by the extraordinary enthusiasm of the crowd: " the crowds were pressing upon him to hear the words of God." (Luke 5:5)

2. The second call is prepared directly by the miraculous draught of fishes, so plentiful, so sudden, and after the fruitless labor of an entire night. This miracle reveals the following dispositions: Acknowledgment of their own inability, and consequently humility, " the whole night through we have toiled and have taken nothing." (Luke 5:5)—Faith: that very helplessness of theirs afforded an opportunity to confess and increase their faith: " but at thy word I will lower the net." (Luke 5:5)— Great reverence for Christ and keen knowledge of Him, together with the consciousness of their own unworthiness: " Depart from me, for I am a sinful man, O Lord." (Luke 5:8)

3. Finally there is the very call with the words, " Do not be afraid " (Luke 5:10); this supposes indeed the natural lowliness of the disciple, who naturally thinks he must fear; and on the

other hand the greatness of Christ who calls. Yet at the same time the call expresses that Christ, by His own free choice, bans every cause of fear, and invites them to continue their companionship and following. This sense of the words "Do not be afraid" is clear from the opposite words "depart from me."

"Henceforth thou shalt catch men." (Luke 5:10) This reveals the object of the call, and kindles the wish to stay on in Christ's company. Peter, then, will deal with men, and be superior to men; he will "catch men," bringing the slaves of the devil to the liberty of the children of God, bringing those dead by sin to the life of grace; and the draught which the Son of God promises will be most plentiful. The condition of the following is hinted at vaguely: "Do not be afraid" to be with me, who am poor and preach poverty.

II. The two disciples who were called *follow* Christ.

Laying aside all fear they follow Christ, leaving for a time their ships, with the intention, however, of returning to them, as is clear from the words, "They brought the ships to land" (Luke 5:11)—of course, to keep them. In this way the disciples show already spiritual poverty, making greater account of Christ than of all their things, ready to give them up as soon as Christ calls them to do so.

C. THE THIRD CALL: "TO FOLLOW FOREVER"

I. *Christ calls.*

The Apostles had come to know well the loveliness of the Lord; now He speaks but a few words to them, as He is walking by the sea of Galilee. As He has long ago been recommended by miracles, He does not now add a new one, but He merely alludes to the miraculous draught of fishes, saying: " I will make you fishers of men." (Matt. 4:19) On the other hand Christ does not merely suggest, but demands: " Come, follow me! " He tells them to abandon their former occupation forever: " I will make you fishers of men." At the same time the Lord clearly promises the graces necessary for this effect: " I will make "; it will be His work.

II. Being called, *both follow*.

" And immediately they left their nets and their father, and followed him." (Matt. 4:22) They had been casting the nets into the sea; they leave immediately, without drawing them out and putting them away.

D. REFLECT ON THE GENTLENESS OF THE CALL

I. From its most desirable *object*.

The Messiah, the Son of God, the Lamb of God: therefore the call includes all excellence and grace; it means knowledge of, and familiarity with, this Messiah, partnership with Him in life, occupation and glory.

II. From the *means* employed.

External means of every kind, such as being reared in the midst of the Chosen People, the teaching of the Baptist, the enthusiasm of the people, and in the case of St. Peter, his brother's invitation; then the appearance of Christ, His glance and way of speaking, the suitable time and great care, miracles, and, to crown all, the actual call.

Internal means, grace that enlightens the mind, sets the heart on fire, and draws the will to Christ.

III. From the *manner*.

1. It is *gentle* and considerate—the call is made three times in succession, the previous call preparing the next one; as to the object: first to some knowledgè, then to follow in some way, and finally to follow for ever; as to the motives: first the attractiveness of Him who calls, then the excellence to be acquired, and lastly the duty imposed.

2. It is also *strong:* Christ, when calling, always obtains the end He has directly in view.

IV. From the *origin and aim* of the call.

It comes from the Savior's heart, so excellent, loving, lovable, and tender; it aims at the fulness of peace which is first given to the Apostles who are called, and through them to countless others, finally consummated in the glory of heaven.

SECOND POINT: The Call of Sts. Philip and Matthew

I. *St. Philip.*

1. Christ is calling. It seems that Philip was not present when the Baptist pointed out Christ, that he was only, like other Israelites, full of expectation of the Messiah; moreover, as Jesus found him near the same place as Peter and Andrew, Philip seems to have been a disciple of the Baptist. No miracle is employed; no suggestion of the eventual vocation; only the words, " Follow Me! " A single look, joined with a most efficacious inner grace.

2. Philip follows.

He is most gently and clearly enlightened to know Christ's

excellence and the obligation of complying with His call, " without doubting, or being able to doubt."

Philip is filled with sure confidence that he will receive all the necessary grace; at the same time he is drawn so as to render doubt morally impossible.

Philip freely yields to so gentle and strong a grace; aye, beyond what grace demanded of him, he went and brought others also to the Savior.

II. St. Matthew.

1. Christ calls.

It seems that St. Matthew had not received any previous instruction; " sitting in the tax-collector's place," (Matt. 9:9) he was by no means well disposed, but rather all absorbed in an altogether different occupation, engrossed with money matters, and hardly free from every attachment to temporal goods. He too is called by a single word, " Follow me!," a single glance, joined with inner grace.

2. Matthew follows.

He too is most gently and clearly enlightened to know the vanity of his past life, the dangers of his state as a publican, the excellence of Christ and of the call that is offered, and the necessity of following.

Matthew is also filled with sure confidence of obtaining the necessary grace, deeming all sacrifices easy; at the same time he is most gently and strongly—nothing doubting, and leaving no room for doubt—impelled to renounce the world and to follow Christ.

Matthew freely yields to so gentle and strong a grace; rising up immediately, and leaving all things he followed Christ.

THIRD POINT: The Calling of the Other Apostles of Whose Particular Call the Gospel Does Not Make Mention.

I. The *other Apostles,*

we may safely take it, are using their natural powers freely and tranquilly. (Cf. Sec. 175)

1. By their *intellect* they knew Jesus was the true Messiah from the writings of the prophets, the witness of the Baptist, the words and deeds of Jesus. Hence they knew that the only way to serve God, and to procure their own salvation, was to follow Christ; they all realized that all other things, such as human relationship, occupation and possessions are of far less value, and accordingly, that they must be left if the Messiah demands it.

2. By their *will* they were kindled with an ardent desire to know Jesus more intimately, and to cling to Him as closely as possible. Day by day they became more indifferent to everything else, and so they reached spiritual poverty; in humble and diligent prayer they asked God for light, begging Him to move their wills and bring to their minds what they should do to promote His praise and glory. (Cf. Sec. 180) In the meantime they joined Christ as much as circumstances allowed.

II. The *course taken by Christ* in their case.

1. Christ might, indeed, have ended all this labor of election by a single light, as in the case of St. Matthew, but He preferred the co-operation of His chosen ones, and by slowly ripening their choice He increased their merit. All these salutary thoughts and impulses were, in fact, proceeding from Christ who, with interior grace, was stirring up and assisting the activity of nature.

2. Consider the *freedom* of man's activity, helped by God in this way. No violence is done to the natural powers, light is given gradually, doubts are allowed to crop up, but they are solved; the affections become more intense, purer, and stronger.

Consider how calmly one acts under the influence of grace. Christ continually checks the disturbances caused by the devil; God is always ready to aid us with His consolations and inspirations and make things easy for us. But *we* must give " good account " of His helps.

3. The Lord rewards co-operation with each grace by a more excellent grace; at length He gives them the Apostolic Vocation, which the Apostles would not have dared to ask for; and Apostleship will prove the source of countless more excellent graces: " He called to him men of his own choosing." (Mark 3:13)

Part II

AFTER GIVING three points for the contemplation on The Vocation of the Apostles, St. Ignatius takes the unusual step of adding: " Three other points must also be considered." We have here the outline of another exercise, presenting the apostolic vocation under a threefold and most efficacious motive. First it removes any possible *diffidence* coming from the thought of our own lowliness; secondly it excites the *desire* to share in so great a dignity; thirdly it inspires *confidence* that necessary gifts and graces will be given us. Thus, the present contemplation directly views the choice of the apostolic life, and it may well be omitted in the case of those who have thus far, during the course of the retreat, experienced no call to embrace that state of life. By the same token, in selecting or arranging the mysteries which follow, the director should consider whether or not the retreatant has felt any call to the apostolic life.

Three other points must also be considered:

1. *That all the Apostles were uneducated and from a humble condition of life.*

2. *The dignity to which they were so gently called.*

3. *The gifts and graces by which they were raised above all the Fathers of the Old and New Testaments.*

First Point: The Condition of Those Who Were Called

I. *In comparison with others who might have been called.*

The Apostles are nearly all Galileans, not Judeans; they are fishermen and publicans, not members of the higher classes; they are poor, not rich. Many others are superior to the Apostles in talent, experience, intelligence, manners, and virtue. Yet the Apostles, not those others, are called even though the latter may have co-operated better with the grace of a vocation.

II. *In comparison with Christ.*

The Apostles are nearly all Galileans, and of obscure condition; Christ is a Jew, a son of David, a King, and a Teacher; He is by far their superior in talent, knowledge, virtue, and grace. He is most holy; they are stained by personal as well as original sin; they labor under ignorance of mind and malice of will; and even after their call the Apostles did many blameworthy things. Christ is the God-Man; they are mere men. One thing recommended the Apostles: their good will at the time, and their co-operation with the previous graces.

SECOND POINT: The Excellence of the Apostolic Calling

I. As companions of the *life of Jesus*.

The Apostles were called to live with Jesus, to see and touch Him, as had been granted to Mary and Joseph, and as is the privilege of the saints in heaven. They are called to be, not servants, but friends, disciples, brethren; to be witnesses of the Lord's words, deeds, and miracles; to have a more intimate knowledge of His most lovable Heart, and to be conformed to It in the highest degree.

II. As companions of the *dignity of Jesus*.

The Apostles were called to share in the same mission which Christ had received of the Father; they share also in His authority as King, Shepherd, and High-Priest. The Apostles have, therefore, royal, pastoral, and priestly authority. They will sit with Christ as judges on the Day of Judgment.

III. As companions of the *power of Jesus*.

The Apostles are called by their new power to preach the whole teaching of Christ. Men must hear them; they will receive the great power to loose and bind under pain of sin, to offer sacrifice and to hand on to others their priestly dignity. The Apostles received all these powers with a view to the reconciliation, sanctification, and eternal glorification of men.

THIRD POINT: The Special Gifts of the Apostolic Calling

I. *On the part of Christ.*

The Apostles enjoy intercourse with Christ, an intercourse so eagerly longed for by the saints of the Old Testament, so joyfully relished by holy Simeon, and reserved for the next life in the case of the other saints.

The Apostles receive His instruction in spite of their slowness of understanding, and at the same time plentiful grace to profit by that teaching, to keep it in mind, and to impart it faithfully to others.

II. *On the part of the Holy Spirit.*

The Apostles receive abundant grace to advance in all virtue; later on there was added confirmation in grace. They received the fulness of the Spirit and of His gifts to perform their office as teachers, pastors, and priests. These powers of the Apostles are absolute both as regards place and time, embracing whatever is included in the end of the Church: teaching, sacraments, government, and special extraordinary gifts: all of these are to last " till the consummation of the world " in the Apostles and their successors.

CHAPTER XXV

The First Miracle, Performed at the Marriage Feast of Cana in Galilee

Cf. John 2:1-11; *The Exercises*, Sec. 276

★

BY THE mysteries of the Hidden Life and the Finding in the Temple St. Ignatius had showed to us two states of life open to our choice, namely, that of the commandments only and that of the commandments plus the counsels. This suggests the question whether other mysteries, perhaps, were selected for a similar reason. We suggest that the two mysteries of the Marriage at Cana and the Cleansing of the Temple were chosen to illustrate the reform of life in the state of matrimony and in the ecclesiastical state. At Cana we see Christ and the Apostles invited to share in the goods of matrimony, and in return Christ assisting His hosts in their need. This teaches on the one hand liberality towards the Church and the poor, and on the other hand trust in God, in which Christian couples should excel. In the Cleansing of the Temple, the holiness of the ecclesiastical or clerical state is defended, and a special warning is given against avarice, the " rich " money-lenders being cast out, while the " poor " sellers of doves are gently admonished. Hence, we apply these two mysteries to the reform of life in the state of matrimony or in the ecclesiastical state.

First Point. *Christ our Lord and the disciples were invited to the marriage feast.*

Second Point. *His Mother calls attention to the shortage of wine, saying to Him, " They have no wine." (John 2:3) She bids the servants, " Do whatever he tells you." (John 2:5)*

Third Point. *He changed the water into wine, " and he manifested his glory, and his disciples believed in him." (John 2:11)*

FIRST POINT: Christ Is Invited.

I. Consider that marriage is the state of intimate *communion of life* and all its goods, " and they shall be two in one flesh " (Gen. 2:24); with it is connected corresponding *gladness,* symbolized by the *wedding-feast.*

II. Consider that the benefits of this state are not restricted to the married couple alone; they must *be extended* to the children, the relations and friends: this extension, too, is signified by the wedding-feast.

III. Consider that among those invited to share in the benefits of the new state in the wedding-feast, are above all *Christ* and His *Apostles:* Christ in the person of *the poor,* the Apostles in the person of *the ministers of the Church.*

IV. Consider that in this way the married state becomes really an imitation of the state of original justice, when the first couple walked in paradise in God's company; and that the married state is full of *gladness and peace,* which are the special feature of the state of the redeemed.

SECOND POINT: Mary's Intercession

I. Temporal goods are necessary for a family, but this does not mean that they may not be scanty at times. God allows families to suffer difficulties for special reasons. Families then must be mindful of spiritual poverty and trust in God.

II. " *They have no wine.*" (John 2:3) Consider that Mary cherishes such families with special tenderness, since she is their special patroness, appointed by her Son. Mary has an eye for their temporal needs and is ready to appeal for her Son's help.

III. " *Do whatever he tells you.*" (John 2:5)

1. The family in need of temporal goods must do nothing against the word of Christ by trying to mend their condition by unlawful means.

2. They must carry out every word of Christ and lead a pious Christian life.

3. They must follow the admonitions of Christ given for those in adversity, and persevere in patience.

4. Though they may not rashly expect a miracle, let them keep a living trust in Jesus and the Blessed Virgin.

Consider that Jesus is so pleased with such families that He even makes haste to hear them: " My hour has not yet come." (John 2:4)

THIRD POINT: Christ Brings Relief.

I. Jesus comes to the rescue of the family in need. His is an easy means: all He requires is water; His provision is plentiful: filling six waterpots of stone, containing two or three measures each; moreover, the wine is of the best quality. Reflect on Christ's omnipotence, whereby He can remedy all troubles promptly and fully; see the liberality with which He helps at the silent wish of the family, and the explicit request of His Mother.

II. Jesus had come to Cana, in appearance humble and poor; omnipotence manifests His glory and divinity. Since He is God, one must believe Him when He teaches, trust in Him when He promises, and obey Him when He commands.

CHAPTER XXVI

Christ Casts the Sellers from the Temple

Cf. John 2:13-22; *The Exercises*, Sec. 277

★

First Point. *With a whip made of cords He casts all those who sell out of the Temple.*

Second Point. *He overturned the tables and scattered the money of the wealthy money-changers who were in the Temple.*

Third Point. *To the poor venders of doves He said kindly, " Take these things away, and do not make the house of my Father a house of business."* (John 2:16)

FIRST POINT: The Holiness of the Ecclesiastical State

I. *The temple.*

1. Reflect on the *purpose* of the temple.

It should be the *house of God*, where God dwells in a special manner. The temple, by a special consecration, has been dedicated to God. The temple should be a *house of prayer:* being the house of God, it is meet that it be the place for intercourse between God and man. The temple should be the special place of *sacrifice*, for it is the appointed place for the worship of God, and the chief act of worship is sacrifice

2. *The holiness of the temple.*

As house of God, the temple must be reserved for God; therefore everything profane or unholy, whether sinful or only worldly, must be excluded.

As a house of prayer, it must breathe the stillness suited for prayer.

As a house for sacrifice, it must be pervaded with the devotion that is essential to worship.

3. The *ecclesiastical state is also, in a sense, a temple.*

a. Its *purpose* is to be in some way a *house of God.* The ecclesiastical state has a special connection with God; He lavishes special graces on it, and He consecrates it in a special manner to Himself by means of holy orders.—The ecclesiastical state should also be like a *house of prayer:* for the soul set in this state is joined more intimately with God, in order to converse with Him more familiarly and with all its powers.—It should, lastly, be like a *house of sacrifice,* since it is a state directly ordained for offering the holy sacrifice of the New Law; it is most intimately united with the Redeemer hidden in the Blessed Sacrament; and it is a state devoted to the sacrifice of one's own life.

b. Its *holiness:* From the ecclesiastical state must be excluded everything profane or unholy, and still more everything sinful, above all whatever savors of *greed;* for greed opens the way to everything worldly, and it altogether retards perfection; it must be a state of calm recollection, and not of distraction through cares about worldly things; it must be a state of devotion which sanctifies even the most ordinary actions.

II. *The sellers.*

Inwardly they pay no heed to the holiness of the temple; outwardly they make a noise which is out of keeping with that holiness; they are guilty of the sin of avarice or greed, altogether unmindful of God's presence, and incapable of prayer and worship. They behave in this way during the greatest feast of the Jews, and so they turn the attention of very many away from the holiness of the temple, and give the greater scandal.

Compare with the sin of the sellers in the temple the inner and outer *defects of churchmen,* and the scandal attaching to the same.

III. *Christ.*

1. Of course Christ is inwardly convinced of the holiness of the temple, and so He burns with zeal for His Father's house; His Heart, so meek and humble, becomes incensed at the sight of the transgressions. There is no room for indulgence, though the transgressors belong to the people beloved above all others, and though the Lord has, on other occasions, witnessed many great sins without resorting to violent means. He now chooses a most efficient, violent, and painful means, the scourge or whip; and He does so at once.

2. Christ shows no less *zeal in safeguarding the holiness of the ecclesiastical state.* Accordingly the priest must not promise himself such indulgence for his transgressions as Christ not seldom shows for sinful laymen, especially at the hour of death. Nor must the priest put his confidence in graces granted to him in times of fervor. What then must the priest do? He must remove the fault and the scandal, before Christ seizes the whip!

SECOND POINT: Churchmen Must by No Means Give Preference to the Rich.

I. *The money-changers.*

Their trade is but very remotely connected with divine worship, nor is it limited only to cases relating to worship; they do not act from a motive of necessity—for they are rich—but from greed of gain; they ply their trade in the holy place, the temple, where they spend the whole day, making noise and disturbing the worshippers.

II. *Christ.*

1. The Lord shows them no indulgence. He does not allow them to stay; He does not admonish them with gentle words, rich though they be, though they may help, and probably have helped, the priests and though their anger may do the priests no little harm.

2. Aye, the Lord deals more severely with the rich than with others: He uses the whip against the persons of the money-changers, overthrows their tables, and pours out their cherished money, thus making it more difficult for them to return to their former trespasses.

3. Christ does so because their sin is the greater, on account of their better instruction and their meaner motive, because their mind is more estranged from divine worship, because the scandal whereby their greed opens the way to every kind of vice is greater. Moreover Christ is doing so to expose the priests who tolerate such trade in the temple.

4. Christ hates greed in the ecclesiastical state; He hates greater attention for the rich, in preference to the poor: where these abuses obtain, there is luxury, ambition, and pride.

THIRD POINT: Special Consideration Should Be Shown by Churchmen to the Poor.

I. *The sellers of doves.*

Their trade is more closely connected with worship, for doves were used as victims; the trade is undertaken under stress of some necessity, for those people are poor; there is far less noise and scandal connected with it, and it does not last so long, for when the owners have disposed of their scanty stock, they go home quietly.

II. *Christ deals mildly with these people.*

The Lord shows the scourge without using it; He does not upset their cages or baskets, but lets them take their things away in order; He adds mild words: " Take these things away " (John 2:16); He follows up these words with some instruction prompted by burning zeal and sweet charity, full of fervor, unction, and sweetness; He points out the dignity of the temple, the house of His Father, which must not be made a house of traffic, lowering it from such high dignity to so deep a degradation.

Christ would have the poor treated with love, even when they are doing wrong. While blaming them, one should instruct and admonish them: severity must be tempered with mildness.

CHAPTER XXVII

The Sermon on the Mount

Cf. Matthew 5; *The Exercises*, Sec. 278

★

ST. IGNATIUS presents Christ as uttering the Beatitudes
" to His beloved disciples apart," whereas the Gospel implies that they were addressed to a large crowd. The idea
is that the Apostles especially were to take Christ's teaching to heart and manifest it not only in word but also in
deed and example. This should be made clear to anyone
who has decided to choose the apostolic life.

In this mystery Christ teaches humility, but only the
second kind explicitly, not yet the third. This appears from
the third point: " He shows Himself not a transgressor of
the Law but a fulfiller." The whole teaching of this point
is that all sins are excluded, not only exterior sins but also
interior, not only grave sins but also light ones.

In the first point the Beatitudes should be considered
not separately, but *in toto,* otherwise, the matter would
be too great. Viewed summarily, the Beatitudes teach rejection of our natural inclination for objects which are
either indifferent in themselves or commonly considered
as such, e.g., material possessions, revenge, pleasure. This
kind of rejection is equivalent to detachment.

Christ exhorts His disciples " to use their talents." The
mention of " talents " here recalls what was said in the
Vocation of the Apostles about " gifts and graces by
which they were raised." (Cf. Sec. 275) The phrase " to

use their talents " is given as synonymous with Christ's saying, " Let your light shine before men." The talents are the light received, and so are to be used for the glory of our heavenly Father; at the same time, they are our light, because they are given to our free will. Nature, apart from these gifts, is like a wick or lamp waiting to be kindled by divine favors. The light shines when the talents are received, made our own, and pass into act, into good works which are to be seen by men and referred to the glory of our Father. They are to be seen by all men. What the Apostles have to do is to spread Christ's doctrine, by word certainly, but still more by example. This subordination of our whole activity to the glory of the Father, what else is it but humility as understood by St. Ignatius?

By the Sermon on the Mount Christ the King promulgates the *law of His Kingdom*. Hence this contemplation is akin to the meditation on the Kingdom of Christ. What was there stated metaphorically " whoever wishes to join me, etc." (Cf. Sec. 95) is explained here without metaphor, namely, the moral law which Christians are to observe. Since the Kingdom of Christ is both within us and outside of us, we have in the first point the law which should govern our attachments, the law of detachment; in the second and third points we have the law which should govern our exterior life, the law of good example, and in the third point we have the law of life. In all these St. Ignatius is dealing only with duties and attachments concerning our neighbor (Commandments 5 to 10), and not our duties to God or our parents. This manner of explaining St. Ignatius' arrangement of the Sermon is suggested by a comparison with the meditation on the Kingdom of Christ.

First Point. *He proposes the eight beatitudes to His beloved disciples apart: " Blessed are the poor in spirit . . . the meek . . . the merciful . . . they who mourn . . . they who hunger . . . the peace-makers . . . they who suffer persecution."* (Matt. 5:3-10)

Second Point. *He exhorts them to use their talents: " Let your light shine before men, in order that they may see your good works and give glory to your Father in heaven."* (Matt. 5:16)

Third Point. *He shows Himself not a transgressor of the Law but a fulfiller. He explains the commandments not to kill, not to commit adultery, not to swear falsely, and commands us to love our enemies: " I say to you, love your enemies, do good to those who hate you! "* (Matt. 5:44)

FIRST POINT: The Eight Beatitudes

I. To *whom* does Christ speak?

To His disciples; they are men of humble condition and little education; whatever they will become later, it will all be the result of grace.

To His beloved disciples, whom He had gently called to so great a dignity, and who would, later on, be honored with so many gifts.

He speaks to them apart: the instruction is for their own immediate use, but through them Christ has also in view those whom they will convert.

II. *What* does Christ say?

1. The eight virtues mentioned in the Beatitudes mean the rejection of our natural inclinations to objects indifferent in themselves, or which were held to be so by the Jews: wealth,

revenge, pleasure, food, zeal for self-interest, self-indulgence, stubbornness, favor with men.

2. Christ declares that this rejection is the surest way to the Kingdom of heaven, the eternal realization of every need and good. The Kingdom of heaven will satisfy these natural inclinations more abundantly, filling the hungry, etc. The poor will be happy even in this life; they will be the happier, the more efficiently they control inordinate inclinations.

3. Christ shows that this rejection gives the right of citizenship to that blessed city of Jerusalem which He will presently gather together.

N.B. See also the same teaching expressed *negatively* by St. Luke: " But woe to you rich . . . woe to you who are filled . . . woe to you who laugh now . . ." (Luke 6: 24-25)

1. Christ warns against indulging in those inclinations.

2. He declares that such indulgence excludes from higher gain, " you are now having your comfort . . . you shall hunger . . . you shall mourn and weep." (Luke 6:24-25) Accordingly for such even the present life contains woe that must rightly be lamented, and that deprives the soul of peace.

III. *Who* utters the Beatitudes?

Consider how all this teaching comes from the lips of Christ: " And opening his mouth." (Matt. 5:2) The teaching, then, is from God Himself, from the Incarnate Word, and consequently is infallibly true, full of sweetness and of grace. Lastly, this teaching comes from the most humble Heart of the Savior, for " the things that proceed out of the mouth come from the heart." (Matt. 15:18)

Consider also how this teaching, as the summary and program of His whole doctrine, is mentioned in the very first place; how He stresses it, pointing out the contrast: " Blessed " and " Woe! "—further, by the enumeration of the several inclinations, and by repeating the declaration: " Blessed " and "Woe!"—It is also emphasized by the diversity of images under which He expresses one and the same happiness, one and the same damnation: " Theirs is the kingdom of heaven; they shall possess the land," etc.

SECOND POINT: On the Good Use of One's Talents

I. " *You are the light of the world.*" (Matt. 5:14)

Of yourself you are the small, insignificant wick of a lamp, owing to your mean condition; but you are the light through my free gift; nevertheless you are truly a light, so that the brightness with which you shine is truly yours, with all its splendor and blessing. The Apostles will be the light by the doctrine which they will preach, by the Christlike life they will manifest in word and work, and by the direction of others to whom they will show the path. They are to be the light " of the world." Reflect on the greatness of this call, through which the Apostles are made the light set upon the candle-stick, the city towering high on the top of a hill; see also the benefits this implies, since it embraces all men.

II. " *So let your light shine before men in order that they may see your good works.*" (Matt. 5:16)

1. " *Let it shine.*" It is the light given by God when it appears in our lives it stamps us as His followers. It is a talent of which

you must, some day, give an account. It must shine in proportion to the light you have received; "before men," hence it is given for the salvation of the human race.

2. The light of the Apostles must shine *by their works*, and especially by the example of their lives. It must show the affections of the heart; a pharisaical observance of the law, with a perverted inner disposition of the heart, is not enough; the example of the Apostles must express the *law of Christ*, which is the rule for living one's life correctly.

III. "*That they may . . . give glory to your Father in heaven*." (Matt. 5:16)

1. Do not seek your own glory, for that would be to cheat God; self-seeking begets pride and hinders grace; Christ, too, did not seek His own glory.

2. Seek ye the Father's glory: for this alone you were created; this alone is the aim of God, and of Christ from the moment of the Incarnation: Glory to God in the highest! It is becoming that the Apostles seek exclusively the goal which their Master is seeking: only thus will they find peace, and be for others the messengers of true peace.

THIRD POINT: The Perfect Fulfilment of the Law

I. Consider that Christ demands perfect observance of His Law.

1. That fulfilment must be perfect in regard to *keeping what is prescribed*:

Speaking in general, His Law excludes not only exterior sins but also interior ones; not only grievous sins but also small ones. It demands not only the first kind of humility but the second as well.

In particular Christ forbids not only murder but also every kind of hatred, with the obligation of full reconciliation; not only adultery but every voluntary sexual indulgence; not only divorce with a bill of rejection but every kind of divorce, " save on account of immorality " (Matt. 5:32); not only perjury but every deviation from straightforward speech; not only is revenge forbidden but we are ordered to return good for evil; Christ demands love not of friends only but even love of our enemies.

2. As for the supreme *rule of observance:*

" You therefore are to be perfect." (Matt. 5:48) This means that the Apostles must be free from venial as well as mortal sin, and from every disorder in the heart: " As also your heavenly Father is perfect." The model of our perfection is the unstained perfection of the Father; the motive is that we are God's children, and hence must become like Him; we are destined for heaven, and hence must be ever more and more free from stain.

II. Consider *how insistently Christ recommends perfection.*

Christ does so *repeatedly* and *emphatically:* " Do not think that I have come to destroy. . . . I have not come to destroy, but to fulfill." (Matt. 5:17)—He confirms this recommendation by an *assurance:* " For amen I say to you, till heaven and earth pass away, not one jot or one tittle shall be lost from the Law till all things have been accomplished." (Matt. 5:18)

Christ inculcates it also by *threats* and *promises:* " Whoever does away . . . shall be called least in the kingdom of heaven; but whoever carries them out and teaches them, he shall be called great in the kingdom of heaven . . . unless your justice exceeds that of the Scribes and Pharisees, you shall not enter the kingdom of heaven." (Matt. 5: 19-20) From the general statement He comes down to *particular cases*, and again distinguishes various applications of these. By constant *antithesis* He lays stress on the perfection which He requires: "You have heard that it was said to the ancients . . . But I say to you . . ." (Matt. 5:21)

CHAPTER XXVIII

Christ Calms the Storm

Cf. Matthew 8:23-27; *The Exercises*, Sec. 279

★

THERE FOLLOW now seven mysteries, the first five of which are placed in a different order from that followed in the Gospel. Thus the Calming of the Storm is followed immediately by the Walking on the Sea. There is an evident affinity between these two mysteries: both took place on the Sea of Galilee, and both teach us not to fear, but to trust in Christ: something we must do if we are to fight Lucifer. In both mysteries the disciples show fear and are reproved for their " little faith " by Christ, who finally removes the cause of their fear. We are invited in these mysteries to consider more deeply who Christ is: " What kind of man is this . . ? " " Truly thou art the Son of God." (Matt. 14:33)

There is, however, a difference in these two mysteries. In both there is a storm. In the former the disciples' lack of trust is corrected by a miracle; in the latter we see them, now better instructed, calmly rowing. Then a new cause of fright presents itself, not this time the effect of natural causes, but from the spiritual world: " A Ghost! " (Matt. 14:26) Again, the faith of the disciples falters, and again it is restored by the word of Christ; indeed, St. Peter profits by the occasion to rise to faith of miracles. But this gives rise to a new occasion for fear, which causes St. Peter to sink. In all this we see a certain evolution. The lesson is always trust, not only when any kind of danger threatens but also when every kind of natural aid is missing. Thus, these two mysteries most effectively teach what was inculcated in the first two points of the second part of the Two Standards, namely the need of trust, which usually leads effectively to action and is needed in the first place for a generous choice.

First Point. *While Christ our Lord was asleep in the boat on the sea, a great storm arose.*

Second Point. *His terrified disciples awaken Him. He reprehends them for the little faith they have, and says to them, " Why are you fearful, O you of little faith? "* (Matt. 8:26)

Third Point. *He commanded the wind and sea to cease, and they obeyed, and the sea became calm. And the men marveled, saying, " What manner of man is this, that even the wind and sea obey him? "* (Matt. 8:27)

First Point: The Tempest

I. Christ was asleep at sea.

1. The sea is a restless, barren element, full of dangers, not suited for a lasting abode in contrast to the shore or land which is firm, fertile, safe and covered with fixed dwellings. This is an image of the present life which is restless, wretched, passing, full of dangers, in contrast to the everlasting and blissful life in heaven.

2. Christ was on the sea: Christ our Lord, the God-Man, the Lord of land and water, of time and eternity. By His Incarnation He had come down from the shore of eternity to the sea of mortal life, subjecting Himself to all the changes of this life, yet retaining at the same time mastery over it. At present He

is on the ship with the disciples, able to have compassion with their needs and to rescue them from danger; therefore nothing could happen to them except by Christ's permission; while they were with Christ all things would turn out for their safety, and they required only confidence in Him.

3. *Christ was asleep:* The Lord did not show any visible effect of His divine presence, nor of His human presence either; nevertheless, the mere fact of His bodily presence was an absolutely sufficient pledge of safety: the ship that carried Him could not perish.

II. *There arose a great storm.*

1. *The storm:* God allows, as a result of natural causes, a storm to spring up against the Apostles; He will also allow storms to arise against us, whether as the outcome of the laws of nature, or of our corruption or that of the world, men, and the devil. God will allow this in order to stir up in us faith, trust, humility, and in order the more strikingly to manifest His power; in this way He weans us more and more from all attachment to earthly things, and He invites us to share more fully in the riches of the supernatural life hidden in Himself.

2. The tempest was *great:* This was due to the violent commotion of air and water. The storm struck fear in the Apostles' hearts, fear for their very lives. For us, too, there are tempests in store, great ones as well as small, when there will be need of great faith, trust, and humility; Christ will use great power to rescue us, and the fruit in true life will be great.

3. Consider how the Apostles had absolutely nothing to fear in that storm, however great it was, since they had Christ, even Christ asleep, with them in the ship: " There arose a great storm on the sea . . . but he was asleep." (Matt. 8:24)

SECOND POINT: Christ Is Awakened.

I. *His disciples, frightened, awakened Him.*

1. *They awakened Him:* In misfortune we must have recourse to Jesus, and awaken Him by prayer; we cannot save ourselves, but He is the Lord having both the power and the will to save, and He wishes us to come to Him. In fact, He allows dangers for this very purpose. Why are we so often overcome by temptation, or overwhelmed by desolation? Because we do not awaken Christ by prayer. This is the only true danger.

2. *Frightened:* The Apostles made too much of the danger, and not enough of Christ; so fearful were they that all their trust in Christ disappeared; this is evident from *their words,* " we are perishing." (Matt. 8:25) They declare absolutely that they are lost: Master, doth it not concern Thee that we perish? These words show want of reverence.—The same is clear from *their actions:* they seem to suppose that Jesus cannot help them if He is not awake; that is why they arouse Him vigorously.

II. *Christ reproaches them* for the little faith which they had, saying: " why are you fearful, O you of little faith! " (Matt. 8:26)

1. *Why are you fearful:* Where Jesus is there is no reason to fear, because His power is able to remove any danger however great, surely, wholly, easily, instantaneously; and because His Sacred Heart is watchful for our safety. Therefore he wrongs the power or the love of Jesus, who is frightened, while he has Jesus with him in the ship.

2. *You of little faith:* It betrays lack of trust to fear when you have Jesus with you, however great dangers threaten even your lives. In spite of their poor condition, little prudence, and virtue the disciples of Christ, who have Him in their ship, must have the greatest faith and trust.

3. Jesus does not give help until He has strengthened the weak faith of the Apostles: our little faith is often the cause why we are not heard.

Third Point: The Tempest Is Stilled.

I. *He commanded the winds and the sea to cease,* and, so ceasing, the sea became calm.

1. Rising up from His humble couch, and solemnly standing up, the Lord commanded. Usually so humble and lovable, He now uses words expressing the fullest authority, bidding the winds and the waters—elements altogether rebellious against the will of man—be quiet, wholly and instantly. " And there came a great calm." (Matt. 8:26)

2. Reflect, then, on the power of Christ's word, when He commands, or when He counsels and advises. " I can do all things in him who strengthens me." (Phil. 4:13) This applies also to the state of life to which Christ calls me, in spite of all difficulties, and to perseverance in that state in spite of any temptations whatever.

II. At this the *men wondered,* saying, " What manner of man is this, that even the wind and sea obey him? " (Matt. 8:27)

1. At once after performing the miracle Jesus sits down, again humble and lovable; yet under the appearance of humility is ever hidden the ready fulness of majesty and power, whereby He can easily rescue us from all dangers.

2. Rendered attentive by this miracle, the men inquire, who is this man of so humble appearance: What manner of man is this whom the wind and water obey?—I also must know the Savior more and more intimately, in order to understand His divinity, and in order to trust most fully that He is both able and willing to help me in all things.

CHAPTER XXIX

Christ Walks upon
the Waters

Cf. Matthew 14:22-33; *The Exercises*, Sec. 280

★

First Point. *Whilst Christ our Lord remained on the mountain, He commanded His disciples to go away in the boat, and after He had dismissed the crowd, He began to pray alone.*

Second Point. *The boat was buffeted by the waves. Christ came toward them walking upon the waters, and the disciples thought they saw an apparition.*

Third Point. *Christ says to them, " it is I, do not be afraid."* (Matt. 14:27) *St. Peter at His command walked upon the waters and came to Jesus, but when he doubted, he began to sink. Christ saved him and reprehended him for his little faith. They entered into the boat and the wind ceased.*

First Point: The Apostles Are Sent away into the Ship.

I. *The Apostles are sent away.*

Christ knows the storm is coming, yet does not keep the disciples from going into the ship; for He wishes to guide them through trials to true life. Nay, He ordered them to go away from Him, thereby showing that His visible bodily presence, as was the case in the preceding miracle of the stilling of the storm, was not at all required to save them. Accordingly, whether Christ is present in body or not, the Apostles are perfectly safe from every danger.

II. *Christ at prayer.*

1. The safety of the Apostles is due to Christ's prayer. He who prays is the Son of God Himself.—He sets about praying: applying each and every faculty of His soul, making acts in due order, repeating, increasing, and changing these acts.—How does Christ pray? Having dismissed the multitude, He commenced to pray alone, He is on the mountain, united to God alone, withdrawn from all the rest, and by reverent behavior of the body He shows this solitude of His mind.—When does He pray? At the very time when the disciples, having gone up into the boat, are sailing on the sea.—For whom is He praying? For His disciples.—For what is He praying? " That they may have life, and have it more abundantly " (John 10:10); and that they may profit by the present trial.—What is the result of His prayer? Ponder the infinite excellence, and the infallible efficacy of Christ's prayer: the Apostles cannot perish while Christ is praying for them.

2. The sea is the world, this inconstant, changeable life; the mountain is heaven, where Christ is at the right hand of the Father, interceding for us: they are safe in any storms whatsoever, for whom Christ in heaven is interceding and praying.

Second Point: Christ Comes near His Disciples.

I. *The little boat was tossed about by the waves.*

Consider how the Apostles continue steadily at the work. They were laboring in rowing, about twenty-five to thirty furlongs, until " the fourth watch of the night," (Matt. 14:25) without showing any signs of fright or alarm. This is the fruit of the temptation through which they had passed in the preceding mystery; note the utility of temptation. All this time Christ goes on praying, and His prayer obtains for them the grace of endurance and calm.

II. *To which Christ came walking on the water.*

1. From the mountain Christ watches the labor of His disciples: He is omniscient. In His exceeding kindness He sets out to strengthen them, without being asked, forestalling all their expectation, while they were still in the midst of the sea. Christ walks on the sea: He is omnipotent.

2. Consider how absolutely safe from all danger the Apostles are in the midst of the waves, while Omnipotence most kindly hurries to their help.

3. Nevertheless He would have passed by them. Christ wants to be called by prayer; if they had not called, He would have passed by; He must be called by prayer, that He may come by consolation.

III. *The disciples thought is was an apparition.*

1. Consider the unreliability of man's judgment when upset by distrust: at one time it thinks Christ to be an apparition, at another time it mistakes a devilish apparition for an angel of light. See the unreliability of man's virtue, however well tried otherwise; the foolishness of distrust which looks upon Christ hastening to help, as if He were an empty vision, and trembles, although Christ, who exercised His authority over the storm, is also able to exercise His authority over an apparition.

2. Christ is not angered at this mistake of distrust, nor does He withdraw, because the will of the Apostles, in spite of their doubts, is still sincerely clinging to the Master.

THIRD POINT: Christ Makes Himself Known to the Disciples.

I. Be of good heart, it is I, *fear not!*

The sound of the voice helps the Apostles to discern

the speaker's form. "It is I," therefore not a vision, but I who command wind and water, who snatched you from danger on another occasion; I who love you so well, who have called you, and have already overwhelmed you with so many graces. Accordingly, "fear not": while I am at your side, there can be no ground for fear.

II. *St. Peter.*

1. Just now Peter was, with the other disciples, plunged in faint-heartedness; now, at Christ's voice, he rises to the very peak of faith, the faith of miracles. See how quietly the grace of Christ can raise us from lowest despondency to the highest virtue. At the words, "it is I," there revive in Peter's mind faith and trust in Christ. Hence, "if it is thou"—you can bid me walk upon the water, and if you order it, I can do it; therefore "bid me come to thee over the water." (Matt. 14:28)

2. Christ rewards such faith with the favor of a miracle. The word "Come" proceeds from the same authority that had pronounced the "let it be made" of creation, and that laid down the laws of winds and seas; that word brought to Peter's mind the grace of the Apostolic call conferred thereby, together with so many graces. By the word "Come" Peter received the grace to obey, and the forces of nature were suspended.

3. With his look fixed on Jesus, Peter walks by faith upon the water; but when his attention was drawn away from Christ, and turned to the strong wind, he once again slips from the height of faith to the depth of fear: as he begins to fear, he also begins to sink; yet Peter is still sustained to some extent by the power of Christ that the sinking may not be for his destruction but for his salvation. Thus the imminent danger caused Peter again to look to Jesus; he once more rises to genuine faith

acknowledging the fulness of power in Jesus, and with the cry, " Save me," he appeals to the Master's kindness.

III. *Christ.*

1. The Lord does not at all reject Peter when he is unsteady in faith, but, stretching forth His all-powerful hand, He frees Peter from the danger to his life. Aye, by adding a gentle rebuke, He frees Peter yet more from wavering and faintheartedness, and He fills the disciples with an abundance of true life and liberty.

2. Having gone up into the boat, Christ now, without speaking a word, without stretching forth His hand, by a mere act of the will, soothes the wind and in no time brings the boat to the shore. (Cf. John 6:21)

3. By this striking miracle the Apostles understood most fully what is the ultimate reason of the great power and kindness of Jesus, namely His divinity; and they acknowledged it by adoring Him and saying, " truly thou art the Son of God." (Matt. 14:33)

CHAPTER XXX

The Apostles Are Sent to Preach

Cf. Matthew 10:1-16; *The Exercises*, Sec. 281

★

THIS MYSTERY increases *trust*, as it shows the power of Christ not only over storms and apparitions but over the devils and all manner of disease. It shows this power not merely exercised for the good of the disciples but communicated to them to use.

As in the Two Standards, the disciples are sent forth, though not as yet throughout the whole world, for Christ said, " Do not go in the direction of the Gentiles." (Matt. 10:5) They will receive their universal mission only after the Resurrection. At present, too, their power is limited to casting out devils from men's bodies and curing all bodily ailments. After the Resurrection they will receive in addition the greater powers of teaching and baptizing, of feeding Christ's sheep, forgiving sins and curing ailments of the soul. The meditations develop more fully ideas which are contained in germ in the mysteries.

They are to preach the kingdom of heaven, which, as we learned from the Sermon on the Mount, is to be obtained by abnegation of natural inclinations, and especially by poverty and humility: " for theirs is the kingdom of heaven." (Matt. 5:3) What is the kingdom of heaven except the kingdom of Christ?

First Point. *Christ calls His beloved disciples and gives them power to cast out devils from the bodies of men, and to heal their infirmities.*

Second Point. *He teaches them prudence and patience, " Behold, I am sending you forth like sheep in the midst of wolves. Be therefore wise as serpents and guileless as doves."* (Matt. 10:16)

Third Point. *He tells them how they should go, " Do not keep gold, or silver, or money in your girdles."* (Matt. 10:9) *" Freely you have received, freely give."* (Matt. 10:8) *And He told them what to preach: " And as you go, preach the message, ' The kingdom of heaven is at hand! ' "* (Matt. 10:7)

FIRST POINT: The Sending of the Apostles.

I. *Christ calls His beloved disciples.*

They are the same beloved ones to whom He had before shown so great love in preference to others: Christ is faithful in His love. At first He had called them to follow Him; they did follow Him. Following Christ, they came to understand His virtues, especially prudence and patience, His method of conduct and preaching, and His miracles. At present He calls the disciples to a kind of apprenticeship; by this call Christ bestows on them understanding of what they are to preach, and eloquence to explain it. He holds ready the graces to be granted to the preachers as well as to the hearers.

II. *Christ sends them.*

Who sends? The Son of God, who has divine authority.
Whom does He send? Men of such plain and poor condition.

To whom does He send them? "To the lost sheep of the house of Israel" (Matt. 10:6): They are His sheep acquired as "the fruit of the loins" of Abraham, Israel, and the other patriarchs. These sheep were lost, having fallen into sin through the cunning of Lucifer; and as a consequence they were entangled in manifold sickness of the body, and even frequently enslaved by diabolic possession.

For what does He send them? To preach, even as they had heard Christ preach, with His words enlightening the minds and rousing the wills. The aim of this preaching is to lead men to Christ the Savior, to bring back the sheep, to heal and free them.

III. And *He gives them the power* to cast out devils from human bodies, and to cure all diseases.

This preaching meets an obstacle in men's slothfulness, and in the devil's cunning. To counteract this, Christ gives to the Apostles, *as their own*, the power of miracles: it extends to all evils affecting men's bodies, whether coming from the forces of nature or from evil spirits. The Apostles are to judge which miracles, and how many, they shall perform. The power given now is a pledge of the fuller power to be bestowed later, to loosen also the spiritual fetters of Lucifer.

SECOND POINT: The Inner Disposition of the Apostles

I. *The future condition of the Apostles.*

1. "*Behold, I am sending you.*" (Matt. 10:16) Consider the Sender's wisdom, omnipotence and kindness: accordingly the Apostles will have, in every trial, as the previous mysteries have

shown already, the supernatural help of Christ ready at hand, and will be safe " in the midst of wolves." Such help, however, will not upset the nature of things: wherefore the Apostles must walk with such caution as is required by their dangerous surrounding.

2. " *As sheep in the midst of wolves.*" (*Ibid.*) The Apostles must be sheep, as Christ Himself is the Lamb of God; unarmed, meek, humble, patient, peaceful; aye, they must be prepared to be slain in the end.

The wolves are of Lucifer's herd: fierce, violent, ravenous, filled with special dislike and hatred of the sheep, exceedingly strong in number and in craft for doing harm; therefore the ruin of those sheep will be even more imminent than was that of the Apostles when tossed in the midst of the tempest.

II. *The virtues to be practiced.*

Christ does not send His dear lambs into the midst of the wolves without giving them useful hints.

1. They must observe *prudence,* proceeding warily, approaching and gaining entrance noiselessly, like serpents, not urging everything at the same time, trying to become all things to all men. Their prudence, however, must be that of simplicity, not cunning. They are to be like doves, without guile, not tempting and laying snares, but going straight to the end.

2. They must have patience under adversity: this is the same as humility. Christ foretells insults, tortures, and death in store for them; the Apostles shall be betrayed by their nearest friends, be brought before courts, scourged, and put to death. Let them remember that " no disciple is above his teacher, nor is the servant above his master. It is enough for the disciple to be like his teacher, and for the servant to be like his master." (Matt. 19:24-25)

THIRD POINT: The Outward Behavior of the Apostles

I. *The manner of their going.*

1. In the person of the preacher poverty is prescribed: "Do not keep gold nor silver." (Matt. 10:9) Such possessions pave the way for Lucifer's snares; the lack of such possessions is the safest protection of humility, and of every virtue. Christ was without these things, and so must be the Apostles who are to preach poverty.

2. Their ministry of preaching must be done freely: "Freely you have received, freely give." (Matt. 10:9) Consider what great graces had been freely given the Apostles; consequently they must give them freely, since their labor to communicate these gifts is to be rewarded not by those who receive, but by Christ who gave them. Thus greater glory is given to the Father from whom all good gifts proceed.

II. *The matter to preach.*

"The kingdom of heaven is at hand." (Matt. 10:8) Its king is the king of heaven and Christ the Son of God; it was founded from heaven on earth, and it leads to heaven where it goes on without end; this kingdom is the reward of God's servants, the heirloom of the children of God, the prize of them that fight; between the kingdom and hell there is no other choice: therefore all must needs enter the kingdom of heaven; its law is the law of heaven, most just, wise, and holy. It is at hand. Make haste to enter it!

Consider with what cheerfulness the disciples ought to obey Christ's most liberal and honorable call.

CHAPTER XXXI

The Conversion of Magdalene

Cf. Luke 7:36-50; *The Exercises*, Sec. 282

★

IN THE Gospel this mystery comes before the three just explained. Their affinity is seen more clearly in the order adopted by St. Ignatius. There " little faith " is blamed; here " saving faith " is praised. There the persons present ask: " What manner of man is this, that even the wind and sea obey him? " (Matt. 8:27) or they confess: " Truly thou are the Son of God." (Matt. 14:33) Here they say within their heart (though St. Ignatius does not quote these words): " Who is this man, who even forgives sins? " (Luke 7:49) There is also a gradation: in the two previous mysteries physical evils, such as shipwreck, drowning possession by the devil are removed; in this one a moral evil, sin, is removed.

First Point. *Magdalene, carrying an alabaster vase full of ointment, enters the house of the Pharisee where Christ is seated at table.*

Second Point. *She stood behind our Lord near His feet, and began to wash them with her tears, and wiped them with her hair. She kissed His feet, and anointed them with ointment.*

Third Point. *When the Pharisee accused Magdalene, Christ spoke in her defense, saying, " her sins, many as they are, shall be forgiven her, because she has loved much . . . But he said to the woman, ' Thy faith has saved thee; go in peace.' "* (Luke 7:47, 50)

FIRST POINT: Magdalene Comes In.

I. *Jesus.*

He is the true life because He is God; " in him was life "; (John 1:4) as man He has the fulness of grace, and by the Father's decree He is the sole source of supernatural life for us. Hence His Sacred Heart longs for nothing else from the very beginning of His mortal life: " That they may have life, and have it more abundantly." (John 10:10) All His thoughts, desires, and actions are centered on this; all His teaching and miracles aim only at this, and so does even the law of self-denial. Fired by this desire Jesus went to the Pharisee's house, and sat at table, ready to impart life also to the Pharisee, provided that he has the necessary disposition.

II. *The Pharisee.*

He is an Israelite, prominent among his fellow-citizens, blessed with earthly goods, well versed in the Law, distinguished for its outward observance, a champion of his nation's freedom: he is therefore distinguished in all that men commonly make much of.

Nevertheless our Pharisee lacks the dispositions necessary for receiving supernatural life, without which all other things are of no value. He lacks humility, since he is proud, trusts his own judgment, and judges others. He lacks faith: he invited Jesus, not because he acknowledged Him as the Messiah, for he does not even consider Him as a prophet. Accordingly he receives the Lord with no special mark of honor, giving Him no water for His feet, no oil for His head, nor does he salute Him with a kiss. The Pharisee does not expect any grace from Christ: why, indeed, should he, since he deems himself to be in every way perfect? He invited the Master only out of curiosity. Lacking the necessary dispositions, the Pharisee, though sitting close by the Sacred Heart, does not receive any grace; quite near the fire he remains cold; touching the source of light and life he remains blind and dead.

III. *Magdalene.*

She is called " a sinner," one stained by sin, not by one or a few only, but her life had been most sinful; she was known throughout the town for her sins, branded with the name " the sinner." And whereas she was spiritually dead, she was moreover the occasion of death to others. She is very far removed from the life of Christ.

Nevertheless she enters now, without an invitation from the Pharisee, who would never admit such a woman into his house. Magdalene had heard of Christ's teaching, miracles, and kindness; this was the first grace, and the abandoned sinner did not reject it. From this came a second grace, a desire of curiosity to see and hear the great prophet. There followed a third grace, fear lest the prophet should see the bottom of her heart. Thence arose a clear knowledge of and sincere shame for the sins she had committed; there arose also trust that He who had declared Himself to be the Son of God, would not only penetrate the secrets of the heart, but would also have the power and the will to remit her sins. Thus there springs up an eager desire to obtain life, and a hope that day after day becomes surer, together with true sorrow, ardent love, and a firm purpose of amendment.

As a proof of her changed frame of mind, she brings an alabaster vessel with precious ointment: once it was an enticement to licentiousness, but now it shall be devoted to the feet of the Savior. Consider how the grace of Christ stirred up all these good feelings in the heart of Magdalene, leading her a long way from death to life.

SECOND POINT: Magdalene Anoints the Lord.

I. *Jesus.*

This first sign of faith, sorrow, and love does not move Jesus to turn to the woman, as she comes in; yet the Sacred Heart rejoices at her coming, and He cherishes and increases the same feelings in the heart of Magdalene.

II. *Magdalene.*

The *place* to which she withdraws shows her humility: she does not stand near, or before, but behind the Lord; nor by the head, but at His feet.

Words of hers: none are heard, so great is the consciousness of unworthiness; the violence of the inner contrition chokes her voice; and so intense is her love which tells her that Christ sees all without any words.

Her actions: she began to wash His feet with tears of sorrow; she " wiped them with the hair of her head," and " anointed them with ointment: " (Luke 7:38)—as many proofs of her thoroughly firm purpose; then " she kissed the feet " with ardent love.

Consider the constant increase of faith, love, and sorrow given to her soul by the grace of Christ, and see the life of grace overcoming the death of sin.

THIRD POINT: Magdalene Is Justified.

I. *The Pharisee.*

Lacking faith and charity, the Pharisee judges haughtily about what is being done; he accuses Magdalene of irreverence, and Christ of ignorance and of falsely claiming prophetical authority. See how easily and grievously they err in their judgment who have strayed from faith and charity.

II. *Jesus.*

1. *He speaks in her defence.*—Christ proclaims the law concerning the proportion between love and gift: men, who see only the outward gifts, and not the inward love, are accustomed to measure love by the presents; God, who searches what is within, proceeds the opposite way, granting inner pardon in proportion to the love displayed.

Having laid down this law, Christ declares that the woman has been granted *remission* of many, *i.e.*, all her sins, in proportion to *her great love;* He praises her remarkable *faith* and the *salvation* she has obtained thereby: she has obtained the *peace* which is the fruit of the Incarnation.

Consider how important for salvation is true faith and love; how fortunate must therefore have been Magdalene, the sinner, to learn from the mouth of Truth in person, that her faith and love were true, and that her salvation was certain.

2. By *the very same action Christ defends Himself*: for He shows that He knows the innermost thoughts of the Pharisee,

and He thus refutes the accusation of ignorance. By exercising the power to remit sin (which also shows His power of reading hearts), He establishes His prophetic authority: thereby He invites the bystanders seriously to examine the question: " Who is this man, who even forgives sins? " (Luke 7:49)

III. *Magdalene.*

She goes in peace: having received pardon of her sins, and the salvation of her soul; she enjoys supernatural life; she is filled with sweetest peace after the anguish of a life spent in sin.

She perseveres in peace: the life of grace just received is never again lost; as a faithful disciple she follows Christ as He goes about the country; she has a place under the cross with the Mother of Jesus; after the Resurrection she is visited first of all the disciples; having spent her life in penance and charity she dies in peace.

CHAPTER XXXII

Christ Feeds the
Five Thousand

Cf. Matthew 14:13-21; *The Exercises*, Sec. 283

★

IN THE Gospel this mystery comes before the Walking on the Water. As placed here by St. Ignatius it continues the gradation which we noticed in the four previous mysteries, and it increases the feeling of *trust* inculcated in the Two Standards and those four mysteries. There was shown in them, more or less, the *negative* side of the goods found in Christ, namely, protection against evils of nature, devils, and sin. Now we see the *positive* goods given us by Christ: in the feeding of the five thousand is foreshadowed the spiritual food to be offered the faithful through the Church's ministries by doctrine, government, and above all by the Holy Eucharist; in the Transfiguration shines forth the glory of life everlasting; in the raising of Lazarus Christ stands before us as " the resurrection and the life." These, like the previous mysteries, invite us also to study more closely the *person of Christ*: the feeding of the five thousand does not do so explicitly, unless we connect it to the confession made by St. Peter in the previous mystery; the Transfiguration does so by the words of the Father: " This is my beloved Son, in whom I am well pleased " (Matt. 17:5)—the raising of Lazarus, by the words of Christ: " I am the resurrection and the life; he who believes in me, even if he die, shall live . . . . Dost thou believe this? " (John 11:25-26) From what has been said it will be seen that, regarding the order in which St. Ignatius places the mysteries for the stilling of the storm to the Transfiguration, we are inclined to favor the opinion that the author's sole idea is to reveal Christ to us more intimately and to increase our faith.

First Point. *Since it was getting late, the disciples asked Jesus to dismiss the multitude of people who were with Him.*

Second Point. *Christ our Lord commanded them to bring the loaves of bread to Him, and ordered the people to sit down. Then He blessed the bread, broke it, and gave it to the disciples who gave it to the multitude.*

Third Point. *" And all ate and were satisfied; and they gathered up what was left over, twelve baskets full of fragments."* (Matt. 14:20)

FIRST POINT: The Eagerness of the Crowd

I. *The multitude.*

1. These many people are the kingdom of heaven gathered around their King, listening to His teaching, and witnessing His miracles.

2. When Jesus crossed the lake in a boat, many followed Him on foot. Seeing them like sheep that had no shepherd, Jesus once more taught, healed, and spoke of His kingdom. And the people listened, regardless of time, food, and their return journey.

3. Really, this multitude hungered after justice, and they were now to receive their fill from Christ.

II. *The disciples.*

They ask our Lord to dismiss the crowd, following thereby human prudence. However their request obtains something far greater, for Christ, by a striking miracle, feeds the five thousand. We must always persevere in prayer, even if our prayers seem to have no effect at all, or not the effect desired.

SECOND POINT: The Nature of the Miracle about to Be Performed

I. *Christ* resolved to refresh the crowd with *heavenly bread.*

Jesus is the *true life,* giving life through His Divinity. He is also the *bread of life;* His doctrine nourishes our intellectual life; His grace, sensibly manifested by miracles, wins for us eternal life; His flesh He gives to us as daily bread.

II. *Further intention of Christ.*

1. Jesus means to use the Apostles as the ministers of this miracle, and thus to indicate beforehand the office which will be given them afterwards, the office of being the ministers of all supernatural life.

2. Christ would thereby teach us that true life is not separated from us by a great interval of time or place, but that it is present everywhere and at all times; that the bread of life is broken for us by the disciples.

III. *The part of the disciples.*

1. The Apostles are used as ministers of this miracle: they bring the bread: for no bread is allowed, but that brought by

their hands; they arrange the crowd: only they who sit down in the order assigned by the Apostles are admitted to the banquet of the miraculous food; they distribute the bread which Christ has blessed: His blessing is the source of the multiplication, yet the multiplication does not take place before the bread has passed through the Apostles' hands.—" He broke." Consider how few and small those fragments are, which are to be multiplied and magnified in the hands of the Apostles.—And He " gave them to his disciples, and the disciples gave them to the crowds." (Matt. 14:19) See the multiplication of the loaves in the ministers' hands, and notice that only what they distribute is multiplied.

2. All this points beforehand to the time when the same disciples shall be the ministers of the whole supernatural life: preaching Christ's doctrine as the supreme teachers, governing the whole Christian life as supreme pastors, and administering the sacraments as supreme priests. Consider how holy are the lips and the hands of the priest!

THIRD POINT: The Multitude Is Fed.

I. *The Multitude.*

1. The whole five thousand and more had their fill and the fragments left over filled twelve baskets: Consider how good and abundant was that bread and how completely it renewed their strength. Yet its effect lasted only a short time; its taste was soon forgotten, its abundance exhausted, the strength it gave lost.

2. Consider the far more numerous crowd which the ministry of the Apostles will later refresh all over the earth until the end of time with the bread of true life, the teaching and sacraments of Christ. Consider how satisfying is this bread, superior to all earthly nourishment; its abundance, affording such fulness as excludes every further hunger, is unsurpassed. " He who comes

to me shall not hunger," (John 6:35) and " He who eats this bread, shall live for ever." (John 6:59)

II. *Turn your eyes to Christ.*

He is the bread of life, the source and origin of all our life. Reflect how from His lips proceeds the infallible teaching preached by the Apostles; how His graces and sacraments are given to us by their hands. We hear His voice from their lips.

CHAPTER XXXIII

The Transfiguration

Cf. Matthew 17:1-9; *The Exercises*, Sec. 284

★

First Point. *Jesus took with Him His beloved disciples, Peter, James, and John, and He was transfigured before them. His face became resplendent as the sun, and His garments like snow.*

Second Point. *He spoke with Moses and Elias.*

Third Point. *When St. Peter said that they should build three tabernacles, a voice was heard from heaven, saying, " This is my beloved Son . . . hear him."* (Matt. 17:5) *When the disciples heard this voice, they fell down for fear, their faces to the ground. Jesus came and touched them, and said to them, " Arise, and do not be afraid . . . . Tell the vision to no one, till the Son of Man has risen from the dead."* (Matt. 17:7, 9)

First Point: Christ Is Transfigured.

I. *Christ.*

1. *" Jesus took with Him His beloved disciples, Peter, James, and John."* Christ *had loved* these three with the same love as the other Apostles, who were called from the world to such a sublime dignity, and instructed by His teaching, example, and many miracles. Christ had loved, with quite a special love, Peter, who was to be the head of the Church, James, who was to be the first of the Apostles to shed his blood for Christ, John, the disciple beloved above the rest, who was to take charge of the Mother of Christ. At present the Lord shows them a special

love by *taking them with Him as companions* on the way to the mountain, and as witnesses of His transfiguration. Later He will take the same three as companions in the Garden, and witnesses of His agony. At last the three will be, with all the others, His companions in heaven, sharing in His never-fading glory.

2. *He was transfigured:* Christ was habitually united with God the Father by the hypostatic union, by grace, and by prayer. When He was in prayer, Christ was transfigured. That close inner union with God had an outward effect and sign in the transfiguration, which means a temporary change of His outward appearance.

3. Consider the beauty of the transfigured Savior: His shining face, His white garments, His body elevated above the ground: all signs that His mind and will were withdrawn from sensible objects and raised to God.

4. *Where* was Christ transfigured? Not in some place among the crowd, but in a *solitary* place, on a high *mountain,* raised above the changes of public life, and nearer to heaven.

II. *The Apostles.*

1. All of us who follow Christ must be transfigured at least spiritually; we must " put on the new man, which has been created according to God in justice and holiness of truth." (Eph. 4:24) Thus the three Apostles, too, were to be transfigured; aye, like Moses and Elias, they might have been the companions of Christ's bodily transfiguration, temporarily, if they had shown themselves worthy of so great a grace.

2. The Apostles, however, do not pray, but *sleep.* Consider those men not using any means to be transfigured with Christ, oppressed by heavy sleep.

III. This transfiguration is an image of the *state of the contemplative life*.

Few men only are called to this state. It is a high and excellent life, nearer to heaven than to earth; it means not going about with Christ among men, but enjoying the company of God on the mountain, and being transfigured there with Christ when He so wills. This life, however, is not a time for *sleeping*, but a time for *praying*; it is continually intent on purifying the soul and uniting the mind with God.

SECOND POINT: Christ Speaks with Moses and Elias.

I. *Moses and Elias*.

1. Moses, the great servant of God, had asked: "Show me Thy face"; God had answered him: "Thou canst not see My face: for man shall not see Me and live." (Ex. 33:20)

Elias had been told: "Go forth, and stand upon the mount before the Lord: and behold the Lord passeth, and a great and strong wind before the Lord overthrowing the mountains, and breaking the rocks in pieces: the Lord is not in the wind. And after the wind an earthquake: the Lord is not in the earthquake. And after the earthquake a fire; the Lord is not in the fire. And after the fire the whistling of a gentle air. And when Elias heard this, he covered his face with his mantle," for he knew that the face of the Lord could not be seen without harm. (III Kings 19)

Both of these men had descended into limbo without having seen the face of the Lord; there for many centuries, they had prayed and waited that they might be allowed to see the face of the Lord. At long last they are summoned to see the face of the Lord on Mount Thabor. They deem it an ample reward for so many prayers and years of waiting.

2. *They are transfigured* with Christ, both "appearing in glory." (Luke 9:31) Generous souls, who seek God with their whole heart, shall be transfigured together with Christ.

II. *Christ.*

1. The Savior *speaks* with generous souls; He communicates to them His plans, and the sentiments of His Heart: not in a doubtful and dark manner, but surely and clearly.

2. The chief topic of the conversation was "his death, which he was about to fulfill in Jerusalem" (Luke 9:31), the mystery of the cross, the shameful death He would undergo, and the necessary connection between the cross and glory: "Did not the Christ have to suffer these things before entering into his glory?" (Luke 24:26)

Watch with what ecstasy the transfigured Christ speaks of the cross, so that the cross seems to be transfigured in His mind and His mouth.

III. *They who lead a contemplative life*

are not necessarily all transfigured, nor constantly. There are long nights of desolations and trials, without any light, violent storms, consuming fires, and but seldom the rustling of the gentle breeze, happy light, and heavenly intercourse. There are true and false transfigurations: the touch-stone is the cross, *i.e.*, perfect self-denial and obedience. Let all, however, diligently apply themselves to inner transfiguration, withdrawing the mind from created things, and transferring it to God.

THIRD POINT: The Sloth of the Apostles Is Reproved.

I. *The Apostles.*

When Moses and Elias " were parting from him " (Luke 9:33), and when the transfiguration of Christ was nearing its end, Peter awakes with his comrades, and is dazzled by the brightness. A drowsy soul, that is not generous, wishing to be with Christ yet at the same time to enjoy perpetual ecstasy, loses itself in weak, inefficient, ridiculous means. Unmindful of the redemption of mankind which must be accomplished, of the Church that has to be founded, of the Gospel to be announced throughout the world, Peter is carried away by a single desire to enjoy for ever the consolation of the transfiguration. So he suggests that they should make three tabernacles; he assumes that Christ will stay for ever with Moses and Elias on the mountain. Peter does not understand in the least " his death, which he was about to fulfill in Jerusalem." (Luke 9:31)

II. *God.*

1. The heavenly Father makes Himself known to the three Apostles after the manner in which He used to manifest Himself in the Old Testament, not face to face, but in a cloud, and by a terrifying voice. This is the way to call back souls that are not generous with God, that do not go straight to Him, but use some double-dealing.

2. " This is my beloved Son . . . hear him." (Luke 9:35) This is the only way to obtain a lasting transfiguration. Follow Christ speaking, as He walks by the way of the cross. But of what does He speak? The mystery of the cross, the necessity of suffering.

III. *Christ.*

Jesus touches the Apostles lightly, addresses them kindly, inspires them with confidence, under His usual appearance, most friendly and forgiving. He allows them to keep secret, for the time being, the vision at which the Apostles were so severely reproved. As He comes down from the mountain, He instructs them more fully concerning " his death, which he was about to fulfill in Jerusalem." (Luke 9:31) Christ speaks patiently and meekly, though He is well aware that the disciples do not at all understand what is being said.

IV. As regards the *contemplative life,* note:

1. Dislike for apostolic labors, love of a quiet life, and a desire for extraordinary graces are not signs of a call to the contemplative life.

2. The contemplative man does not live comfortably in tabernacles; but he keeps nightwatch in a cave or in the open air. Let him listen to Moses and Elias, present in the cloud, and to the utterances of Holy Scripture; let him above all listen to the voice of God, speaking through the Church and Superiors, to be led thereby to Christ, in whom is all wisdom, perfection, and glory.

3. Christ *comes down* from the mountain: He must accomplish among men the work entrusted Him by the Father. The three Apostles *come down* too: he who has definite obligations to fulfil among men, and he who has no signs of a true vocation to a life of contemplation, may, if he likes, retire for a while to the mountain, in order to enjoy God in solitude; but afterwards *he must come down* from the height, and he must not try to fix his permanent abode on the mountain.

CHAPTER XXXIV

The Raising of Lazarus

Cf. John 11:1-45; *The Exercises,* Sec. 285

★

First Point. *Mary and Martha inform Jesus of the sickness of Lazarus. After He was informed of this, He delayed for two days that the miracle might be more evident.*

Second Point. *Before He raised him, He asked faith of both Mary and Martha, saying, " I am the resurrection and the life; he who believes in me, even if he die, shall live."* (John 11:25)

Third Point. *Jesus raises him after He had wept and said a prayer. The way in which He raised him was by a command, " Lazarus, come forth! "* (John 11:44)

FIRST POINT: The Miracle Is Delayed.

I. *Christ is informed about the sickness of Lazarus.*

Consider the *faith* of Martha and Mary: first from the *fact of sending* news to Christ, their very simplest remedy being recourse to Him; then from *their words,* " Lord, behold, he whom thou lovest is sick " (John 11:3); by the word, " Lord," they profess Christ's authority; by the words, " he whom thou lovest," they acknowledge His readiness to help; by saying, " he is sick," they only mention the fact of sickness, without adding any petition; they leave the whole matter confidently to Christ's love for Lazarus. This does not imply any distrust; they do not say: " Save us, we are perishing." (Matt. 8:25) Their message breathes the serenity, trust, resignation, and peace enjoyed by those who have obtained true life in Christ:

by Lazarus, in the pains of sickness and in danger of life, as well as by his sisters, in anxiety for their brother's safety.

II. *Christ remained in the same place two days.*

1. Jesus truly loved Martha, Mary and Lazarus. He wished not only for their eternal salvation but also to give them proofs, in this life, of His special love by granting their prayers and soothing their grief. But above all else Christ had in view the Father's glory: this required that the answer to their petition should be put off, not on account of any fault committed by Lazarus or his sisters, but that their faith and trust might shine forth more clearly, that God might be glorified by a more evident miracle, that we might be taught more distinctly that in Christ is the fulness of true life.

2. For these reasons Christ remains in the same place, subordinating the love of these persons to the glory of God. Consider how Christ, during the whole of those two days, watches the resignation, sufferings, and agony of Lazarus; how He suffers with him, yet allows all for the glory of God. Jesus watches also the faith and grief of the two sisters, sympathizing with them. But, in view of God's glory, He permits them to suffer. Consider, during the same time, that Lazarus wavered not in his faith, trust and resignation. Not for a moment did he doubt Christ's love. Finally he died, at peace with God. The sisters abounded in faith, humble trust, and prayer; with resignation they did not harbor any impatience or bitterness against Christ, as if He had neglected their brother.

SECOND POINT: Faith Is Demanded.

I. *Christ is the resurrection and the life.*

Consider the *fulness of life* which Christ enjoys with the Father and the Holy Spirit, a life that is eternal, infinite, holy, and happy: " In Him was life." Christ is the author of all angelic and human life. Consider the original excellence of this life in nature, grace, and virtue, and see its completion in glory; consider also the excellence of the immortal life of the body in paradise, " For God made not death." (Wisd. 1:13)

Reflect that sin, in angels as well as in men, is spiritual death, through which came also the death of the body into this world. (Rom. 5:12) See, in the course of so many centuries from the Creation to the Redemption, the struggle between life and death. At length the Son of God became incarnate: in Him was life, the fulness of true life, the fulness of divinity, of all grace and virtue, to be completed by the fulness of glory. But the purpose of the Incarnation was to make men share the fulness of life, on earth and in heaven, in all grace, virtue, and glorification.

The manner, established by God for our receiving life, was that life should wrestle with death, and by His death restore all to life. Accordingly Christ is not only life, but also *resurrection:* He will rise again from the dead by the fulness of life that He possesses; and He merits in His earthly life, and achieves also in due time, our own resurrection. The power of raising to life is always possessed by Christ, and He uses this power in certain cases, according to the good pleasure of the Father.

II. *Faith is the condition of life.*

" He who believes in me, even if he die, shall live." (John 11:25) Faith, living faith of course, is the only condition for sharing the life and resurrection. Christ does not require any other. It is necessary: Christ insists on it absolutely; it is sufficient: death itself is overcome by it; it is universal: it procures any and every good of true life, God's glory in the widest sense: " If thou believe, thou shalt behold the glory of God." (John 11:40)

Contemplate this faith in Martha and Mary, when they have recourse to the Lord, in His absence, by a messenger; and again when they go to meet Him, on His arrival. " Lord, if thou hadst been here my brother would not have died." (John 11:21) And Martha adds a special profession of faith: " Yes, Lord, I believe that thou art the Christ, the Son of God, who hast come into the world." (John 11:27)

THIRD POINT: Lazarus Is Raised from the Dead.

I. *Jesus weeps.*

Jesus weeps on account of the sad condition in which He finds the persons He loves: Lazarus is dead, the sisters and their friends are overwhelmed with grief; He weeps also for their past sufferings. The Jews rightly attribute these tears to the love Jesus bore to those persons: " See how he loved him! " (John 11:36) Gather all the tears that the Redeemer has shed, wailing in the manger, mourning for Jerusalem, praying in the Garden, and through all His life, for us: and these tears are but the first-fruits of the cross.

II. *Jesus prays.*

In this prayer Christ expresses His gratitude for having been heard: " Father, I give thee thanks that thou hast heard me." (*ibid*. 41) This supposes the previous prayer of Jesus, when He had asked for a clear confirmation of His mission and teaching, through the striking miracle of the resurrection of Lazarus. The purpose of this confirmation was, " that they may believe that thou hast sent me." (*ibid*. 42) Christ wishes that faith be consolidated and increased in souls. The reason is that faith is the condition of true life, and He ardently wishes for nothing but that they " may have life, and have it more abundantly." (John 10:10) See how eagerly Christ longs to communicate life to you; how He is at one with the Father in this; how He allowed, for this purpose, the death of Lazarus, the grief of the two sisters, and His own tears. He is ready to shed His own blood for the same purpose.

III. *Jesus commands.*

1. *Who commands?* He who had called light out of darkness, He who had ruled the winds and the sea, He who, with gentle voice, had pronounced the pardon of Magdalene, He who, even without speaking, had soothed the waves, and multiplied the loaves for the five thousand men.

2. *How does He command?* " He cried out with a loud voice." (John 11:43) Even those far away could hear it and it expressed at once the firmness and the greatness of the effect that was to follow. He used no words of entreaty, but words of command.

3. *What does He command?* He commands one who has been dead four days to return to life immediately. Thereby Christ proves His divine mission and dignity, the truth of His teaching, including the doctrine on humility and the cross as the condition of true life. He gives a proof that He is the resurrection and the life.

Reflect how greatly this miracle gives glory to God, and peace to men of good will.

CHAPTER XXXV

The Supper at Bethany

Cf. Matthew 26:6-10; *The Exercises*, Sec. 286

★

IT SEEMS to us that the present contemplation has a special affinity with that on the Three Classes of Men, whereby we are urged to a generous disposition in the choice of a way of life.

First Point. *Our Lord eats in the house of Simon the leper together with Lazarus.*

Second Point. *Mary pours out the ointment upon the head of Christ.*

Third Point. *Judas murmurs with the words, " To what purpose is this waste? "* (Matt. 26:8) *But Jesus defends Magdalene again, saying, " Why do you trouble the woman? She has done me a good turn."* (Matt. 26:10)

FIRST POINT: Christ at Supper

I. *Jesus.*

The Son of God, the resurrection and the life, is consumed with the desire to communicate life according to each one's disposition; He is sorry that the showing forth the glory of God by the raising of Lazarus has become a scandal for very many; yet at the same time He is glad at the company and faith of those with whom He is taking supper: He binds every one to Himself by His friendliness, instructs them by His words, enlightens and inflames them by inward grace.

II. *Simon.*

He was a generous, whole-hearted disciple of the Lord. On hearing that Jesus is sought for by His enemies, Simon invites Him to supper, thus making a profession of the most lively faith; and hearing the Lazarus also is exposed to persecution, Simon invites him as well. He does so quite openly, to make it known to very many.

III. *Lazarus.*

His former faith, love, and resignation have been wonderfully increased by the favor of the resurrection. He does not avoid the Jews who crowd around him, even to the danger of his own life; for the sake of professing the faith he comes courageously, in the sight of all, to the supper at Simon's house.

IV. *Martha.*

Her faith and love, too, have been marvelously increased by the miracle of her brother's resurrection. Though she is a noble lady, she undertakes, for the sake of professing her faith, the part of a servant, and that too, in another's house. The Heart of Jesus is overjoyed to be in the company of such generous souls.

SECOND POINT: Mary's Anointing

I. *The feelings of Mary.*

Here is a lively faith: she feels with her sister " I believe that thou art the Christ, the Son of God." (John 11:27) Here is an ardent charity: she " loved much " when yet a sinner; she loves now even more ardently after having received so many favors. Hers is a great desire to offer some more excellent compensation for the past sins. Here are the fulness of peace and joy. Reflect how all these dispositions of Mary have become more mature ever since her conversion; they are more firm, more noble, and more peaceful.

II. *The actions of Mary.*

She anoints the Savior after the fashion in which honorable guests used to be anointed. Yes, she does so with an altogether extraordinary reverence and devotion, as shown by the fine quality of the ointment she uses and by its great quantity. She anointed not only the head, but the feet as well, doing so with her own hands, as a noble lady, and then using her hair to wipe the feet. Add the circumstance that she rendered all this homage publicly, in the presence of guests when it would soon be known at large, not without danger to herself. Notice in all these actions the calm grace of ripe virtue: Mary is not now carried away by the impulse of a novice as formerly, when she was reclaimed as a sinner. Reflect on the feelings of the Heart of Jesus, rejoicing at the company of such a generous woman.

THIRD POINT: The Departure of Judas

I. *Judas murmurs.*

Recall the graces formerly bestowed on Judas among the beloved disciples of Christ. Now he has so far fallen away as to be devoid of all charity. His love for Jesus has little by little changed to indifference, as greed of money engrossed his mind. He has no longer faith: true, he declares that Jesus is just; he sees all the time the proofs of the Master's omniscience and omnipotence; all the same this has now lost all practical efficacy. Judas declares Jesus guilty of waste, and Magdalene too, whose faith he is no longer able to appreciate. From inward indignation (beyond which the Pharisee on the previous occasion had not gone), Judas goes on to open blame: he tries to deceive the others, and even Jesus, with a pretended zeal for the poor. Thereby Judas is giving scandal to the rest, and leads them by his example to grumble: he has become the model of the ungenerous soul.

II. *Judas is corrected.*

Consider how the heart of Jesus does not cease to love the erring Apostle. Christ deeply grieves at his conduct and constantly offers His grace to him. A public correction is, however, necessary, because of the imminent danger for the salvation of Judas, and the scandal to the other disciples. Jesus gives him a clear reproof, proclaiming that Mary " has done me a good turn " (Matt. 26:10) and so declaring that it is not right to trouble her. At the same time the reproof is gentle: " Why do you trouble the woman? " (Matt. 26:10)—" Let her be—that she may keep it for the day of my burial." (John 12:7) Jesus softens the reproof by pointing out that His death is near, in order thereby to soften the heart of the Apostle and to excuse more fully the lavish use of the ointment.

III. *Judas is hardened.*

This very gentle reproof only serves as an occasion for Judas to consummate his treachery. Judas takes the reproof as an insult, and he fancies he has a right to avenge it. Knowing beforehand that he cannot be any longer tolerated in the company of Jesus, and that he may be expelled from it, Judas claims the right to be the first to desert from the Savior; deeming the waste of the ointment his own loss, Judas takes it upon himself to procure a compensation. He resolves therefore to avail himself of the invitation of the Pharisees for his own private gain, and he sells the Savior to them. Consider how the sadness of Jesus was increased beyond all bounds at seeing an Apostle thus fall away from true life!

CHAPTER XXXVI

Palm Sunday

Cf. Matthew 21:1-17; *The Exercises*, Sec. 287

★

To THE question " Why did Christ choose to ride on a beast of burden? " the Gospel of St. Matthew provides this answer: " Now this was done that what was spoken through the prophet might be fulfilled, ' Tell the daughter of Sion: Behold, thy king comes to thee, Meek and seated upon an ass, and upon a colt, the foal of a beast of burden.' " (Matt. 21:4-5) The Vulgate (Zach. 9:9) has " poor " instead of " meek "; the Hebrew word includes the meanings poor, meek, peaceful; in short, poor and humble. Hence in this mystery we contemplate the entry of Christ the King, decked with the emblems of poverty and humility. The purpose of this entry is peace; this is self-evident, and is made quite clear from the declaration of Christ: " If thou hadst known, in this thy day, even thou, the things that are for thy peace." (Luke 19:42)

Therefore the connection of this exercise with the Kingdom of Christ and the Two Standards is evident. Note, however, that single mysteries contain these meditations not yet fully developed, but partially and germinally. Thus we find expressed, in Christ's triumphal entry, poverty and humility, but not His love for humiliations. He showed His humility not in accepting reproaches, but in His meekness; the reproaches will appear in the mystery on the Passion. We learn, then, in this mystery something of Christ's plan, but not His entire plan.

This mystery is also connected with the third week, at the end of which in particular Christ is constantly shown as King and in the course of which shine forth poverty and humility, brought there to the climax of the third kind. The present contemplation is more or less a connection between the second and third weeks; it repeats concisely the teaching of the second week and prepares for that of the third.

First Point. *Our Lord sends for the ass and the foal, saying, " loose them and bring them to me. And if anyone say anything to you, you shall say that the Lord has need of them, and immediately he will send them."* (Matt. 21:2-3)

Second Point. *After the ass was covered with the garments of the Apostles, Jesus mounted it.*

Third Point. *The people came forth to meet Jesus, and spread their garments and the branches of trees in the way, saying, " Hosanna to the Son of David! Blessed is he who comes in the name of the Lord! Hosanna in the highest! "* (Matt. 21:9)

First Point: The Entry Is Prepared.

I. The Blessed Trinity decreed from eternity that, towards the end of His public teaching, Christ should enter Jerusalem in a manner expressing both the royal dignity and special feature of His kingdom. This decree was promulgated by the prophet: " Tell the daughter of Sion: Behold, thy king comes to thee, Meek and seated upon an ass, and upon a colt, the foal of a beast of burden." (Matt. 21:5; Cf. Isa. 62:11; Zach. 9:9)

II. *Christ* obediently accepts the decree and sets about carrying it out. He orders two disciples, according to His authority, to bring to Him the ass and the colt, without asking the owner; this may have been done to save the man from the displeasure of the Pharisees. Christ shows Himself also as a prophet saying: "immediately he will send them." (Matt. 21:4)

III. It was also decreed by the Blessed Trinity that *Christ should be received as King,* and Christ Himself demands it now as His own right.

IV. *Jerusalem* is eagerly looking forward to the King-Messiah, but they picture Him with wealth and pomp; this expectation is due to the attachment, instilled into their souls by Lucifer, for riches and honors. Consequently they fail to recognize Christ as the Messiah, and reject Him. The Master, however, makes poverty and humility a condition for accepting Him as Savior and Redeemer. See how necessary is the law of the cross, since it is the necessary condition of salvation.

SECOND POINT: Christ Enters the City.

I. *The Person who enters.*

"Behold, thy King will come to thee, the just and Saviour." (Zach. 9:9) Recall the titles of Christ's kingship, His royal endowments and loveableness. Recall the extent of His kingdom which includes all men, all outward and inward things. Remember the provinces of His kingdom: earth, purgatory, and heaven; also the nature of the kingdom: it is above all spiritual, to be begun on earth and accomplished in heaven. Whereas the King shall be clothed with glory in heaven, He now enters Jerusalem clothed, not with glory, but with justice, about to bring salvation to His subjects: negatively this means redemption from sin, and positively true life and peace.

II. *The manner of entering.*

1. "He is poor (humble), and riding upon an ass, and upon a colt, the foal of an ass." (Zach. 9:9)

The entering itself shows Christ as *King*, for it is a royal and a triumphal progress. The nature of the kingdom is disclosed: the kind of mount, an ass, shows the meekness of the rider rather than His majesty; it is neither His own nor hired, but lent; the emblem of poverty rather than of pomp. Instead of precious hangings the Apostles laid their coarse, well-worn garments on the beast of burden. The apparel of the King and of His retinue is *poor*.

2. This manner of entering the Holy City expresses the condition of salvation: "Blessed are the poor in spirit, for theirs is the kingdom of heaven." (Matt. 5:3) It expresses the *law of the kingdom*: love of God, with its indispensable complement of detachment. God has also decreed this law, and Christ demands it: they who do not accept this law are not Christ's own.

THIRD POINT: Christ Is Received.

I. Consider that *many did not receive* Christ in a becoming manner.

Judas is a living sham as he walks with the exulting disciples. The Pharisees are "moved with indignation" and become hostile. Many others, even after seeing so many miracles, refuse to believe; many of the chief men who "loved the glory of men more than the glory of God"

(John 12:43) only pretend faith. To all of these the cause for scandal was Christ's poverty and humility. Reflect how foolishly all those men reject so great a king for so trifling a reason.

II. Consider how *many others did receive Christ.*

Having learned from the raising of Lazarus that Jesus was the Messiah, they renounce the prejudice they had conceived against His poverty and humility; they receive the humble and poor Jesus as Messiah and King and profess their faith in Him by deeds, signs, and words: " And the crowds that went before him, and those that followed, kept crying out, saying: ' Hosanna to the Son of David! Blessed is he who comes in the name of the Lord! Hosanna in the highest! ' " (Matt. 21:9) They do not wait till He enters the City, but they go out to meet Him. They salute Him with a quite unusual display of honor. They acknowledge Him as Son of David and Messiah. They wish Him all blessing from God. Indeed, they distinguish themselves in His service, with the whole city looking on, with the Pharisees standing by, full of rage, from the city-gate right into the temple.

III. *We, too, must join Christ.*

Let us go to meet Christ; let us surrender our persons and all our possessions to His service and good pleasure; let us join His company, and imitate His life and manner of life. By this way let us go as far as Christ goes, right into the city of the world, even to the height of Mount Calvary. Let us be convinced that this is the way to go through life " in the name of the Lord "; let us realize that by so doing we shall thus give glory to God and peace to men. As spiritual Crusaders, clothed with the dress and livery of Christ, let us enter the Holy City, the heavenly Jerusalem.

Renew the offering made in the meditation on the Kingdom of Christ.

CHAPTER XXXVII

Jesus Preaches in the Temple

Cf. Luke 19:47-48; *The Exercises*, Sec. 288

THIS MYSTERY, like the two preceding, leads the exercitant from the second to the third week.

★

First Point. *He was teaching daily in the temple.*

Second Point. *After His teaching, since there was no one in Jerusalem who would receive Him, He returned to Bethany.*

FIRST POINT: Christ Teaches in the Temple.

I. *Where is He teaching?*

In the temple designed by David, built by Solomon, rebuilt by Zorobabel, which had constantly been the scene of so many manifestations of the divine favor. There the Infant Savior had presented Himself as a victim, and begun His life of sacrifice; there the Scribes and Pharisees (now after the death of Simeon, and Anna, and the Doctors gathered round the boy of twelve years of age) the Scribes and Pharisees, I say, are now profaning the chair of Moses; the temple has become a den of thieves, owing to its constant profanation by sellers and buyers, etc. . . . .

II. *Who is teaching?*

He who is the light of truth, and the life of grace; whose words are truth and life; whose Heart embraces the hearers with the most ardent love; whose words are made more efficacious by the inner working of grace in the hearts of the hearers, demanding, however, our free acceptance of His grace.

III. *Whom is He teaching?*

The Apostles, who have been gained already for life and truth, but who are as yet uncertain in truth and unsteady in life; and among them Judas who is sitting in darkness and in the shadow of death.

The people, who share in a lesser degree even than the Apostles in the truth and life; the people hold Him to be a prophet, but do not acknowledge Him as the Son of God; they follow Him with attention and admiration, but do not rise to complete self-surrender; some indeed through invincible ignorance, and others through wilful ignorance, through human respect, and through worldly attachments.

The Pharisees and Priests, who deliberately resist life and truth, prepare to attack truth with insidious questions, and plot against life.

IV. *What is He teaching?*

The Kingdom of heaven, by various parables. The judgment that threatens those who refuse to believe.

V. With what *perseverance* is He teaching?

" He was teaching *daily* in the temple " (Luke 19:47); day after day, therefore, with great constancy, with ever equal patience, insistence, and zeal; without allowing Himself to be deceived by the vain protestations of the Apostles, the barren admiration of the crowd, and the deceitful reverence of His adversaries and of Judas; lastly, without allowing Himself to be deterred by the lowering spiritual darkness, or the foreseen partial barrenness of His preaching.

SECOND POINT: Jesus Retires to Bethany.

I. *After His teaching.*

1. *The Pharisees* are incensed with anger and hatred, they rage against Him with looks, words, and secret plotting; nevertheless they " do not stretch forth their hands against Him " (Cf. Luke 22:53): not from want of malice, but because His hour, appointed by the Father, has not yet come.

2. *The people* show yet greater reverence and admiration for His words and signs; in spite of this no one holds out a friendly hand to Him; from fear of the Pharisees " there was no one who would receive Him in Jerusalem ": none of those who had been moved inwardly, or who had hailed Him as He entered the City, or who had experienced His benefits.

3. This was repeated *" daily,"* beginning from the very day of the triumphal entry: " And when he had looked round upon all things [in the temple], then, as it was already late, he went out to Bethany with the Twelve." (Mark 11:11)

II. *He used to return from Jerusalem.*

The way back led the whole length of the triumphal road, where every stone and every crossing would remind Him of the fickleness of popular favorite. He would gaze at the city, overwhelmed with so many favors, destined for severe judgment. He would pass by the withered fig-tree, the image of His chosen people; His mind would dwell on all the earlier journeys to Jerusalem, beginning from the presentation in the temple, when He was forty days old, and He would weigh their scanty fruit. Christ was doing so " daily," beginning from the very day of the triumphal entry.

III. *To Bethany*.

1. There the hands of all are extended: Lazarus and Simon to give Him hospitality, Martha to serve Him, Mary to honor Him with special signs of love, Judas to betray Him! The Heart of Jesus, in return, is expanding to bestow an abundance of graces on all, and even to pardon Judas. Contemplate in detail the supper that closes each day at Bethany.

2. After supper Jesus used to withdraw, " but as for nights, he would go out and pass them on the mountain called Olivet." (Luke 21:37) In prayer the Lord seeks strength to continue His preaching; even at prayer He knows before hand that next day's preaching will be without immediate fruit; in prayer He comforts Himself with the consideration of the Father's will, of our own instruction, and of the profit that some at least of His hearers will reap after the coming of the Holy Spirit. Strengthened by this prayer, and refreshed by a short sleep, He goes back to preach once more in the morning. Christ was doing so daily, from Palm Sunday onwards.

Third Week

The contemplations of the third and fourth weeks serve chiefly to *confirm* the Choice that has been made: the third week shows the condition of the perfect following of Christ, the third kind of humility; the fourth week sets before our eyes the reward of such a following. From this can be seen their close connection with the meditation on the Kingdom of Christ.

Now we see Christ suffering all injuries, reproaches and poverty. Here we are taught what is meant by being content to eat, drink, dress, and act as Christ does. (Cf. Secs. 95 sqq.) Indeed, in order that nothing at all of Christ's trial should be overlooked by us in this place St. Ignatius advises us in this manner: " I will take care not to bring up pleasing thoughts, even though they are good and holy . . . . Rather I will rouse myself to sorrow, suffering, and anguish by frequently calling to mind the labors, fatigue, and suffering which Christ our Lord endured from the time of His birth down to the mystery of the passion upon which I am engaged at present." (Sec. 206)

Furthermore, we are led on to the third kind of humility by considering not only the persons, words and actions in the mysteries, but also by considering " what Christ our Lord suffers in His human nature (Sec. 195) . . . . how the divinity hides itself (Sec.

196) . . . that Christ suffers all . . . for my sins "
(Sec. 197).

The consideration of the tortures and reproaches
that Christ suffers, and suffers willingly, is naturally
an efficacious inducement to follow Him in all reproach. Throughout the second week we had been
urged not only to know and love the Lord, but also
to follow and imitate Him. A still greater motive is
given in the Passion when we consider that Christ
suffers all for " my sins " and me. The contemplation
of Christ's Passion, His goodness to us by the institution of a Church that will hand His life on to us, all
this gives us many motives for following Christ, especially the motives of gratitude to such a loving
Lord and shame for ourselves who have been so cruel
to Him.

The third prelude of this week tells us " to ask for
sorrow, compassion, and shame because the Lord is
going to His suffering for my sins." (Sec. 193) This
prelude thus continues the work of the previous
weeks, for, in the meditation on sin which was made
in the first week, we asked: " What have I done for
Christ? What am I doing for Christ? What ought I
to do for Christ? " (Sec. 53) Those sentiments had
been intensified throughout the second week and
fortified with great love of Christ and the desire to
imitate Him. Now we are led to answer that question
and the only answer can be had in a firm resolve to
practice the third kind of humility.

By leading us to the practice of the third kind of humility St. Ignatius shows us the entire scope of the exercises, namely to make us want to share all Christ's poverty, all His insults, all His injuries. The culminating point is reached in the meditation on the Passion.

The special feature of the mystery we are now to consider is expressed in the words: " ask for sorrow, compassion, and shame because the Lord is going to His suffering for my sins." (Sec. 193) It is a contemplation of our Lord as He begins His Passion, preparing for the torments of the following day, bidding farewell to His disciples. It is truly the *Last* Supper. The eating of the Paschal Lamb appears as the viaticum; the washing of the feet as the last instruction; the institution of the Holy Eucharist as the final and memorial gift.

CHAPTER XXXVIII

The Last Supper

Cf. Matthew 26:20-30; John 13:1-30; *The Exercises*,
Sec. 289

★

First Point. *He eats the Paschal Lamb with His disciples, to whom He predicts His death: " Amen I say to you, one of you will betray me." (Matt. 26:21)*

Second Point. *He washes the feet of the disciples, even those of Judas. He begins with St. Peter, but St. Peter, considering the majesty of the Lord and his own lowliness, does not want to permit it, and says, " Lord, dost thou wash my feet? " (John 13:6) St. Peter did not know that Christ was giving an example of humility in this, and therefore, Jesus said to him, " For I have given you an example, that as I have done to you, so you also should do." (John 13:15)*

Third Point. *He institutes the most holy Sacrifice of the Eucharist, the greatest proof of His love. He says to them, " Take and eat." (Matt. 26:26) When the supper was finished, Judas went forth to sell our Lord.*

FIRST POINT: Christ Eats the Paschal Lamb.

I. *The journey to the Cenacle.*

The time.

It is the greatest *Pasch* prefigured by so many others, on which Jesus is to be sacrificed as a lamb for my sins, so that God should spare me, the sinner. For Jesus there will not be granted a " passing of the chalice " or Phase.—It is *the hour and power of darkness,* when He will be given over to the hatred and cruelty of darkness, in order that I may be freed from them.—*" His hour "* (John 13:1), *" My time "* (Matt. 26:18), *i.e.,* the time for the suffering and death decreed by the Father, on account of my sins; accepted by the Son at the Incarnation, the presentation, the baptism . . . .

The route.

From *Bethany* to *Jerusalem.* At Bethany were staying so many followers devoted to Him; there He had daily been taking pleasant meals with them and with His beloved disciples. (Ps. 54:15) Jerusalem, the city of peace, had become a Babylon, a city of confusion and darkness, the abode of cruel beasts.

The journey.

With the words, *" Go into the City "* (Matt. 26:18), Jesus generously embraces this journey with all the effort of His will. He uses His omniscience in order to prepare the place of the Supper, which was but one step removed from the Passion. Christ avails Himself of the service of two chosen apostles: Peter, the future head of His Church, and John, the disciple beloved above all the others; the Master gives them an excellent opportunity to understand something of the mystery of His Passion.

II. *The Paschal Supper.*

1. While eating the paschal lamb

Christ sees in His mind all the graces which had been given the Chosen People ever since the exodus from Egypt. Sadly He notes that nearly all of them had been made vain through sin.

He sees the destiny reserved for Himself on account of those sins, a destiny which was prefigured by this paschal lamb. He sees also the great neglect awaiting Him in the tabernacles throughout the world.

2. While drinking the chalice,

the symbol of union, Christ sees in His mind the former paschal suppers, especially those which He had celebrated with Mary and Joseph; also His constant intercourse during the last three years with His Apostles and other devoted persons, in particular those at Bethany.

3. Throughout all this Christ is reflecting:

a. That all is over now, that this is His *Last* Supper: " for I say to you that I will eat of it no more, until it has been fulfilled in the kingdom of God . . . . I will not drink of the fruit of the vine, until the kingdom of God comes." (Luke 22:16, 18)

b. Christ reflects that this is the Supper at which He must say farewell to His disciples, previous to a violent separation from them. For this reason He had before longed, with the most ardent desire of His Heart, to unite by this Supper, for the last time, all His disciples with Himself: " I have greatly desired to eat this passover with you before I suffer." (Luke 22:15)

c. At the same time Christ is tortured by the consciousness that He is, at this Supper, conversing intimately for the last time with one of His loved disciples; and that He will be without that disciple for all eternity. Notice the baseness of this treachery: " He who dips his hand into the dish with me, he will betray me " (Matt. 26:23); notice its atrocity: the Son of God affirms with a repeated oath " Amen, amen, I say to you, one of you will betray me " (John 13:21); see its destructiveness, since that disciple, after three years' instruction, can only be given this certificate of his progress: " It were better for that man if he had not been born." (Matt. 26:25)

SECOND POINT: Christ Washes His Disciples' Feet.

I. *When* does He wash their feet?

" Knowing that the hour had come for him to pass out of this world to the Father " (John 13:1) He gives His last instruction, His testament.

" Having loved his own who were in the world, loved them unto the end " (John 13:1); therefore this action is prompted by a most ardent love. The last instruction dwells, not on superfluous or less necessary things, but on what is really of paramount importance.

When the supper was done; consequently with a Heart sated with sadness owing to the imminent separation from His own.

" The devil having already put it into the heart of Judas Iscariot, the son of Simon, to betray him " (John 13:2); therefore Christ is not in the least deterred from His purpose by so black an ingratitude.

II. *What* is Christ doing?

He wishes to give to His followers a last, and consequently also a most necessary, *instruction*. The Master wishes to give this lesson in the manner that will make it enter more deeply into the mind, not only by words, but chiefly by *example*: " I have given you an example, that as I have done to you, so you should also do." (John 13:15)

Now He wishes to give them an example of *humility*: He had taught this first of all virtues by His Incarnation; He had again inculcated it by so many mysteries of His life; He was to confirm it in the end by the most abject humiliation of the cross. Humility is the foundation of the whole of salvation; it is utterly hated by Lucifer; it is the chief ornament of the Redeemer's Heart. He gives the example of humility by a striking *act of humiliation*, for such acts are a safe way to acquire the habit of humility; consequently He chooses a "*mean and low service*," that refers to the cleanness of the body, not to that of the soul, not to the head, but to the feet: a service usually performed by slaves. To render this service " He rose from the supper "; notice that these are well-nigh the last steps made by the Savior's holy feet, while yet free from fetters. He " laid aside his garments, and taking a towel girded himself. Then he poured water into the basin and began to wash the feet of the disciples, and to dry them with the towel with which he was girded " (John 13:4-5); these again were well-nigh the last actions done by the Savior's holy hands, before they were bound and nailed to the cross.

And these actions are performed by Him who " came from God," who is therefore " God of God "; by Him who " goes to God," soon to be glorified above all the angels; by Him " to whom the Father had given all things into His hands," the Savior, the Teacher, the King of the whole human race.

III. *Of whom* does the Lord wash the feet?

Christ gives an example of the *humility* to be observed *among equals;* for He teaches the Apostles that which they must do to one another. The Apostles are in a sense equal to one another. Christ gives them an example *a fortiori:* " If, therefore, I the Lord and Master have washed your feet, you also ought to wash the feet of one another."

(John 13:14)—Christ gives an example of observing humility even *towards equals who are bad*: He washes the feet of Judas, who was equal to the others in apostolic dignity, and the others, too, ought to wash the feet of Judas.— Christ gives the example of observing *humility towards superiors,* though they may happen to be less perfect, as was Peter, whose fall was foreseen.—He gives also the example of observing *humility towards inferiors,* for all of the Apostles are inferior to Christ, who is the Lord and Master.

IV. *What result* does Christ obtain?

The immediate result of this so affectionate and eloquent instruction was very meager indeed, overwhelming the Heart of Jesus with sadness. St. Peter " knew not " the meaning of the lesson, and betrayed his ignorance by his words; the majority of the others also " knew not," but they prudently held their peace; Judas hardened his heart. Nor was the sadness of Jesus relieved by the foresight of the future fruit, for this too was to fail in many.

THIRD POINT: Christ Institutes the Holy Eucharist.

I. *Christ consecrates.*

1. *Who* is consecrating?

Consider, outside the Cenacle, the world wrapped in darkness and the shadow of death; persecuting with mortal hatred Christ, the true life. Inside the Cenacle, see around Jesus, first Judas: he too is a son of darkness and death; then all the other Apostles: they are weak in faith and charity. In the center behold Christ, the true life, and the bread of life by His grace and teaching.

2. *What* is He consecrating?

He blesses and breaks the bread; He blesses the chalice. He acts in a similar manner as He had acted when multiplying the loaves; here also He gives food, agreeable, satisfying and abundant. By the words, " This is my body "; " this is my blood . . .", (Matt. 26:27, 28) He brings the substance of His body and of His blood under the appearances of bread and wine. In manifold ways He displays His omnipotence, wisdom, and other divine attributes.

II. *Christ gives*.

1. *To whom?*

He is giving to His beloved disciples. Reflect here on the graces bestowed on them from the moment of their vocation; they are now completed by this grace. The offices to which they have been called are now strengthened by this gift, especially the office continually to renew and dispense this food. Christ is also giving to Judas: review his graces and his fall!

2. *How* does He give?

By way of food: under the appearances of food and drink for the body, Christ gives food for the soul; under the divided appearances He gives food that is undivided and whole.

3. *What* does He give?

His most sacred body: this body is united to the soul, and with the soul to the divinity; it contains the abundance of every grace; it had been given and fitted to Him by the Father (cf. Hebr. 10:5); it had been given, by the overshadowing of the Holy Spirit to the Blessed Virgin to be conceived and formed; Christ was to give and deliver it soon to be crucified for us. This body is most holy owing to its very special relations to the divinity, owing to the gifts of created holiness, and owing to its power to effect holiness in ourselves.

b. *His precious blood:* that blood was the principal means of spreading sensitive life in the most holy body; it was also, in the Sacred Heart, to be the principal support of the spiritual and supernatural life; in virtue of the hypostatic union, and moreover by the acceptance of God, that blood is sufficient to redeem the whole world: for this end it will be shed shortly.

III. *Christ institutes the Holy Eucharist.*

1. *The institution itself.*

By the words, " Do this in remembrance of me " (Luke 22: 20), Christ gives to His Apostles the power to do, in every place and at any time, that which He has done Himself. Accordingly He brings it about that He gives us His continual *presence,* that He is continually our *food* of the supernatural life, and our never-failing *sacrifice* which perpetuates, in an unbloody manner, the bloody sacrifice of the cross.

Christ, then, institutes the Holy Eucharist " as the greatest sign of His love ": greatest *in duration,* for it will last on till the end of the world; greatest *in extension,* for it will be in every place " from the rising of the sun even to the going down " (Mal. 1:11); greatest *in significance,* for it signifies love under the aspects that are most proper to love: it belongs to love to wish to be present near the beloved, to wish to be useful to him and serve him, to wish to be sacrificed for the beloved. Now what lover is more present near the loved ones than our Redeemer in the Holy Eucharist? Who is more their servant than He who takes the apearance of food to nourish them? Which sacrifice is more perfect than the one which is performed, not in one place and for a few hours, but always and everywhere? This sign is lastly the greatest *in effectiveness,* giving the greatest glory to God in the highest and continually appeasing Him, giving peace on earth to men of goodwill, and continually giving them true life and applying to them the fruits of the Passion.

2. *The conclusion of this mystery.*

a. *Judas*. Already Satan had entered into him; darkness and death became his light and life. " He went out," in body, from the Cenacle; in will, from the family of the Apostles. " He went out "—the so dearly beloved disciple, who was called to so great offices—in order to sell, for thirty pieces of silver, Christ the Lord, the truth and the life.—" Now it was night " (John 13:30). Consider the physical night lowering over the Cenacle, and *the spiritual night enshrouding the traitor's* soul; see also the night of sadness that overwhelms the soul of the Savior.

b. *Christ*. The Lord concludes with an exhortation. He speaks out to the Apostles, the future ministers of life, the fundamental principles of true life: " Now this is everlasting life, that they may know thee, the only true God, and him whom thou hast sent, Jesus Christ." (John 17:3) He recommends union with Himself: " I am the vine, you are the branches." (John 15:4) " This is my commandment, that you love one another as I have loved you." (John 15:12) The consequence of obeying this commandment is union with God: " Yet not for these only do I pray, but for those also who through their word are to believe in me, that all may be one, even as thou, Father, in me and I in thee; that they also may be one in us, that the world may believe that thou hast sent me." (John 17:20-21) Reflect how appropriately Christ utters these principles, how happy He is to utter them, even though He is filled with sadness in the face of His approaching Passion.

CHAPTER XXXIX

From the Last Supper to the Agony

Cf. Matthew 26:30-46; Mark 14:32-44; Luke 22:39-46;
The Exercises, Sec. 290

★

THIS MYSTERY sets before us a special suffering of Christ, the interior agony of His soul. It continues throughout His Passion, but is more closely examined here as it is the only one present. St. Ignatius refers to the words " my soul is sad, even unto death," only in the third point of the meditation. The words were actually spoken by Christ when He entered Gethsemani, but Ignatius places them later. He is justified, however, inasmuch as the words remain true throughout the Passion and in the third point they describe perfectly the intensity of the agony of His soul, shown exteriorly by the bloody sweat.

First Point. *When the Supper was finished, and after the hymn was sung, Jesus, full of fear, goes forth with His disciples to Mt. Olivet. He left eight of them in Gethsemani, saying, " Sit down here, while I go over yonder and pray."* (Matt. 26:36)

Second Point. *Accompanied by St. Peter, St. James, and St. John, He prays three times to the Father, saying, " Father, if it is possible, let this cup pass away from me; yet not as I will, but as thou willest."* (Matt. 26:39) *" And falling into an agony he prayed the more earnestly."* (Luke 22:43)

Third Point. *So great was the fear that overwhelmed Him that He said: " My soul is sad, even unto death." (Matt. 26:38) And He sweat blood so copiously that St. Luke says, " And his sweat became as drops of blood running down upon the ground." (Luke 22:44) This supposes that His garments were saturated with blood.*

FIRST POINT: The Journey to the Garden

I. *What Jesus is doing.*

" *When the Supper was finished* ": Christ did not cut short the Supper and the instruction after it because of His mental agony, neither did He stall, desiring to keep in the company of His Apostles and feel their consolation.

" *And after the hymn was sung* ": Christ does not omit anything that adds to His Father's glory; rather He gives us an example of attention and devotion to prayer.

" *Jesus . . . goes forth* ": with quiet step, showing His deliberate intention; with firm step, showing His determined will; with calm voice, showing His resolve and readiness to suffer. " *To Mount Olivet* ": this was His usual place for prayer. Even in such desolation Christ does not omit prayer. The place was known to Judas, and the Lord foresaw that the once beloved disciple would accomplish there the betrayal of his Master, and his own ruin; in that place the chalice prepared by the Father was waiting for Christ. Every step of His repeats and confirms the generous " go ye " with which He had set out on the journey from Bethany to the Supper at Jerusalem.

II. *What Jesus is feeling.*

1. All *His perfections* are now, as it were, conspiring to torture Him: the vision of the divine essence manifests the inner-

most deformity of sin; the vision of God's decrees shows the irrevocable decree of the Passion; the vision of the future reveals each and every suffering, together with people's indifference for the most holy Passion; His intuition of hearts lays open His enemies' wickedness, the betrayal by Judas, and the cowardice of the Apostles.

2. There was added a special sadness from the work of the foundation of the Church: the Apostles were to be the cornerstones. Notice the number of them that accompany Him: there are only eleven; one has by this time been miserably lost. See their dispositions: they are full of fear on account of Christ's sayings about His betrayal, which they could not understand; on account of their imminent separation from Christ; on account of the impending Passion which had been foretold; on account of the world's hatred to which He had alluded. And the disciples were not trying to resist this fear by watching and prayer; rather, they tried to neglect it by vain self-reliance, building their nest in another man's house.—Lastly Jesus feels, as already present in its causes, the *coming fact* of the denial and desertion: it would follow with moral necessity from such a disposition of mind, and it had been foretold by the inspired oracle: " You will all be scandalized this night because of me; for it is written, ' I will smite the shepherd, and the sheep of the flock will be scattered.' " (Matt. 26:31)

III. *What Jesus is saying.*

Although Christ quite clearly foresees the uselessness of His warning, He never desists giving it to the Apostles, as that duty belongs to Him as Teacher. He declares distinctly the effect that will follow from their cowardice: " You will all be scandalized in me "; the universality of this effect: " All you "; its nearness: " this night "; its certainty: " For it is written."

However this pointing out of the coming event provokes empty protests from the Apostles, and above all from St. Peter, so that Christ may learn also by experimental knowledge that of which He was already aware by His foreknowledge of the future, and His insight into hearts.

Although Christ foresees that it is useless to repeat the warning, He nevertheless forewarns Peter in particular concerning the imminent scandal, and the threefold denial that very night. He confirms the warning with a solemn assertion: " Amen, I say to thee." (Matt. 26:34) But this warning only makes Peter still more confident, and he brings all the others to the same presumption

Lastly, Jesus admonishes the Apostles, by His own example, to prayer: " Sit down here, while I go over yonder and pray " (Matt. 26:36) ; yet again He knows beforehand that the warning is lost on them.

SECOND POINT: The Prayer in the Garden

I. *Beginning of the prayer.*

Jesus wished to forearm at least the three most beloved Apostles against the threatening temptation; He therefore took them closer to Himself, to teach them near at hand by His own example; He recommends them prayer more insistently, though He knows that the warning will be useless. Notice how the circumstances that would naturally draw Him away from prayer accompany Him to the very threshold of prayer. However much He is the Son of God, now, clothed in the form of a servant, He goes for this reason to pray; He does not allow Himself to be distracted from prayer, but He does pray to the Father; He chooses a more secluded spot, " going forward a little " (Matt. 20:39) as far as a stone's cast, He stands with utmost calm and reverence in the place of prayer, then He kneels down, folds His hands, now lifting up His eyes, then casting them down, He moves His lips.

II. *The object of the prayer.*

There hovers before Christ's eyes the cup of the Lord's wrath, " deep and wide " (Ez. 23:32), and full to the brim: it contains all the sufferings, both of the mind and of the body, that He is to endure in the Passion; all the sins of the whole world that He is to have on Himself; all the future ingratitude of men: nevertheless the chalice is presented by the Father's hand, prepared by His holiness and justice, and decreed by His will.

The chalice presented in this manner stirs up in the Redeemer's soul feelings of sadness, of fear, and of loathing or disgust; for it contains everything that is sad, dreadful, and repugnant to natural appetite; yet it stirs up at the same time the feeling of reverence towards the hand of the Father who presents the chalice.

III. *The perseverance in prayer.*

Consider that these reluctant feelings began gently, and that Christ met them with prayer; they go on in spite of the prayer, and Christ perseveres, praying three times; and when, from dryness of desolation, He had no other prayer ready at hand, He " prayed a third time, saying the same words over " (Matt. 26:44); those feelings are ever increasing, and Christ likewise increases the insistence of His

prayers, " He prayed the more earnestly " (Luke 22:43);
He cries to the Father " with a loud cry and tears " (Hebr.
5:7) so that His human nature begged: " Father, if thou
art willing, remove this cup from me; yet not my will
but thine be done." (Luke 22:42) No matter how arduous
the torments He yields to the wishes of the Father; He
offers us the perfect example of obedience.

THIRD POINT: The Agony in the Garden

I. *The slothfulness of the disciples.*

During the prayer Jesus came to His disciples, because
they were His own, entrusted to His care; because He
loved them, and eagerly wished—little as they deserved it
—to fortify them against the impending temptation; at
the same time He foresees that He will find them sleeping,
and that they will not in the least profit by His warning.

He " found them sleeping " (Luke 22:46): they are
heavy with sorrow of the heart; Christ is pained Himself,
because He finds so little sympathy, docility, and gratitude; He is pained for the sake of the disciples, because
they will most certainly succumb to temptation.

And He said: " Could you not, then, watch one hour
with me? " (Matt. 26:40) Christ speaks words of gentle
reproof; and yet He again exhorts them to prayer more
explicitly: " Watch and pray." (Matt. 26:41) He stressed
the reason and the necessity for this: " That you may not
enter into temptation. The spirit indeed is willing, but the
flesh is weak." (Matt. 26:41) And then He admonishes
them once more by His example of prayer.

Consider the feeling of utter abandonment in the soul
of the Savior, forsaken by the disciples and His Father.

II. *The Agony of Christ.*

1. *In His soul:* Jesus was reduced to saying: " My soul is sad, even unto death " (Matt. 26:38); so great is the sadness He bears that it can almost separate the soul from the body; these words, spoken on entering the Garden, were the more true when our Lord was in agony.

2. *In His body:* Consider the bloody sweat, which has occurred in but very few persons, and only those in a state of extreme agony; consider the abundance of the bloody sweat, as it breaks forth everywhere from the pores, soaking the garments, and trickling down in drops upon the ground.

3. *The fruit of the prayer of the Agony:* " There appeared to him an angel from heaven to strengthen him." (Luke 22:43) The angel was sent by the Father; he was perhaps one of those who had come to Christ's Nativity, who had ministered to Him after the temptation in the desert. The angel was not to hinder the sacrifice as was done formerly by the angel appearing to Abraham; but the angel strengthened our Lord; the one who was lower supported Him who was higher.

He would impress on Christ's mind that the Passion was indeed decreed by the Father, for it is a real comfort to have a confirmation of a truth already known otherwise; he recommended the chalice to Christ's will, pointing out that it was given by the Father, and that it would give life to the world. As a result of the angel's comforting the will of Christ was strengthened; it completely subdued the lower nature, and absolutely accepted the chalice. With firm step Jesus now goes towards the disciples, and He speaks to them in a steady voice: " Rise, let us go! " He repeats the generous " go ye," which He had uttered when setting out from Bethany for the Passion.

CHAPTER XL

From the Garden to the House of Annas

Cf. Matthew 26:47-58; Mark 14:44-54, 66-68;
Luke 22:47-57; John 18:1-23; *The Exercises*, Sec. 291

★

AMONG THE more general points given by Ignatius for the third week is this: "To consider how the divinity . . . leaves the most sacred humanity to suffer so cruelly." (Sec. 196) This consideration strikes us vividly in the mystery in which Christ resigns Himself to His enemies. Thus He allows Judas to kiss Him and men to seize Him as a robber. At the same time, ever mindful of His duty as Teacher, He reminds both of His divinity; Judas by words which show His omniscience, the guards by words which cause them to fall to the ground. In the second point we are shown how Jesus does not allow Himself to be defended by human means, but opposes His enemies only by meekness.

First Point. *Our Lord allows Himself to be kissed by Judas, and to be seized as a robber. He says to them: " As against a robber have you come out, with swords and clubs, to seize me. I sat daily with you in the temple teaching, and you did not lay hands on me." (Matt. 26:55) When He said, "Whom do you seek? " (John 18:7), His enemies fell to the ground.*

Second Point. *St. Peter wounds the servant of the High Priest. The meek Lord says to him, " Put back thy sword into its place." (Matt. 26:52) And He healed the wound of the servant.*

Third Point. *Deserted by His disciples, He is led to Annas. There St. Peter, who had followed Him afar off, denied Him once. Christ was struck in the face and asked, " Is that the way thou dost answer the high priest? "* (John 18:22)

FIRST POINT: Jesus Is Seized.

I. *The Lord allows Judas to kiss Him.*

1. *Judas: his person, words, actions.*

a. Judas was *one of the twelve.* Review the graces given him, his spiritual downfall, and his visit to the high priests.

Consider his *intention to betray:* it is unjust, for it is a question of ruining an innocent person; it is ungrateful and shameful, for the disciple betrays his Master, and the shamefulness of his cunning in a way reflects on the Master and Lord who had chosen and loved him; it is cruel, for Jesus is handed over to His worst enemies, with evident danger to His life.

b. *" Hail Rabbi! "* Consider how contrary these friendly and respectful words are to the inward intention of betraying. Consider the shamelessness of these words, uttered publicly before witnesses who knew that intention. Compare the salutation uttered now with the same salutation spoken formerly by Judas, when offering himself as a disciple.

c. *The Kiss.* Of its very nature a kiss is a sign of friendship; here, however, it comes from the heart of an enemy and a traitor; it is the signal given to the attendants, pointing out Christ as an evil-doer, and inviting them to seize the desperate man, and carry Him off with every precaution; it is an actual denial of Christ's perfections, on which their friendship was based, of the Lord's holiness, since Judas points Him out to the mob as a criminal, of the Lord's omniscience, since Judas assumes that the Master will be deceived by a false show of love, of the Lord's omnipotence, since Judas implies that such a fraud can be attempted without risk of punishment.

2. *Jesus: His person, actions, words.*

a. The Son of God, the Savior of the world, who is now worn-out by the awful agony, and therefore feels more deeply the wrong and insult inflicted on Him. Jesus thoroughly sees, feels, and detests the treason of Judas; at the same time He has full power immediately to confound the traitor, and to escape his cunning.

b. Jesus refrains from every use of His omniscience and omnipotence; He allows Himself to be kissed gently, offering His cheek.—Why so?—Because that betrayal is part of the chalice which He was ready to accept from the Father's hand; because Christ freely chooses to bear the shame of that treason, together with all the subsequent Passion, for me, that I too may bear something for Him; because Jesus loves me, not with words and the tongue, but in deed and truth.

c. " Friend, for what purpose hast thou come? " (Matt. 26:50) Or what is the same: " Judas, dost thou betray the Son of Man with a kiss? " (Luke 22:48) Jesus fulfils the part of a good teacher towards Judas, by recalling His omniscience, by pointing out the wickedness and gravity of the betrayal, and by warning Judas against it: Jesus is truly a kind and meek teacher.

II. *Jesus allows Himself to be taken by the attendants.*

1. *The soldiers and servants.*

They were sent by the high priests on a mission to seize one suspected of false teaching and wicked fraud; in reality, however, they were sent to seize one whom their superiors envied and hated. They are to arrest the Lord and deprive Him of liberty; they make all the preparations that are usually employed in the arrest of the criminal of the worst sort; they therefore seize Him at night and lead Him carefully; as they have to do with a most desperate fellow their number must be large, armed with swords and clubs. All observe deep silence, lest the culprit smell some danger and escape.

2. *Jesus: His person, words, actions.*

a. Christ is the King, the son of David, the priest according to the order of Melchisedich, the strong God; Christ is a man most innocent, most worthy of liberty, against whom that display of force is most insulting; yet now the Lord is disgraced by the kiss of Judas, and therefore in opinion of the attendants no longer above suspicion.

b. Jesus protests that He is no robber seeking to escape, but a teacher who sat every day in the temple. The Lord deeply feels the shame of all that display of force. He states that He is not yielding to the swords and clubs, but to the will of His Father, who allowed that hour.

c. By the words, " I am he! " (John 18:5), Jesus strikes down His adversaries with His almighty power; on the strength of His authority He bids them let the disciples go unmolested. Then He allowed Himself to be taken, showing Himself as meek and humble as a lamb.

Second Point: Malchus Is Healed.

I. *St. Peter: his person, words, actions.*

a. Peter is prompted by love for his Master; yet a very imperfect love, since it is spoiled by presumption and excitement, and not made firm by diligent prayer. Accordingly Peter cannot enter in the spirit of Christ and accept the chalice gladly. Peter thinks the chalice must be rejected by all means.

b. " Lord, shall we strike with the sword? " (Luke 22:49) Peter sets about a foolish plan: with only two swords to take up the fight against an armed band, to beat off the wrong and insult that form part of the chalice offered by the Father.

c. The imprudent plan is carried out most awkwardly: Peter inflicts a slight wound on one Malchus.

II. *Jesus: His person, words, actions.*

a. The Lord opposes only meekness, both to Peter's excitement and to the enemy's violence.

b. Doing His office as teacher, Jesus declares that He renounces all human means: " Put back thy sword into its place; for all those who take the sword will perish by the sword." (Matt. 26:52) Human means are quite superfluous, considering that Jesus has at His command legions of angels, most efficient in number and power; the Passion must, of a necessity, be undergone, since it is the chalice offered by the Father, and foretold in Scripture. At the same time Christ declares His firm will to undergo the Passion: " Shall I not drink the cup that the Father has given me? " (John 18:11)

c. Jesus heals the ear of Malchus, showing thereby that He undergoes the Passion quite freely, and that He has sufficient power to avoid it, if only He so wills. At the same time He shows the utmost meekness to Malchus, the enemy, whom He heals by a miracle, and to Peter, giving him by the same miracle a lesson in meekness.

THIRD POINT: Christ Is Brought before Annas.

I. *Deserted by His disciples, He is led to Annas.*

1. *The disciples: their persons and actions.*

a. After so many benefits and so many warnings the disciples have forgotten their many professions of fidelity; when they see that Jesus is unwilling to repel force by force, they despair of His cause and even of His person; they no longer do anything, not even so much as to utter a word in His defense; they refuse to follow Him and go with Him to death. All are the same!

b. The Apostles now flee from the sight of the opponents who had just been struck down on the ground by the Master's word; they run away from the Almighty, their friend, yet they do not know whither to go. They think any place safer than that where He is. Reflect on the weakness of nature deprived of more abundant grace.

2. *The attendants: their persons, words, actions.*

a. The servants and soldiers think even worse of Jesus than before; they imagine that He has been captured unawares and that He had been badly mistaken in His choice of followers; they interpret His meek look and the pallor of His face, caused by the dreadful agony in the garden, as a sign of fear and of a bad conscience. Moreover, as they had been struck down by His word, they are all the more furious to avenge that insult on a man who will not offer resistance.

b. They burst into shouts of joy and jeers.

c. They bind Him carefully and tightly. They drag, push, and jeer Him as they go first down the valley of Cedron, then up the slope to the house of Annas, the High Priest. There Christ will be accused of blasphemy. He will not be judged, but will be dragged thence to further humiliations, and finally to the cross.

3. *Jesus: His person, words, and actions.*

a. Now abandoned, the Lord grieves for the disciples' sin and their ingratitude to Him. Christ feels the contempt of His guards; He tastes all the bitterness of His abandonment: They who had protested that they would go with Him to death are far away; at each step the fetters, shouts, and blows make the Master realize how empty were their promises: the Shepherd is now alone in the midst of the wolves; He bends under the weight of the words of Scripture which, as He well knows, must be fulfilled, and He feels their fulfilment already.

b. Christ goes along meekly and in silence, praying for His torturers and His disciples; by His grief He merits for the disciples the grace that they may recover, after a short interval, from their desertion, and that the recollection of their weakness may confirm them afterwards in His following.

c. Christ refrains, for the time being, from giving more liberal grace to the Apostles; He allows Himself to be dragged along. He bears all because the Scripture must be fulfilled; because the shame and sorrow of that desertion is a drop of the chalice offered Him by the Father, because He loves me!

II. *The denial by St. Peter.*

1. St. Peter follows the Lord, drawn by love and pushed by presumption; he *follows afar off*, held back by fear. The *Heart of Jesus* is anxiously and sadly watching Peter as he follows from afar, but for good reasons Jesus does not give the Apostle at once more abundant grace.

2. After receiving so many benefits above all the other Apostles, St. Peter ought to have taken up the defense of His accused Master; on the contrary, he denied Him, although it had been but a short while ago when he had pledged his loyalty by the fervent declaration: " Even if I should have to die with thee, I will not deny thee! " (Matt. 26:35) Upset by the casual question of a poor servant girl, Peter denies Christ.

Jesus is grieved at this denial, which was a bitter drop of His chalice; yet He does not at once give the grace of conversion, because the denials which were still to follow had been decreed and foretold by the Father.

III. *Christ is struck before Annas.*

1. *Annas* had lawful judicial authority, but his mind was prejudiced and hostile; as the father-in-law to Caiphas, he was joined to him not only by affinity, but also by malice. *Jesus* does not refuse an answer to the high priest, who asks with lawful authority. He answers with words that were indeed sufficient, even though few. He could have solved at once all the accusations by an answer of His, or He could have softened the enemies' hearts by His grace; but Christ does not do so, because He has resolved to drink to the full the cup offered Him by His Father.

2. A servant strikes Him. As a result of the words spoken, Jesus is given a lesson in reverence towards the high priest; the lesson comes from one of the servants, concerning a matter evident even to the lowest, requiring no explanation from the self-appointed teacher: the argument used is a physical blow, as though Christ would not be able to grasp a more subtle one; the lesson is given publicly, amid the general applause of the bystanders.

3. *Jesus* keeps to His part as a *teacher:* He teaches the one who struck Him with a few gentle words; He teaches us what we ought to think of insults, and how we ought to bear them. He, who had struck down by His power those who had sought Him in the Garden, does not now strike down the servant who strikes Him. He hides His divine nature; His sole will is to please His Father, to save me from my sins.

CHAPTER XLI

From the House of Annas to the House of Caiphas

Cf. Matthew 26; Mark 14; Luke 22; John 18;
The Exercises, Sec. 292

★

IT SEEMS to us that St. Ignatius emphasizes in this contemplation the *Redeemer in bonds*, but the agony of Christ's soul, the unjust condemnation and the humility of His position are also included.

First Point. *They led Him bound from the house of Annas to that of Caiphas, where* St. *Peter denied Him twice. When our Lord looked upon him, he went out and wept bitterly.*

Second Point. *Jesus remained bound the whole night.*

Third Point. *Those who kept Him bound scoffed at Him, buffeted Him, covered His face and struck Him with the palms of their hands, and asked Him, " Prophesy to us, O Christ! who is it that struck thee? "* (Matt. 26:68) *And similar things they said, blaspheming Him.*

FIRST POINT: Jesus Is Dragged Bound from Annas to Caiphas.

I. *The Lord is dragged*.

On the way to Caiphas the previous sufferings of Christ continue and increase: weariness, shame, and insults. He is dragged through the streets, those streets through which He had passed but a few days previously in triumph, hailed by all as the Son of David and the Messiah. At present *the Lord is bound*, accused of the blasphemous crime of having falsely claimed the honor of Messiah, and He has not been absolved of the charge by the first judge.

II. *Christ is cross-examined.*

1. *The Judges.*

The high priest had been divinely appointed to judge anyone who should claim to be a prophet or the Messiah. Caiphas, however, is an unjust judge; already before the trial he had made up his mind to destroy Jesus. Similarly the other priests and scribes were raging with hatred against Jesus, and they too were quite determined not only not to release Him from His bonds, but also to make His captivity a prelude to His death: all of them were such that they should rightly have been rejected as judges. The legal process consisted in this, that evident false witnesses were summoned one after another, not in order that the case should be investigated, but that the accused might be quite certainly destroyed. The very trial was evidently unjust.

2. *Jesus.*

It would have been easy for Christ, considering His wisdom, to refute the charges; He could have done again what He did in the Garden, *viz.*, strike down the accusers by His almighty power, or melt their hearts by a single look, as in the case of St. Peter. But the Lord holds His peace; He wishes to *remain bound;* His tongue and arm and eye are held by the far stronger *bond of charity:* at the Incarnation both His divine and human nature were bound by charity, and His whole substance is bound in the Holy Eucharist under strange appearances: all actions of human life are under restraint; charity has disarmed Christ.

III. *The Lord is condemned.*

1. The high priest, disgusted with the false witnesses, and setting aside the charges that could not be proved, adjures Christ and puts a question which it was undoubtedly his right to put: " I adjure thee by the living God that thou tell us whether thou art the Christ, the Son of God." (Matt. 26:63)

2. Jesus answers clearly to the just question: " Thou hast said it." (Matt. 26:64) He foresees, however, that He will be condemned because of His answer. He answers so because He is obliged to declare His identity. He adds that He will one day appear as the universal judge and by this warning the Lord mercifully reminds the unjust human judges of the future account they must render.

3. The judges reject this grace. Christ had affirmed His dignity of Messiah and universal Judge; the judges declare it a blasphemy and Christ a false Messiah, a false prophet, who has sacrilegiously violated what was holy above all else to the Chosen People. They pronounce Him guilty of death!

Consider how repugnant blasphemy, an insult uttered against God, and especially so wicked a blasphemy, is to Christ who is God; reflect on the Lord's utter abasement in this humiliation.

IV. *Christ is denied a second and a third time.*

1. Consider how of all men Peter would have been able to bear witness in favor of Christ in His fatal predicament: Peter knew the Lord more intimately than all the others, and he ought to have spoken because he was aware of Christ's authority; he had received innumerable benefits, had again and again professed his loyalty.

2. Peter denies that he knows Christ; he denies the Lord a second time, and he does so once more under an oath with a

curse. Peter acts from fear, not of a judicial inquiry, but at the casual remarks of some servants.

3. Jesus bound with chains unbinds, by a glance of His, the chains of confusion and fear that held the Apostle's mind enslaved; by that single look Peter is recalled to penitence.

SECOND POINT: Jesus Remained Bound All That Night.

I. The Lord is *bound*,

that is, deprived of liberty: an image of the slavery into which we fall through sin; He remains bound in order to atone for our abuse of liberty, and to restore us to the liberty of the children of God.—Jesus is deprived of rest in body as well as in mind: an image of the misery into which we fall through sin; He remains bound to atone for our sensuality and sloth, and to restore us to happiness and peace.—Jesus is exposed to the gaze of all: an image of the ugliness of sin; He remains bound to atone for human respect and want of sincerity, and to rescue us from the shame of the judgment day.

II. But Christ is bound much more by His own free will.

He accepts the bonds willingly and *perseveres in chains*, praying all the while that our fetters may be loosed. This is going on the whole night, a time consecrated by nature to relax the bonds of duty, to allow rest, and to exclude the sight of others. Consider how long that night must have been for the Lord, how heavy those bonds, how unbearable that watching, how wearying those ever malign looks!

III. Jesus, the infinite liberty, is restrained by bonds.

The endless happiness is not allowed the comfort of rest; the uncreated light is calling with His sighs for the dawn of day; eternity complains of the slow progress of the hours: all this is done in order that He who suffers thus may in very truth be for us a Jesus, a Savior, a Liberator!

THIRD POINT: The Bound Jesus Is Mocked.

I. *He is mocked*.

Those who held Him captive had no right to inflict insults on Him, for they were not judges; neither had they received an order from the judges; they were soldiers and servants. They mocked the Lord, striking Him as one who had forfeited all right to respect. They covered His face and hit Him, asking: "Prophesy, who is it that struck thee?" (Luke 22:64) Thus they insult Him as a false Messiah and as a false prophet. "And many other things they kept saying against him, reviling him." (Luke 22:65) They spat in His face. Christ was unjustly condemned for blasphemy, and He was insulted by blasphemy.

II. These things were done *to Him, in addition to others,* by the guards.

In the meantime Jesus is allowed no liberty, no rest, no privacy. He is insulted first by some of the servants, then by others, then by the priests and scribes who seek Him out, finally by some of these in the crowd that had gathered. As soon as some tire of their sport others are ready to take over, trying to surpass their predecessors in coarseness; as the latter fall out, the first come back for another turn. Reflect on the coarse abuse given Jesus during the whole night.

III. *The behavior of Jesus.*

Jesus remains in a kind of hell, seeing on all sides the sneers of His enemies, hearing the awful blasphemies, feeling the spittle and blows. The engineers of that hell were two: hatred of sin, and unspeakable love for me. Let charity bind together the stones of that hell and lock its doors; by charity the mouth, hands, and eyes are held bound for Christ.

CHAPTER XLII

From the House of Caiphas to the House of Pilate

Cf. Matthew 27; Mark 15; Luke 23; *The Exercises*,
Sec. 293

★

IN THIS and in the two following mysteries are primarily set forth the *wrongs* suffered by the Savior. The first events in which Pilate figures may be summarized under the following heads: Christ is accused, declared innocent, rejected in favor of Barabbas. Here we see the wrongs done to *His innocence*. Then comes the episode of Herod: Christ is sent to Herod, questioned by him out of curiosity, treated by him with contempt. Here we see the wrongs done to Christ's *wisdom*. The final events at Pilate's Court show the wrongs done to Christ's *royal dignity*. Notice how well the meditation on the Kingdom of Christ is related to these.

First Point. *The whole multitude of Jews took Him to Pilate, and accused Him before the governor, saying, " We have found this man perverting our nation, and forbidding the payment of taxes to Caesar."* (Luke 23:2)

Second Point. *After Pilate had examined Him several times, he said: " I find no guilt in this man."* (Luke 23:4)

Third Point. *Barabbas, the robber, was preferred to Him: " Away with this man, and release to us Barabbas! "* (Luke 23: 18)

First Point: Jesus Is Brought before Pilate.

I. *The Lord is dragged along.*

1. *Who?* Jesus, the Son of God; therefore Majesty itself, Holiness itself, Truth itself, Justice itself; the King, Teacher, and Judge of the world; He who had been seized as a robber, struck before Annas as one who despised the nation's religion, condemned and mocked before Caiphas as a blasphemer and a false Messiah.

2. *By whom?* The whole multitude of the Jews: now not merely a few servants, but the priests, scribes, and all the elders; and together with them an endless multitude either of those that went with the procession, or that lined the roads and looked on; the crowd is ever swelling, all raging against the Lord like mad wolves.

3. *To whom?* To Pilate, the representative of the authority in obedience to which Jesus had been born at Bethlehem. Pilate wields secular authority, a pagan authority, usurped by force. The Jews consider the governor's person as unclean, and meet him as seldom as possible. At present Pilate is to be the judge of the life or death, the shame or honor of Jesus.

4. *How?* They drag Jesus along, bound and worn-out as He is, with the greatest violence. And it was morning: at once, as soon as it was daylight, with pressing hurry, adding words of hatred and mockery.

5. *For what purpose?* In order that He may be sent to the cross as an evil-doer. Their hearts are already shouting: Crucify Him, crucify Him!

II. *Jesus is accused before Pilate.*

At first the Jews ask that Jesus should be condemned as a criminal; their only proof is their own witness: " If he were not a criminal we should not have handed him over to thee." (John 18:30) When Pilate declined to do so, they come out with accusations that are altogether different from those with which they had charged Jesus shortly before, at the Sanhedrin; and the charges are such that they would be deemed an honor rather than a shame in any other respectable person. Two of the accusations were false: " We have found this man perverting our nation, and forbidding the payment of taxes to Caesar " (Luke 23:2); another charge was ambiguous: He says that " he is Christ a king." (Luke 23:2) In addition to this they bring forward many other things, minor points, of course, not selected with any regard to justice, but with the intention of inciting the governor against Jesus. They gamble with the honor and life of Jesus.

SECOND POINT: Jesus Is Examined by Pilate.

I. *Pilate.*

The Roman governor examines the case of Jesus again and again; he recognizes the innocence of the accused from what he had already seen before, namely, that Christ had been delivered up to him through envy; from the obviously false charges that were brought forward; from the circumstance that nothing had been heard before in regard to the principal charges, which could not possibly have been but most public; from the clear answer whereby Christ cleared Himself of the third charge about being a king. At last Pilate proclaims the innocence of Jesus: " I find no guilt in this man." (Luke 23:4) The sense of these words is pointed: Jesus has not been guilty of a crime by declaring Himself to be a king; otherwise Pilate would have investigated further into this matter.

II. *The Eternal Father.*

Consider the Eternal Father invisibly seated on His throne of judgment: the Father has, so to speak, transferred this throne to court of Pilate. Round His throne stand the angels, singing " holy, holy, holy," covering their faces on account of the sins of Jerusalem and of the whole world. The purpose of the Father's judgment is that God should receive glory, and men obtain peace at the price of the blood of the God-Man. The Eternal Father had laid on Jesus " the iniquity of us all." (Is. 53:6) Accordingly He now declares: " I do find cause in this man; he is guilty of death." And the angels answer: " Amen, so be it."

III. *Jesus.*

1. The Lord concedes what must be conceded, *viz.*, that He is King. He goes on to explain the nature of His kingdom; otherwise He does not say so much as one word in His own defence. Consider what fine statements Christ might have made! Moreover He offers to the judge, who is less guilty than the Jews, a twofold grace: warning Pilate through his wife's dream, and inviting him to inquire into truth and the spiritual kingdom. Pilate, however fails to co-operate with either grace by a more careful investigation.

2. Jesus accepts willingly the condemnation coming from the mouth of the Eternal Father, and He is ready to undergo death for my sins.

THIRD POINT: Barabbas Is Preferred to Jesus.

I. *Pilate.*

After proclaiming the innocence of Jesus, Pilate, from

human respect, does not dare decree at once that the accused be discharged. The weak judge tries to bring about the discharge, due on the ground of justice, as a favor that is granted freely according to the Paschal custom: understand, a favor which the sworn enemies should grant to Christ as a false Messiah, who is now harmless. With a view to wringing this favor from the Jews with greater certainty, Pilate makes a comparison between Jesus and Barabbas, a most desperate criminal. If the Jews prefer Jesus to that man, they do not, on that score, acknowledge the Lord's innocence, but merely His less wickedness. Pilate is gambling with the right, the honor, and the life of Christ.

II. *The Jews.*

The multitude declare that Jesus does not deserve that favor: " Not this man " or that He certainly deserves it less than Barabbas: " But Barabbas." They shout this without any previous legal inquiry, stirred up by the priests. In this they are, however, consistent with themselves and their former wickedness: supposing indeed that Jesus is a blasphemous, false Messiah, then He is, of course, more unworthy of the favor than even Barabbas. The Jews are gambling with the right, the honor, and the life of Christ.

III. The Eternal *Father.*

The Divine Judge proclaims that He will not pardon the sin of " this Man," His beloved Son, in whom He is otherwise well pleased, but who now bears the sins of the world. The Father pardons " Barabbas," that is to say, all sinners who have rebelled against Him. The heavenly

Father is prompted by most generous love: " For God so loved the world that he gave his only-begotten Son." (John 3:16)

IV. *Jesus.*

The Savior does not ask a favor for Himself; He allows the crowd to shout for Barabbas and to cry " Crucify him! Crucify him! " (Luke 23:21) He readily offers Himself as the victim for our sins: " Behold, I come." (Ps. 39:8)

CHAPTER XLIII

From the House of Pilate to the House of Herod

Cf. Luke 23:6-11; *The Exercises*, Sec. 294

★

First Point. *Pilate sent Jesus, the Galilean, to Herod, the tetrarch of Galilee.*

Second Point. *Herod curiously asked many questions, and Jesus answered nothing, though the scribes and priests accused Him constantly.*

Third Point. *Herod and his whole court mocked Jesus, and clothed Him with a white garment.*

FIRST POINT: Jesus Is Sent to Herod.

I. *Who is sent?*

Jesus, the Son of God, bearing our sins; He has been rejected in favor of Barabbas, and thus declared a notorious criminal. His liberty, honor, and life are not protected by law; they are at the whim of favor and politics: He is from Galilee; this is now the only thing worthy of notice about Him.

II. *By whom is He sent?*

By the Eternal Father, that He may drain the chalice. By Pilate, under pretence of respect for Herod's jurisdiction; the governor was wont to ignore it, and to encroach upon it; in reality he would now get rid of the accused whom he dares neither condemn nor absolve; moreover Pilate would thus win Herod's favor by gambling with the liberty, the honor, and the life of Jesus. Accordingly the Lord is dragged along by the attendants, amid an ever growing concourse of people.

III. *To whom is He sent?*

To Herod, a scion of the house which had usurped David's throne, the son of the Herod who had laid a snare for the Child Jesus. In character this Herod is exactly like his father, exactly like Lucifer, and most unlike God, the source of all authority: Herod is notoriously proud, cruel, licentious, and wicked; he has murdered John the Baptist; his power is insignificant, since he is merely tetrarch of Galilee; yet all the while he would try to seem to be influential: hence constant friction with Pilate: Herod was restless from remorse of conscience, and from unsatiable greed for new pleasures.

SECOND POINT: Jesus Is Brought before Herod.

I. *Christ enters the court.*

1. Consider Herod. He sits on a great throne, but he has no true greatness. His throne is precious, but he, rejected of God, is worthless. His throne is massive, but he lacks peace of mind and moral firmness.

Notice the spacious hall, the home of unbridled vanity and spiritual misery. The courtiers, in large numbers, are like their king in dress and in manner; they exaggerate his power and encourage him in his vices. Reflect on the vanity of all things whereby that assembly is no more than a Babylon, a place of confusion.

2. When Jesus comes in no shame for past sins seizes their minds; there is no reverence for the Sovereign Majesty present; there is no desire to obtain true life. The looks betray nothing but a worldly curiosity. Reflect on the shame, the humiliation, and the pain of Jesus.

II. *Christ is examined.*

1. Herod is harboring in his mind feelings that seem to be friendly to Christ; in fact they are insults more atrocious than the taunts of the mob, and more offensive to Christ. Herod, prompted by curiosity, had longed for Christ's coming: " he had been a long time desirous to see him, because he had heard so much about him." (Luke 23:8) Now Herod shows idle rejoicing at the coming of the accused; when he " saw Jesus, he was exceedingly glad." (Luke 23:8) He flatters himself with the absurd hope that Jesus, for the sake of show, and to please courtiers, is going to perform some miracle; Herod hoped " to see some miracle done by him." (Luke 23:8) The king supposes that he can flatter our Lord and so, with nauseating foppery " he put many questions to him." (Luke 23:9) The bland talk contains the silent offer that Herod will set aside all the charges without examination, provided that Christ gives proof of His skill to work miracles, or rather to perform magic tricks. Herod is gambling with Christ's freedom, honor, and life. Consider how hollow is the friendship of the world.

2. *The priests and the scribes.* Notice their numbers and weigh the accusations they make to rouse Herod to glee. The accusations are a torrent of confusion, the one destroying and refuting the other. Notice their perseverence in accusing Christ and the hatred on their faces. Learn from the emptiness of those charges how hollow is the hatred of the world. They, too, are gambling with the liberty, honor, and life of Christ.

3. *Jesus* does not refute the accusations, as He could have done most easily, nor does He yield to the eager and silly suggestions of Herod. He renews His oblation of Himself to the Father.

THIRD POINT: Jesus Is Mocked by Herod.

I. *Statement of the fact.*

" Herod, with his soldiery, treated him with contempt and mocked him." (Luke 23:11) The king despises Christ in his mind, thinking that Jesus is no prophet, that He is unable to work miracles. The king despises Christ in words, calling Him a cheat and a forger; at these words there is applause from the whole crowd, the courtiers, the priests and scribes, the servants and the multitude; the applause spreads from the royal throne through the hall and the lobbies into the streets. Herod lastly despises Christ by actions: " arraying him in a bright robe." (Luke 23:11) The judge neither absolves nor condemns; ignoring altogether the question of justice he declares by deeds that Jesus is a fool; at the same time Herod pays a compliment to the governor by not pronouncing judgment, and heaps insults on the head of the prisoner.

Accordingly Herod declares the Master a fool, the King a fool, the Son of God a fool, the Messiah a fool, the Prophet a fool—a man who lacks the very first requisite that is above all necessary for each and all those offices.— Listen once more to the applause of the whole army approving Herod's wisdom, and of the priests and scribes who would indeed have preferred a condemnation. Reflect on the feelings of Jesus, His humiliation, resignation, and self-oblation.

II. *An examination of the fact.*

1. Reflect what a contradiction there is in this sentence: " Jesus is a fool! "; whether we consider His divine nature or His human nature. Reflect on those who utter that sentence: their ignorance, stupidity, and conceit; their minds are altogether incapable of passing a just judgment concerning Christ. How absurd and wicked then is that sentence, which was pronounced so unanimously and unhesitatingly.

2. Hence reflect in general on the *vanity of all the judgments of the world,* comparing things heavenly with things earthly, and spiritual things with material things: " But the sensual man does not perceive the things that are of the Spirit of God, for it is foolishness to him, and he cannot understand, because it is examined spiritually." (1 Cor. 2:14) Consider that from the Babylon or confusion of the world there cannot come but Babylonian or confused and absurd judgments.

3. Consider how this Babylon of the world shrinks from Christ, and from the humility and poverty that are His; on the contrary the world loves and embraces that which is hateful to Christ: honors, fame, pomp, and pleasures, whereas Christ, in turn, rejects the latter things and embraces the former. The world's judgments are vain, Christ's judgment is true. It is meet, therefore, that they who seriously follow Christ should embrace and reject the same things as Christ.

CHAPTER XLIV

From the House of Herod to That of Pilate

Cf. Matthew 27; Luke 23; Mark 15; John 19;
The Exercises, Sec. 295

★

First Point. *Herod sent Jesus back to Pilate, and because of this they became friends, though before they were enemies.*

Second Point. *Pilate took Jesus and had Him scourged, and the soldiers made a crown of thorns and placed it upon His head. They put a purple cloak about Him, and came to Him and said, " Hail, King of the Jews! " (John 19:3) And they gave Him all manner of blows.*

Third Point. *Pilate led Him forth before all: " Jesus therefore came forth, wearing the crown of thorns and the purple cloak. And he said to them, ' Behold, the man! ' When, therefore, the chief priests . . . saw him, they cried out, saying, ' Crucify him! Crucify him! ' " (John 19:5-6)*

FIRST POINT: Jesus Is Sent back to Pilate.

I. *He is sent back by Herod.*

Consider the *injustice* of this act: the case had been referred to Herod's tribunal, and there no fault was found in Him; in justice the accused should therefore have been set at liberty.

Consider the *shame* of this act: Not only was Jesus not discharged, but He is ordered to pass through the streets in the dress of a fool: the Lord's honor, liberty, and His life as well, are used as means for some private end of Herod, *viz.,* to win Pilate's favor. Jesus is overwhelmed with insults by the priests and the crowd, who are fully aware that anything concerning this man will go unpunished. Jesus is oppressed with sadness, and this increases the joy of the bystanders.

II. *Herod and Pilate are made friends.*

The *priests* rejoice that Jesus has not yet been acquitted, and that the case is going back to Pilate; the fickle Herod was less open to their influence. *Herod* rejoices that his jurisdiction has been acknowledged by Pilate, and that his curiosity to see Jesus has been satisfied; he rejoices, moreover, that he has satisfied the Jews, if not by condemning Jesus, at least by mocking Him. *Pilate* rejoices, not indeed at the return of the troublesome prisoner, but surely at the confirmation of his own sentence concerning the innocence of Jesus, and at the honor done to his jurisdiction by sending the prisoner back to him; he rejoices further at the favor gained with Caesar by winning over Herod so luckily. Pilate and Herod further manifest their satisfaction, and they are fully reconciled. Among so many people that rejoice, *Jesus* alone is consumed with sorrow. See how vain are the rejoicings of the world!

SECOND POINT: Jesus Is Scourged and Crowned with Thorns.

I. *He is scourged.*

Consider the *injustice* of this torture: it is inflicted on a person who has been acquitted by two judges; who has certainly not been convicted of a capital charge. The torture is only less severe than a death-sentence: " I upon examining him [Jesus] . . . have found no guilt . . . Neither has Herod . . . . behold, nothing deserving of death has been committed by him. I will therefore chastise him and release him." (Luke 23:14-16)

Consider the *cruelty* of the scourging: " From the sole of the foot unto the top of the head there is no soundness in him." (Is. 1:6) The torturers, men without feeling, are the more savage as they see that Pilate's plan is to make some concession to the Jews; add to this the hatred of the priests, and perhaps bribes. Jesus is forced to undergo this torture, when His strength was already gravely exhausted.

Consider the *shame* of this punishment: the torture for slaves is inflicted on Him who had declared Himself as King, Prophet, and Son of God, and who was so indeed.

II. *He is crowned with thorns.*

1. Those soldiers were absolutely without any authority; they had not made any enquiry; Pilate's cowardice alone filled them with fury, and, sure of the approval of the Jews, the torments they devised were suggested by their own *wanton cruelty*

They therefore deck Christ, the King, with a king's emblems: a crown and the purple; yet these were not of precious, but of vile material, fit to produce not honor, but shame; not pleasure, but torture. They pay homage to Him also with the honors offered to a king: by gesture, coming and bending the knee; by word, saying: " Hail, King of the Jews! " (John 19:3) by actions, giving Him blows, first one, then another, and afterwards the whole lot of them; and when these are tired, fresh ones take their place, seeking to surpass the previous ones in brutality.

2. Consider the *shame* of this insult. An insult is more bitter when it is inflicted under the appearance of honor; it is the more bitter as it mimics the show of more excellent honor; and it becomes yet more bitter when He on whom it is inflicted can claim that high honor as His birthright and His strictest due. Conclude from these considerations how great was the insult of that shameful mockery of kingship: the purple cloak was thrown not over the bare skin, but over the raw wounds; a weak reed as sceptre was the emblem of His power; the piercing crown formed of rough thorns was the symbol of His majesty; the insults of kneeling and saluting were varied by blows on the Holy Face.

III. *The feelings of Jesus, when scourged and crowned with thorns.*

1. Christ is conscious of His royal dignity "But I am appointed King by him." (Ps. 2:6) Christ knows clearly what throne, sceptre, purple, and homage are His due: and yet He derived no consolation from this consciousness, as He was overwhelmed by utter desolation.

2. The tortures and insults which our Lord suffers show the opinion of the Jews about His kingship, *viz.*, that it was powerless, quite unable to check the torturers, devoid of authority; that it could, without any risk, be treated with contempt to His face, a mere sham kingship, suitably represented by emblems altogether unfit for royal use. All this shows that the Jews were looking forward to a Messiah surrounded with worldly pomp and riches. Our Lord is grieved at the ruin of His Chosen People.

3. Christ sees that this judgment of the Jews, so public and so emphatic, proceeds from a mentality which is utterly ignorant of higher things; they were wretchedly enslaved by concupiscence of the flesh, and of the eyes, and by pride of life; Christ foresaw that this would go on to the end of the world,

for the ruin of many. The Savior prays that, through the merits of His Passion, the Kingdom of God may come into the hearts of the elect.

Third Point: Jesus Is Brought Forth in Public.

I. *He is brought forth.*

With legitimate authority Pilate brings forth Jesus who has been scourged and crowned with thorns. By this action Pilate approves of the executioners' doings, and makes them known to the people. The Most High King therefore goes forth, decked in mockery with the emblems of kingship; the unstained Holiness goes forth bearing the marks of the torture reserved for great crimes. He goes forth from the governor's hall to a place where He can be seen by all.

Consider the mockeries aimed at Him in the hall; the soldiers are glad that their coarse humor has not been punished by Pilate. Hear the loud murmur of the crowd; it strikes the ears of Jesus and becomes more disgusting as He advances from the hall through the galleries; then the cries ring out as He first comes into sight; the clamor is ever swelling until He is now in full sight of all, on the raised platform where He stands: He is saluted scornfully by the universal shout of the mob.

II. *His crucifixion is demanded.*

1. Pilate says: " *Behold, the man!* " (John 19:6) The governor is now appealing only for mercy; he does not appeal to Christ's innocence, which had been repeatedly declared by different judges; he does not now suggest that Jesus should be released in place of Barabbas, a known criminal: granted that Christ is a

blasphemer, sacrilegious, and an imposter; nevertheless He has now been reduced to such a wretched condition that He will no longer be able to pose as a teacher, king, and prophet: granted that He was a rabble-rouser; He is now harmless.

2. They shouted, saying: " Crucify him! Crucify him! " (John 19:6) The Jews declare that only the extreme penalty is equal to the misdeeds of this man. This answer is prompted by the high priests, inspired by hatred and envy, and ultimately by Satan. Listen how at intervals there are heard at first the voices of individual priests, presently the shouts spread wider and wider, till at last all is drowned in the yells of the whole populace.

3. *The words of Jesus* are those of the Holy Week office: " My people, what have I done to thee? or in what have I grieved thee? Answer me! "

CHAPTER XLV

From the House of Pilate to the Cross

Cf. John 19:13-22; *The Exercises*, Sec. 296

★

First Point. *Sitting in judgment, Pilate delivered up Jesus to be crucified after the Jews had denied that He was their king, saying, " We have no king but Caesar." (John 19:15)*

Second Point. *He carried the cross upon His shoulders, and when He was no longer able to do so, Simon of Cyrene was forced to carry it after Jesus.*

Third Point. *They crucified Him between two thieves. The title placed over the cross read: " Jesus of Nazareth, the King of the Jews." (John 19:19)*

FIRST POINT: Jesus Is Condemned to the Cross.

I. *He is condemned.*

1. Consider Pilate, seated as judge by the power given him by the Father for the administration of justice. Pilate wishes indeed to set the Just One free, but at the same time he desires to please Caesar and the Jews. At last, " seeing that he was doing no good " (Matt. 27:24), he washes his hands and declares himself innocent of any guilt in the condemnation of Christ. He sets aside the dream of his wife; he makes light of the promises he had made publicly to set the accused free after the scourging etc. Pilate delivered the Just One to His fierce enemies, to be punished with the most cruel, shameful, and unjust death.

2. Consider the Father, sitting invisibly as Judge, surrounded by the glorious hosts of angels, delivering the Just One to death in vicarious atonement for sinners: His blood be upon you and upon your children!

3. Consider the Jews, who in quite a different sense call His blood upon themselves; see from this the twofold effect of His blood; for some it will be a " laver of redemption and of life "; for others it will be the cause of damnation.

4. Consider Jesus, to whom the Father has given all judgment, appointed as Judge of the living and the dead, now standing before the tribunal as the Lamb of God that takes away the sins of the world; He accepts the judgment of the Father, and that of Pilate. He prays from the bottom of His Heart: " May My blood be upon you, and upon your children, as a laver of redemption and of life."

II. *The King is brought forth.*

1. *Behold the King.*

a. It is not customary to choose as king a man of doubtful reputation. Who is this man? Legally nothing regarding His reputation has been proved. It was not proved before Annas whether or not He was a true or a false doctor of the law; nothing was proved of the many charges brought against Him before Caiphas; at the court of Pilate even the Jews withdrew, by their prudent silence, the accusation of blasphemy; it has not been proved that He did anything against Caesar. He was indeed acquitted of that charge, yet at the same time He was kept in chains; there was no question of proof in the people's choice of Barabbas. The only thing certain is that He has been unjustly crowned with thorns and condemned to the cross. Pilate's job is now over. Having condemned Him, he can wash his hands.

b. It is not customary to choose as king a man who has no title to show. What title can Christ show? The title of Son of

God and Messiah is rejected. Will He be king on the grounds of His origin? He is a Galilean!—On the grounds of His strength? He is bound.—On the grounds of His wisdom? Herod adjudged Him a fool.—On the grounds of respectability? He was judged less worthy than Barabbas.—On the grounds of popular appeal? The people clamor for His blood.

c. With whom will that king have authority? Not with the people, nor with the priests and the leading citizens. The tetrarch of Galilee has despised Him. The procurator of Caesar has condemned Him. Without any authority the soldiers have crowned Him with thorns, and paid Him homage by means of spitting, buffets, stripes, and mockery. All this kingship of Christ seems then to be empty, a mere sham.

2. *" Behold, your king! "*

Hear these words as uttered by Pilate: Behold, He who made Himself king stands now before you in utter misery. A condemned man's misery is greater than that of one who is to be condemned: there is but one step wanting to his misery, execution. Pilate asks them to grant remission of the last step. The governor appeals for mercy, by pointing out that the man can never become an actual king.

Hear the same words, " Behold, your king!," as uttered by the Father, proposing to us Christ as King, decked with the emblems of deepest humility.

3. *" We have no king but Caesar! "*

Surely, " all persons who have judgment and reason will offer themselves entirely for this work." (Sec. 96) They will acknowledge Christ as King, and they will be ready to wear His livery.

The Jews protest that they belong to Caesar's kingdom, one of ambition, violence, and fraud; it will one day perish with all its glory; yet, ere that, it will crush and scatter these very Jews. They also protest that they belong only to this kingdom, that they expect all their happiness from it, that they have nothing in common with Christ's kingdom, which is one of cross and shame. Thereby the Jews show that they have *no* " judgment and reason "; it is indeed evil and bitter to reject the cross of Christ.

SECOND POINT: Jesus Carries the Cross.

I. *What does He carry?*

He is carrying the cross, the instrument of execution reserved for the greatest crimes, the mark of the deepest shame. By carrying it Christ becomes " the reproach of men, and the outcast of the people." (Ps. 21:7) The cross is above all the throne of the King crowned with thorns, and the instrument of our salvation.

II. *Whither does He carry the cross?*

Christ proceeds on the long and tortuous " Way of the Cross ": first through various streets of the City, which He had before entered in triumph; then He goes up Mount Calvary, to die on the cross; but shortly afterwards He will, by the power of the cross, go up into heaven, whence He shall come back, one day, with the cross in glory as the Judge of the world.

III. *Who carries the cross?*

1. *Jesus* who as God is " upholding all things by the power of his word " (Hebr. 1:3); to whom as man the Father has given all things into His hands: He was carried in the womb and on the arms of the Blessed Virgin; afterwards—though He often had not where to lay His head—He was honored by the service of

the Apostles and the pious women; but now He is a King having no servants, and He is forced to carry His cross Himself.

Christ carries the cross " *on His shoulders* " after being crowned with thorns, and torn by the scourges; He carries it as long as His strength does not fail. He carries the cross gladly and willingly: because the cross, decreed by the Father, is the instrument of the world's salvation; because we, too, must go by the way of the cross, and He would teach us by His example.

2. Simon of Cyrene carries the cross, but only because he is forced to do so. Reflect how greatly he lacked judgment and reason, forced as he was to carry so noble a burden, the cross of the Son of God; so useful a burden, one so fertile in merit; so precious a burden, the tree of true life.

3. We should conclude from this that it is an honor for us to carry the cross willingly.

THIRD POINT: Jesus Is Crucified.

I. *He is nailed to the cross.*

1. Our King at last mounts His throne, a hard, bare, shameful cross. The place for His throne is Mount Calvary, a place of shame. The thorns and nails are Christ's crown and jewels.

2. On this throne all the former tortures are increased: The Savior is now deprived of liberty, that He may give us liberty; He is fastened to the cross not merely by ropes but by nails; He is none the less able even now, by His wisdom and omnipotence, to set Himself free from all these fetters.

His *pains* are increased by the torture of the nails added to the pains of the thorns and stripes. Reflect how this pain went on increasing as the blows of the hammer pierced the Son's flesh, and through His Mother's heart wounded His Heart.

The *shame* is increased by the place and the kind of punishment; also from the company of the two thieves: Jesus is joined to them, and thus made equal with them; nay, by occupying the middle place, He appears as the head of those criminals.

Now, when He is raised from the earth, the looks of all are centred on Him more than ever. The last *separation* of death is at hand. His soul is overwhelmed by a still more unbearable *agony*.

II. *The title is put up on the cross: " Jesus of Nazareth, the King of the Jews."* (John 19:19)

Jesus: He had been given this name by order of the Father, through an angel, in view of the cross! By the cross He was now made the Savior from all evil.

Of Nazareth: This end on the cross had been foreshadowed and prepared throughout the life of Christ, even from His infancy: Jesus was born in the greatest poverty. He was brought up in continual obedience, that " after hunger, thirst, heat, and cold, after insults and outrages, He might die on the cross, and all this for me." (Sec. 116)

King: The kingdom of Christ, established by the Father and foretold by the prophets, is intimately connected with the cross, as the condition to be accepted by all citizens of His kingdom.

Of the Jews: That kingdom embraces time and eternity, angels and men, and more particularly the Jews; but when the latter are rejected through their own fault, Christ's kingdom remains. Jesus has no need of us, whereas there is neither salvation nor life for us without Him.

CHAPTER XLVI

Jesus Dies upon the Cross

Cf. Matthew 27:35-52; Mark 15:24-38; Luke 23:34-46;
John 19:23-37; *The Exercises*, Sec. 297

★

*First Point. He spoke seven words upon the cross: He prayed
for those who crucified Him; He pardoned the thief; He recommended St. John to His Mother; He said with a loud voice, " I
thirst "* (John 19:28), *and they gave Him vinegar to drink; He
said that He was forsaken; He said, " It is consummated! "* (John
19:30); *He said, " Father, into thy hands I commend my spirit."*
(Luke 23:46)

*Second Point. The sun was darkened, the rocks rent, the graves
opened, and the veil of the Temple was torn in two from top
to bottom.*

*Third Point. They blasphemed Him saying, " Thou who de-
stroyest the temple. . . . come down from the cross! "* (Matt.
27:40) *His garments were divided, His side was pierced with a
lance, and blood and water came forth.*

First Point: Christ on the Cross

I. *He spoke seven words.*

The body of Christ is covered with blood, the head
wreathed with thorns, hands and feet pierced with nails,
and His strength growing weaker and weaker. The face
turns pale, the heart throbs more slowly, but His will remains unshaken: in all this the humanity is united to the
divinity. The last drops of blood trickle from the wounds,

and His mouth utters the seven words. Oh, how precious are these drops of blood, which make up the full price for the redemption of the world! How sweet are these seven drops of honey, that issue forth from the bloodless lips! Three drops, and three more drops, and yet one more.

II. *Consider the Words separately.*

1. The first three words.

" *Father, forgive them, for they do not know what they are doing.*" (Luke 23:34) In the Sacred Heart of Jesus, there is no feeling of revenge: He prays for them that crucify Him.

" *Amen I say to thee, this day thou shalt be with me in paradise.*" (Luke 23:43) In the Heart of Jesus, filled with reproaches, there is love for the repentant sinner: Christ opens paradise to him.

" *Woman, behold, thy son!—Behold, thy mother.*" (John 19:27) In the Heart of Jesus, consumed by sadness, there is ever the same care to teach and console His own, to provide for their wants, and to make them be one. These are the things to be observed by him who follows Christ in all reproaches.

2. The next three words.

The outward wounds strike the eyes; but there is, moreover, the *inner suffering.* It is profitable for us not to be ignorant of any of Christ's sufferings; therefore, that we might know that nothing in Him is free from the cross, He adds two words by which He calls our attention to certain inner sufferings which are not so obvious.

" *I thirst.*" (John 19:28) The first of these inner sufferings is the thirst that consumes His frame; it arose from lack of drink ever since the Supper, from the exhaustion of His strength, and the great loss of blood. That thirst may be seen from the urgent appeal, " I thirst," made with a hoarse voice; but His thirst is not quenched, the vinegar offered Him makes it worse.

" My God, My God, why hast thou forsaken Me? " (Mark
15:34) The second inner suffering is the *agony* of the mind;
it had ever increased since the time in the Garden; now no angel
is sent to comfort Him, so that Christ at last complains that He
is abandoned by God.

" It is consummated! " (John 19:30) Now we know all the
sufferings of Jesus; He therefore declares that all things are fulfilled which were decreed by His Father, and foretold by the
prophets; that the chalice of suffering and shame has been
drained: all has been settled, not by His own likes and dislikes,
but by the decree of the Father.

3. The last word, *" Father, into thy hands I commend my
spirit."* (Luke 23:46) Hereby Jesus accomplished what He once
said: " I lay down my life that I may take it up again. No one
takes it from me, but I lay it down of myself." (John 10:17)
Freely abandoning life He cried " out with a loud voice, and expired." (Mark 15:37) Christ the High Priest drains the chalice
and on the altar of the cross completes the sacrifice of redemption. He gives glory to God, and peace to man. Christ the King
has conquered His enemies, and gains possession of the kingdom
which shall last forever. See to it that you, too, drain your
chalice, and die in Christ.

SECOND POINT: The Standard of Christ at Calvary

I. *What is done?*

The sun was darkened, the rocks rent, the graves opened,
and the veil of the temple was torn in two from top to
bottom. All these prodigies could not have happened at
the same time except by God's almighty power; and for
no other reason except with a view to the death of Christ.
These effects produced by divine omnipotence at the death
of Jesus are a most solemn testimony given for Him, con-

firming His declarations and teachings, and establishing His divinity.

II. *By whom is this done?*

1. Consider how all orders of creatures participate in this testimony: the heavenly bodies, as the sun is darkened; the earth, as it quaked and rocks were rent; the dead, as the tombs were opened; the things consecrated to the supernatural order, as the veil of the temple was torn.

2. Consider that this prodigious testimony caused the Roman centurion, and others as well, to strike their breasts and say: " truly he was the Son of God." (Matt. 27:54) Consider that this testimony is continued in all the miracles of the following centuries, making countless others profess " truly this is the Son of God."

3. Consider that this testimony comes ultimately from the divinity hypostatically united to Christ's humanity. During the Passion the divinity had hidden itself, but now it shows itself by striking and most marvellous effects: accordingly it is an infallible testimony, and one that cannot be denied.

III. *For what purpose is this done?*

All this is done in order to win faith both for Christ and His standard; to show the " Way of the Cross " as the only way consecrated by God for obtaining salvation; to bring home the lesson that we are to love and imitate Christ's poverty and humility.

THIRD POINT: The Standard of Lucifer at Calvary

I. *What is done?*

Consider that Christ on the cross was all the time exposed to insults, insults such as had been separately foretold by the prophets; therefore they were allowed by the Father for a definite purpose. " They have dug my hands and my feet, they have numbered all my bones, etc." (Ps. 21)

" That the Scripture might be fulfilled which says, ' They divided my garments among them; and for my vesture they cast lots.' " (John 19:24)

" That the Scripture might be fulfilled, ' Not a bone of him shall you break.' And again another Scripture says, ' They shall look upon him whom they have pierced.' " (John 19:36-37)

II. *By whom is this done?*

1. Consider how Jews and Gentiles, leaders and people, combine to insult Christ by word and deed; from hatred, when they blaspheme; from covetousness, when they cast lots; from wantonness, when the side is opened with the lance. Alive as well as dead Jesus is insulted in His honor, His property, His body.

2. Consider how these insults are continued unceasingly in the wrongs and persecutions against the Church, the Mystical Body of Christ; they, too, are aimed at the honor, the property, and the members of the Church.

III. *For what purpose is this done?*

All this is allowed by God to make us understand that poverty and humility are the uniform of Christ the King, and of His Spouse, the Church; that we, who have resolved to follow Christ as our King, must be prepared to suffer the same things.

CHAPTER XLVII

From the Cross to the Sepulcher

Cf. Matthew 27:35-52; Mark 15:24-38; Luke 23:34-46;
John 19:23-37; *The Exercises*, Sec. 298

★

As THE preaching in the temple connected the second and third weeks, so this mystery connects the third and fourth. The sentiments aroused by Christ's Passion are indeed continued in the burial of His sacred body; but if we keep watch with the guards at the sepulcher and with Mary in her chamber, soon the hope of the Resurrection prepares the way for joy.

First Point. *He was taken down from the cross by Joseph and Nicodemus in the presence of His sorrowful Mother.*

Second Point. *The body was borne to the sepulcher, and anointed, and buried.*

Third Point. *Guards were stationed.*

First Point: The Body of Christ Is Taken Down from the Cross.

I. *The Sacred Body of Christ.*

1. Being now separated from the soul, the sacred body is stiff, pale and cold. In a word, it is dead. Consider that death is the punishment given men because of the sin of Adam, through whom sin and death have entered the world (Cf. Rom. 5:12

sqq). Christ, the spotless and sinless lamb, has saved us from sin and opened to us the treasure of God's grace. " Therefore as from the offense of the one man Adam the result was unto condemnation to all men, so from the justice of the one Christ the result is unto justification of life to all men." (Rom. 5:18) Recall Christ's innocence and beauty. Gaze upon His bruised and lifeless body and understand the malice of sin.

2. That very body continues to be united to the divinity, which, of course, hides itself as much as is possible: the touch of the body works no miracle; the lips utter no words of doctrine or mercy; the eyes no longer soften sinners' hearts. Nevertheless the divinity is present and gives an infinite value to that corpse, making it worthy of adoration, and pledging incorruption and resurrection.

II. *Joseph and Nicodemus.*

Previously these two men had faith and charity, but they were somewhat timid; now, by virtue of Christ's Passion, they have become generous and bold; they risk their reputation by publicly professing themselves as disciples of Christ; they give their money, buying linen and spices; they give their strength, as with the greatest reverence they, with their own hands, take down the body of Christ.

III. *Mary.*

The Mother of Jesus is all sorrowful, in greatest need of consolation, worn-out by the anxiety of the last days; she suffers from the sight of the dead body, and from the memories it revives of all that has been done to that body both recently and long ago; she is overwhelmed by the knowledge of the innocence and the divinity of her Son, and the ingratitude and rejection of the Chosen People; she is crushed by the feeling of the separation brought about by death.

Nevertheless Mary is most valiant in her sorrow, and this fortitude of hers is the fruit of her Son's Passion.

" When one is in desolation, he should be mindful that God has left him to his natural powers to resist the different agitations and temptations of the enemy in order to try him. He can resist with the help of God, which always remains, though he may not clearly perceive it. For though God has taken from him the abundance of fervor and overflowing love and the intensity of His favors, nevertheless, he has sufficient grace for eternal salvation." (Sec. 320)

SECOND POINT: The Sacred Body Is Buried.

I. *The Sacred Body is carried to the Sepulcher.*

This carrying reminds Mary of the time when she bore the Lord in her womb and on her arms, when He " went about doing good " (Acts 10:38), when He entered Jerusalem in triumph. All that has come to an end, never to be repeated. It reminds Mary of the hours of the Passion, when the Lord was dragged about by enemies, when she met her Son and accompanied Him on the " Way of the Cross ": all that had been prearranged by God, and foretold long before: it was the sword that should pierce the Virgin's soul. Alas! whereas the divinity formerly showed itself by so many signs, it is now hiding itself as much and even more!

II. *The Sacred Body is anointed.*

This anointing invites us to consider again all the wounds; see from their length, breadth, and depth the foulness of sin, the Majesty of God who was offended, and the love of the Savior. This anointing reminds the Mother of all the tender care she had bestowed on the Divine Child, and all the attention given to the body of the grown-up man. It reminds Mary Magdalene of the twofold anointing by herself of so loving and merciful a Redeemer, who in turn anointed the sinner's soul with His grace.

The anointing is resorted to with a view to preserve the dead body from corruption, and so it is a supreme humiliation for the Son of God.

III. *The Sacred Body is buried.*

1. Burial consists in the removal of the body, as unfit for intercourse with the living; it confirms the lasting separation which was brought about at the moment of death; it is also a last honor shown to the mortal remains, not on account of their present condition, but of the previous life-union with the soul.

2. The *effect* of the burial: between the pious souls of the mourners and the lifeless body of the Savior is thrust a cold stone, that shuts the corpse from sight. Mary then returns home with her companions; she leaves as if her heart were buried in the same cave, keeping no longer anything of her beloved Son except His memory.

Third Point: Guards Are Placed at the Sepulcher.

I. *The guards.*

With Pilate's permission guards are set by Christ's sworn enemies, the priests and pharisees; this is done with the intention of frustrating the saying of Christ: " After three days I will rise again," (Matt. 27:63) and its pretext is that Christ was a seducer, the Apostles cheats, and the whole Christian revelation a jumble of errors. They add soldiers and seals in order to prevent the resurrection by force and authority. These are Lucifer's nightwatches set at the Lord's sepulcher.

II. *The angels.*

From eternity God had decreed the Resurrection of Christ, and it had been announced by the prophets: " It is written: Thou wilt not suffer Thy holy one to see corruption." (cf. Ps. 15, 10); " After three days I will rise again." This word of God is a far stronger protection of the sepulcher than seals and guards. Angels hover round the tomb, waiting for this word to be fulfilled: they had sung to the Savior at His birth, ministered to Him in the desert, and they are eager for the glory of God and the salvation of men. These are the night-watches set by God to guard the sepulcher.

III. *Mary and the disciples.*

They keep watch and pray in the humble house; in faith and hope they look forward to the Resurrection. These are the night-watches enlisted under the *Standard of the Cross,* allied to the angelic guards and far stronger than Lucifer's crew.

Fourth Week

During the fourth week we are " to ask for the grace to be glad and rejoice intensely because of the great joy and glory of Christ our Lord." (Sec. 221) This joy of the lover at the glory of the Beloved will of itself make every sacrifice of ours lighter, and thus it confirms us in the resolution of gaining and preserving the third kind of humility.

However other considerations are to be made by us. We are told " to consider the divinity . . . now appearing and manifesting itself so miraculously." (Sec. 223) Thereby our faith in Christ, the Son of God, is strengthened. When we observe " the office of consoler that Christ our Lord exercises " (Sec. 224), we are inflamed by the hope of having a like consolation. Thus we are reminded of the reward set before us in the meditation on the Kingdom of Christ, both for the following of Christ in general, and especially for following Him by means of practicing the third kind of humility.

The mysteries of the fourth week can be classed as follows:

a) The appearances 1-5, which were granted to individuals, or to a very few, emphasize the fact that we shall be consoled with the glory of Christ in proportion as we have shared His Passion, and recall to mind the meditation on the Kingdom of Christ.

b) The appearances 6-10, which may be called public appearances, lead us to the realization that we cannot follow Christ, save through the Church instituted by Him.

c) The appearances 11-13, which may be called subordinate appearances, are of less importance. It seems that St. Ignatius meant to gather together each and every appearance of Christ recorded either by Scripture or by Tradition in order to impress upon our minds the more deeply the affections desired for the fourth week.

[Father Hummelauer does not treat appearances 10-13 in his work.]

CHAPTER XLVIII

The Resurrection of Christ Our Lord — The First Apparition

Cf. *The Exercises*, Sec. 299

★

First Point. *He appeared to the Virgin Mary. Though this is not mentioned explicitly in the Scripture it must be considered as stated when Scripture says that He appeared to many others. For Scripture supposes that we have understanding, as is written, " Are you also even yet without understanding? "* (Matt. 15:16)

THE ABOVE paragraph represents a departure from St. Ignatius' usual manner of giving points. To the usual first point there is no corresponding second or third; yet according to the title of this exercise it seems that we should first contemplate the Resurrection of our Lord, and then pass on to the first appearance of Christ, that made to the Blessed Virgin. It is quite unusual with St. Ignatius to start a discussion in the points, and his doing so here shows his anxiety about the honor of the Mother of God.

Moreover, St. Ignatius does not so much infer from Scripture than an appearance was granted to the Blessed Virgin, as maintain its implicit assertion, contained in the words, " he showed himself alive after his passion by many proofs." (Acts 1:3) What is missing here about the Resurrection can be supplemented by these words of St. Ignatius: " This is the history. Here it is how after Christ expired on the cross His body remained separated from the soul, but always united with the divinity. His soul, likewise united with the divinity, descended into hell. There He sets free the souls of the just, then comes to the sepulcher, and rising, appears in body and soul to His Blessed Mother." (Sec. 219)

FIRST POINT: The Glorification of the Soul of Christ

I. *The Body of Christ*

remained separated from the soul, stiff and cold, without motion and life; the Sacred Heart was rent asunder: in one word, it was a corpse. Nevertheless the divinity was all the time united with the body; the presence of the divinity did not show itself in any perceptible way, yet it penetrated that lifeless frame with a sort of unction, safeguarding it from corruption and preserving it for resurrection, giving it an infinite price and dignity, and making it an object of adoration for the angels.

II. *The Soul of Christ.*

1. At the first moment after death the consciousness of having accomplished the work of Redemption filled the soul of Christ with the greatest sweetness; the soul that had thought itself forsaken by the Father, and commended itself into the Father's hands, presently awakes in the most sweet embrace of the Father.

2. Accordingly the soul overflows with joy from its *union* with the divinity, from the indwelling of the Three Divine Per-

sons, and in particular that of the Holy Spirit, the Comforter; during the mortal life all these influences had not been felt so keenly as now.

3. Enlightened by the Holy Spirit with the light of glory, the soul of Christ is now *made happy* by the Vision of God, intimately and permanently present. It is made happy by the knowledge of things from the consideration of which it had been tortured during the Passion: all the past, present and future; the secret thoughts of all hearts, and the mystery of the whole Redemption accomplished for the glory of God throughout so many centuries, and in so many countless individuals.

4. Christ's soul enjoys, in the Holy Spirit, the deepest peace; every pain and anxiety that had tormented it before has disappeared. Gone is the pain of separation which tortured Him at the Last Supper. There is now no pain in His soul because of a separation from the body hanging on the cross; the soul knows that that body is united to the divinity which is life, and is preserved for the resurrection which is soon to follow. The soul, then, rejoices, recollecting the words: " After three days I will rise again." There is also no pain left at the separation of the Apostles, for it rejoices with the words: " I will not leave you orphans." (John 14:18) There is no anxiety about the Church He is to found, for it will be firmly established, since the Holy Spirit will " put to shame the strong " by choosing " the base things of the world." (1 Cor. 1:27) Nor is there any uneasiness about the Chosen People, since the new Israel has now been acquired by the blood of the Redeemer. Gone is the agony which had weighed down the Sacred Heart in the Garden and afterwards, for death has been overthrown, the chalice drained, the guilt of sin destroyed, and God's grace acquired.

5. The glory of the divinity, united with Christ's soul, flows over into it, and glorifies it.

SECOND POINT: The Descent of Christ's Soul to the Lower World

I. *The place*

is not the hell of the damned, for those present are not guilty of mortal sin; nor is it purgatory, for the inhabitants are free from every, even the slightest stain and guilt; it is not heaven either, for this remains as yet closed, through the fault of our First Parents.

The place is limbo, the abode of the just souls who wait for the coming of the Redeemer: it is not a land of liberty, but one of detention, not of perfect peace, but of expectation, not of glory, but of twilight.

II. The ones present are the souls waiting for the consolation of Israel.

1. God's Chosen People, the holy Jerusalem, consists of souls freed from every guilt, and decked with virtues and merits.

2. They are waiting: St. John the Baptist and St. Joseph for a few years only; Simeon and Anna for several years already; the Prophets and holy Kings for centuries; Adam and Eve from the beginning of the world. They are waiting steadfastly, patiently, eagerly.

3. They wait for the consolation of Israel. Listen to their prayers: Eternal *rest* give unto us, O Lord: and let perpetual *light* shine upon us!—May we rest in *peace!*—*Deliver* us, O Lord, from the deep pit: make us to pass from death to *life!*

III. *The Soul of Christ.*

1. Christ *descends* to limbo, and by His own glory proclaims Himself to be the Resurrection and the Life. Consider, in the

souls of the just, the affections of adoration, and the gladness corresponding to each one's condition: the Patriarchs are glad at such an offspring, the Kings at such a successor, the Prophets at such a fulfilment of the prophecies, etc. Consider, in the soul of Christ, the apostolic joy at the redemption of those souls, the exultation over His Passion by which that redemption has been achieved.

2. Christ *delivers* those souls: He pours into them the Holy Spirit, the Paraclete or Comforter; at the same time He makes them share in His glory and peace: thereby limbo is suddenly transformed into paradise, and the souls are overwhelmed with the fulness of life, light, rest, peace and liberty. Consider that this glorification takes place in proportion to each one's merits, and these, in turn, are in proportion to the sufferings which each endured after the example of the Redeemer. By this glorification those souls consider themselves abundantly repaid, not only for the sufferings of their mortal lives but also for their long waiting in limbo.

THIRD POINT: The Resurrection of Christ

I. *Coming to the Sepulcher.*

1. Consider the *glorious arrival of the soul* of Christ, escorted by the saints of the Old Testament and the angels, to the body conveyed from the cross to the further humiliation of the burial. *Contemplate the body,* as it was when separated from the soul, quite lifeless, and now moreover with the heart pierced; the body has been anointed all over, to keep off natural corruption; see it wrapped in a linen shroud as if useless for any purpose of life, enclosed in the tomb, cut off altogether from intercourse with the living.

2. Consider the *feelings* with which the just souls of the Old Testament view the sacred body; they adore it, as being united

with the divinity; by the depth of the wounds they measure the painfulness of the Savior's torments, the foulness of sin, and the intensity of God's and Christ's love. Consider also the feelings with which the soul of Christ views that lifeless body, comparing the price of even a single redeemed soul with those very wounds, and rejoicing that He had accepted them all.

II. *And rising again.*

1. Reflect that it is laid down by God's law, that they who share in the cross of Christ shall also share in His glory; that they shall share in it in proportion as they have shared in His Passion: accordingly it was necessary to call, first of all, to a share in that glory that body which had been so closely united to the soul of Christ throughout the whole Passion.

2. Consider that, by divine power, Christ's body was in an instant restored, so as to become a fit instrument for a glorified life: the stiffness of the limbs relaxed, warmth and color came back, the wounds, with the exception of the five wounds, disappeared. Then the soul was again united to the body, the heart began once more to beat, the eyes opened, the lips were unclosed. The glory of the soul forthwith pervaded the whole body: it effected an indissoluble, immortal union of body and soul; it made the whole body bright and shining in its outward appearance, agile in its movements, subtle and impassible in its contact with other objects. Compare the superabundance of this glory, and its eternity, with the smallness and shortness of the sufferings.

3. See how the saints and angels show reverence to Christ's body brought again to life; then, how they go with Christ out of the sepulcher without removing the stone. Listen to the angels who had kept guard around the tomb, intoning a triumphal Alleluja!

FOURTH POINT: Christ's Appearance to His Blessed Mother

I. *Before the appearance.*

1. God's law has it that each one shall be rewarded to the extent and in the order in which one has stood close by the cross; therefore the Blessed Virgin was to be gladdened first of all.

2. Mary was the humble handmaid of the Lord, Christ's Blessed Mother, full of grace, whose soul a sword had pierced, who had beheld her Son persecuted by the diabolic Herod, who had now lost Him by a violent death. What were the feelings of Mary's heart? Inner pain at her Son's torments, a firm faith in the future Resurrection clearly understood from the words of Christ, hope and expectation. By this time the feelings of sorrow had more and more given way to those of hope and eager longing; these had reached their height on the third day that was now beginning to dawn.

II. *During the appearance.*

The Mother recognizes her Son's face and wounds, now radiant with brightness; she recognizes His voice and enjoys His loving embrace. At the same time Mary clearly understands that her Son is now living a life that is blissful, glorious and immortal; that the work of man's redemption is accomplished; that Christ's divinity is proved beyond every doubt before the whole world; that the resurrection of many is assured.

III. *After the appearance.*

The Blessed Mother reflects that she will shortly see her Son appear again, and that, when the rest of her life is over, she will be eternally with Him in heaven. She reviews in her mind the blessings bestowed on her through the whole of her life, and now crowned by this last blessing: in all she acknowledges God's power, holiness and mercy, and once again her " soul magnifies the Lord." (Luke 1:46)

CHAPTER XLIX

The Second Appearance

Cf. Mark 16:1-11; *The Exercises*, Sec. 300

★

First Point. *Very early in the morning Mary Magdalene, Mary the mother of James, and Salome go to the tomb. They say to one another, " Who will roll the stone back from the entrance of the tomb for us? "* (Mark 16:3)

Second Point. *They see the stone rolled back and the angel who says to them: " You are looking for Jesus of Nazareth . . . He has risen, he is not here."* (Mark 16:6)

Third Point. *He appeared to Mary who remained near the tomb after the others left.*

FIRST POINT: The Women Go to the Sepulcher.

I. *The persons.*

1. They were the same *women* who had followed Christ in Galilee, and had ministered to Him; who had stood near the cross, and taken part in the burial: those, therefore, who had adhered to Jesus by faith, hope, and charity. While the Lord was being buried, they had been anxious witnesses. On their return home they had, that very day, prepared spices for anointing the Lord, as a proof of their faith and love. They had rested on the Sabbath out of reverence for the commandment; their minds, however, had all the time dwelt on the sepulcher, and the lifeless body laid therein. On the day after the Sabbath they went " very early in the morning " laden with a large store of precious ointment, according to the intensity of their love and devotedness.

Their purpose is to anoint the body, and thus to show reverence to that body overwhelmed with so much reproach and shame: they would bestow on it the only service now in their power, that of delaying its corruption.

2. *Mary Magdalene* goes before all the others; she is constantly mentioned in the first place by the Gospels; she had received greater mercies, and she adheres to the Lord with firmer faith and a more ardent love. It was she who must have suggested the idea of anointing the body; on her mind was impressed most deeply everything connected with the tomb and the Sacred Body.

II. *Their sentiments.*

1. The women were affected with great *sadness* by the remembrance of Christ's Passion and Death, and by the sorrowful service for which they were then setting out.

They were uneasy with the *worry* of accomplishing the task they had undertaken, owing to the huge size of the stone that closed the monument. To this we may add *fear* of the Jews and of the guards; this fear was yet increased by the quaking of the earth under their feet.

3. Nevertheless they go forward; faith and love get the better of fear; they are so much in need of *consolation,* and also so worthy of it for their faith and love.

SECOND POINT: The Women Are Told About the Resurrection.

I. The women *receive consolation* when " they see the stone rolled back "; their fear and worry become less.

1. The rolled-back stone and the angel sitting on it manifest the *power* of Christ, and the enemy's *impotence:* for Christ is

seen to be stronger than death, and earth, and angels; He is the Lord of miracles and prophecies; neither guards nor seals can check Him in the least.

2. They manifest Christ's *authority*, majesty, and glory as compared with the *idle designs* of the enemies.

3. They also manifest Christ's *wisdom*, in opposition to the *foolishness* of the enemies: He makes the very guards set by His enemies become the messengers of His Resurrection, and the stone He makes His angel's throne; the enemies, with their seals and guards, had wished to keep down God's almighty power!

4. They also show Christ's *charity*; by this very miracle He invites the Jews to faith. They show, too, the *obduracy* of the Jews, when they forge the false story about the disciples stealing the body.

II. The women *receive consolation* when the words of the angel remove the cause of their sadness.

1. Christ is declared to be alive again, " He has risen." The women are allowed to examine the place which they had noted so accurately: " Behold the place where they laid him "; (Mark 16:6) thus they are made to understand fully that the place is the same, and the body is not to be found there: consequently Jesus has really come to life again.

2. The women are honored with a mission to the Apostles: " But go, tell his disciples and Peter that he goes before you into Galilee." (Mark 16:7)

3. They are cheered by the promise of an appearance at some time to come: " There you shall see Him, as He told you." By all this they learn how much the risen Christ is solicitous about them, not less solicitous than He had been during His mortal life.

THIRD POINT: Christ Appears to Mary Magdalene.
John 20:11-18

I. *Magdalene before the appearance.*

1. Formerly Magdalene had been a greater sinner than all the others; later, however, she had been more fervent in love; she stood nearer to the cross, and she is therefore now the first after the Blessed Virgin to be cheered by the appearance of Christ. Her faith was true, but confused, as she had not grasped the mystery of the cross and the Resurrection; hers was an ardent love, but it was now exclusively directed to the fulfilment of her self-made desire to anoint the Lord's dead body.

2. In Magdalene's behavior there is a constant mixture of nature and grace, of faith and error.—From the fact of the stone being rolled back she draws the true conclusion: He is not here; and then she at once adds the false inference: they have taken the Lord away from the sepulcher. Thereupon all the force of her mind is applied to a solution of this problem. As she is unable to stand quietly near the empty tomb, she hastens to the apostles most intimately connected with Christ, Peter and John, though she knows that she is not likely to learn from them any important news. She cannot stay there either, hence she goes back to the tomb. Not knowing whither to turn, she stops at last, and sheds tears over the loss of her Master's body. Soon, unable to find rest, she looks into the tomb, though she knows full well that the body will not be found there.

3. The sight of the angels does not bring home to her the error of her fancy that Christ's body had been stolen, nor does it lead her to knowledge of the Resurrection. To the friendly question of the angels she answers bluntly: "Because they have taken away my Lord, and I do not know where they have laid him." (John 20:13) She turns round and looks about for some trace of the lost body. When a venerable stranger asks kindly

the reason for her tears, she makes no answer; rather she suspects him of the theft, declaring that she, though a weak woman, will gladly take the corpse of her beloved Lord, even though there is no place to which she can decently and usefully take it.

II. *The Behavior of Jesus.*

1. When Magdalene, the sinner, was converted, Jesus was kindled with love for her; this love had increased constantly in proportion to Magdalene's love; for her the Savior shed His blood, and gave His life. From the moment of the death on the cross the glorious soul of Christ was yearning with the desire of consoling her; when come again to life, the Sacred Heart had the same longing; for this purpose He had sent angels to the place of the sepulcher.

2. Jesus sees the faith, the love, and also the error of Magdalene but He is not estranged from her on this account; amidst all her errors He confirms her faith and enkindles her love. Finally He grants her the fullest consolation by His voice, His appearance, the sight of His wounds; He suffers her touch and her kisses.

III. *Magdalene recognizes the Lord.*

1. Reflect on the fulness of love, joy and consolation expressed in this one word, "Rabboni," Master!

2. Jesus allows Mary Magdalene to relish consolation in her own way: she prostrates herself, seizes and kisses His feet, and washes them with her tears; and this for a good while, until He says: "Do not touch me" (John 20:17); or as the Greek reading says more accurately: "Do not press me thus with your hands," for I am not yet ascended to my Father. In the eternity to follow Mary will have the opportunity to embrace her Lord's

feet. Jesus then honors Mary by sending her as His messenger to the apostles.

3. Consider Mary Magdalene hastening to the apostles; she is quite filled with, and joyful at, this thought: " I have seen the Lord, and these things he said to me." (John 20:18)

CHAPTER L

The Third Appearance

Cf. Matthew 28; *The Exercises*, Sec. 301

★

First Point. *The two Marys go from the sepulcher with great fear and joy to announce the Resurrection of the Lord to the disciples.*

Second Point. *Christ our Lord appears to them on the way, and says to them, "'Hail!' And they came up and embraced his feet and worshipped him."* (Matt. 28:9)

Third Point. *Jesus says to them: "Do not be afraid; go, take word to my brethren that they are to set out for Galilee; there they shall see me."* (Matt. 28:10)

FIRST POINT: The Women Go out from the Sepulcher.

I. *The joy of the holy women.*

1. At the removal of their former fears: the stone, the guards, etc.

2. At the renewal of their faith in the Resurrection of Christ. This joy is in proportion to their former sadness; it is about the life recovered by Christ, the fuller understanding of His prophecies, the conversation of the angel, and the honor of being Christ's messengers to the apostles.

3. At the renewed hope for the restoration of the Kingdom of Israel, and the blessings to be given themselves and others; this joy, too, is in proportion to their former dejection.

4. At their rekindled love: for they are now certain that their Master is alive and not far away; they know that they will soon enjoy once more His sight and company.

5. Reflect that this joy was granted by Jesus through the Holy Spirit poured out into their hearts; it is pure and bright from first to last; it produces directly in the soul the will or purpose to fulfil the command received from the angel, and it urges the soul to set immediately about its execution.

II. *The fear of the holy women.*

1. Consider that the Holy Spirit does not proceed violently, but that He changes the previous disposition gradually into a more perfect one. And so, together with a great joy, there is at first great fear in the women's minds, owing to the sudden change from sadness to joy, and owing to the earthquake and the appearance of the angel.

2. Reflect that the Holy Spirit does not resent this fear but adapts His grace to man's weakness: with each step their fear decreases, and their joy increases.

3. See Christ invisibly present, and taking delight in that fear and joy.

SECOND POINT: Christ Appears to the Holy Women.

I. *The time of consolation.*

1. Christ hastens to console the women on the way, as they were wishing to carry the news. He is satisfied with the good will, and does not wait for the accomplished work; when He is not looked for and asked for, He Himself is eager to console His own.

2. In addition to the future appearance promised by the angel, Christ already grants them this visit which had not been promised; and He does not wait till the women have laid aside their fear and are perfect in every way.

II. *The manner of consolation.*

1. *Christ* appears to the holy women, cheering them by His sight, the sound of His voice, the gentleness of His address: all this joined with internal illumination and assistance; He consoles their whole being: mind, will, and sentiments, increasing faith and charity, allaying fear, and bringing joy to its highest pitch.

2. Prompted by these sentiments, *the women* draw near, quite close to Him whom they had imagined to be torn from them for ever; they fall down and adore the Son of God; they choose the lowest place, at His feet, yet they seem not to have touched them from sheer reverence: those feet they had followed, as the Lord went about preaching the Kingdom of God; they had mourned to see them pierced on the cross; then they had washed and anointed them at the burial, and at this moment they behold the same feet with the marks of the glorious wounds. Oh! how vile their spices appear, when compared with the heavenly fragrance of the Lord's feet!

THIRD POINT: Christ Addresses the Holy Women.

I. *He bids them not to fear.*

Do not be afraid to approach and touch Me, who am come to life again, *I am yours!*—Indeed, Christ is ours; He devotes the forces of His body and His soul to our salvation; He is doing so now more efficiently than before, when they were not yet glorified; longer than before, when He had not yet obtained immortality. Ours are the wounds and the heart of Him who sits at the right hand of the Father, and intercedes for us.—" Do not fear " on account of your unworthiness, for you see with what kindness I, in My new life, am seeking you.

II. *The holy women are sent as messengers.*

They are honored in being sent to the Apostles. By the expression ' my brethren ' they are instructed about the close relationship of the glorious Jesus with the Apostles, as well as with themselves. They are gladdened by the promise of yet another appearance; and so, filled with consolation, they at last leave the glorious Savior.

CHAPTER LI

The Fourth Appearance

Cf. Luke 24:9-12; 33-34; *The Exercises*, Sec. 302

★

First Point. *When St. Peter heard from the women that Christ had risen, he went with haste to the tomb.*

Second Point. *He entered the tomb and saw only the linens with which the body of Christ had been covered, and nothing more.*

Third Point. *While St. Peter was thinking of these things, Christ appeared to him. That is why the Apostles said, " The Lord has risen indeed, and has appeared to Simon."* (Luke 24:34)

First Point: St. Peter Goes to See for Himself.

I. *Peter loves.*

St. Peter *believes,* but there is a good deal of obscurity about his faith, especially as regards the prophecies of the Resurrection. Peter *hopes,* for Christ revived his hope when He looked pitifully on the fallen Apostle; yet this hope is kept low by the consciousness of the denial. Above all Peter *loves;* contrition has rekindled love and the pious disposition to believe, ready to admit also the Resurrection.

II. *Peter listens.*

As a result of this pious readiness to believe Peter does not consider the women's words " as idle tales," but he admits at once that there may be some truth in them, though he cannot yet ascertain what it is, owing to imperfect understanding of the prophecies. He wishes and hopes, that the facts agree with the women's words; he realizes not only the possibility of the Resurrection, but also its probability; charity impels him to inquire into the matter as best he can.

III. *Peter goes.*

Complying with divine grace, Peter went, never minding the mockeries of some. He went quickly, urged on by great hope and charity; and the further he advanced the more his hope and charity increased, the stronger grew his joyful expectation, making him hurry the more.

SECOND POINT: St. Peter Believes.

I. *Peter understands.*

On seeing the stone rolled back, Peter at once draws the conclusion that the women's report was true, *viz.*, that Christ was not there; at the same time, from the circumstance of " the linen cloths lying " in order, (John 20:6) he draws the conclusion that Magdalene was wrong when she added that the body of Christ had been taken away by force.—Seeing that the women's report about the removal of the stone was true to fact, he concludes that the other circumstances of the vision, and the conversation of the angels must have been related faithfully; and he draws this conclusion, although he himself does not see any of these things directly.—As Peter then compares that authentic report with the prophecies which had been obscure for him till now, he concludes that the vision was really one of angels, and that Christ has risen indeed from the dead.—Immediately a flood of light clarifies many points that had been obscure so far: what had been said about the destruction of the temple of the body, and of raising it up again in three days (John 3:19); what the Lord had declared on the last journey to Jerusalem, and on the way to the Garden (Matt. 17:22; 26:32); above all what had occurred at the Transfiguration: "And they kept what he said to themselves, discussing with one another what the words, 'When he shall have risen from the dead,' might mean." (Mark 9:9)

II. *Peter reflects with himself.*

Filled with admiration and joy, "he went away wondering to himself at what had come to pass." (Luke 24:12) There is revived in him the most glorious hope of the restoration of the Kingdom of Israel; knowledge of his sin, and sorrow for the same are increased; he feels more keenly how unworthy he is of being consoled by an appearance, and of being made the head of the Church. Accordingly he went away without being in need of any further proof for the Resurrection, without expecting any other consolation, and considering himself quite unworthy to tread such sacred ground. Nevertheless, he walked less and less quickly, the further he receded from the sepulcher and those cloths, the last traces of his dearest Master: at each step the feeling of his unworthiness and his contrition increased. He was, however, not so absorbed in his own affairs as to omit informing others about the Resurrection of Christ; this is clear from St. Luke: "The Lord has risen indeed, and appeared to Simon." (Luke 24:34)

THIRD POINT: St. Peter Sees.

I. *Christ.*

1. *His Person:* The *Lord appears* to Peter, not under a disguise (as a gardener or a traveller), but in His own shape. His presence proves His Resurrection, and the wounds show clearly the connection between the humiliation of the cross and glory. His aspect is cheerful, not grave and sad, as on the way to the Garden; as a friend He grants full pardon for the past, confirms the name Peter (the Rock), given before, as well as the promise He had made concerning the Primacy.

2. *His Words:* From the short remark, " He appeared to Simon," it is not clear whether Jesus spoke to Peter or not. From the record of St. Luke, and that of St. John, one would say that Peter did not tell the Apostles any words of Jesus. All the first witnesses saw the open sepulcher, and the cloths laid by; besides that, the women beheld Christ in His own shape; they did not touch Him, yet they were greeted with a short address, and received a commission. Mary Magdalene beholds Christ, first under a disguise, then in His true shape; she touches Him, hears a few words, and also receives a commission. As for Peter, he sees Christ in His true shape; but he hears no words and receives no explicit commission, it would seem; but he carries out all that the vision implied: " Now there are varieties of gifts, but the same Spirit; and there are varieties of ministries, but the same Lord; and there are varieties of workings, but the same God." (1 Cor. 12:4-5) In all these events there is the same charity, corresponding to each one's character and condition, to the love of Christ, the good of the Church, and our own instruction. We should beware of spiritual envy of the gifts bestowed by God on others.

II. *Peter*

acquires certainty about Christ's Resurrection, and his own full pardon.

He conceives a most firm hope that the Kingdom of Israel will be restored, and that he himself will play a part in it. He entertains humble feelings about his own person, seeing that, without any merit of his own, so many favors are bestowed on him. He is aflame with a generous love: " Yes, Lord, thou knowest that I love thee " (John 21:15); impelled by this love he goes and announces the Resurrection to the Apostles.

CHAPTER LII

The Fifth Appearance

Cf. Luke 24; *The Exercises*, Sec. 303

★

First Point. *He appeared to His disciples who were going to Emmaus and were talking of Christ.*

Second Point. *He reprehends them, showing them by the Scriptures that Christ must die and rise again: " O foolish ones and slow of heart to believe in all that the prophets have spoken! Did not the Christ have to suffer these things before entering into his glory? "* (Luke 24:25-26)

Third Point. *At their request He remains there, and was with them till He gave them Holy Communion. Then He disappeared. Thereupon they returned to the disciples and told them how they recognized Him in Holy Communion.*

FIRST POINT: Christ Appears to the Disciples.

I. *The two disciples.*

1. They had followed Christ with true faith, hope, and charity; but now, owing to the " foolishness " of the cross (Cf. 1 Cor. 1), they have become thoroughly perplexed. They confess that Jesus is a prophet, that His miracles are genuine, and His teaching divine; but they cannot reconcile His greatness with the pitiful end He made. They acknowledge Him as the Messiah, yet they find fault with His failing to restore the Kingdom of Israel. Now, on the third day, His lifeless body is missing; some people claim to have had visions, but Christ is not seen Him-

self, and everything is in a state of uncertainty. The disciples had also become thoroughly sad and despondent: because of all that had happened during the last few days, the present doubtful condition, and—so they thought—the frustration of their hopes: " We were hoping." (Luke 24:21)

2. The two disciples, then, ill at ease in the company of the Apostles, and setting aside even St. Peter's report about the Resurrection, leave the place where they felt more and more oppressed by perplexity and sadness: they try to seek relief in solitary conversation. As they are moved by love for Christ, they cannot help talking about Him. By the grace of Christ this conversation soothes their sadness, and increases their charity.

II. *Jesus.*

1. He bears the marks of the cross, radiating glory, " the power of God and the wisdom of God." (1 Cor. 1:24) These wounds have become the world's law: as long as their splendor lasts, there is no way to glory but by these wounds and the cross.—The heart of Jesus, which was pierced on the cross, is now alive again, and burning with the desire to save the world through the law of the cross. Accordingly Jesus, the good Shepherd, does not abandon the straying sheep, but He lovingly goes after them, and He seeks to teach them the wisdom of the cross, to save them by its power.

2. Jesus proceeds by degrees. Often in desolation, without our being aware of it, He is near us; but our faults and imperfections hinder Him from revealing His presence. He appears therefore to these two disciples, not at first in His own shape but in that of traveller, who, covered with dust, overtakes them on the way. He seems a person worthy of respect and kind, has compassion for the down-hearted disciples, starts a friendly conversation, and by asking them questions brings them to disclose to Him the

whole cause of their sadness; even this alone gives some relief to their oppressed minds.

SECOND POINT: Christ Speaks to the Disciples.

I. *He reproves them.*

1. The traveller upbraids the disciples, saying: " O foolish ones and slow of heart . . . ." Consider the gentleness of voice, face and look with which these words are uttered, so that they charm the listeners and fill them with a salutary shame at their ignorance.

2. The reference to " all that the prophets have spoken," shows a thorough knowledge of Scripture in the speaker, and excites in the hearers a desire to learn, as well as great confidence in such a teacher.

3. The truth, for ignorance of which the disciples were reproved, is concisely stated in the words, " Did not the Christ have to suffer . . . ? " This way of stating the case implies that the matter is so evident that the mere putting it in words compels the assent of the hearer. Finally Christ adds instruction which makes the reproof fruitful.

II. *He teaches them.*

1. *What does He teach?*

He tells them that, according to God's decree, the cross is necessary, and its glory surpassing great: there is an unfailing connection between the two: glory is the reward for the cross, and is in perfect proportion to it. This is shown with complete thoroughness: " Beginning then with Moses and with all the Prophets, he interpreted to them in all the Scriptures the things referring to himself." (Luke 24:27) He explains each text, and compares the texts one with another. Notice the warmth and unction with which He explains the Father's decree ordaining the cross, the ineffable excellence of the glory, the mystery of the cross, revealing in it God's wisdom, God's power, God's mercy, the nature of the spiritual Israel . . . .

2. *How does He teach?*

Jesus apears to the disciples as a complete stranger, knowing absolutely nothing about what had happened, and therefore as one who is free from every bias. He first allows the disciples to speak out quite freely what they think. He puts forward His view, not as His own, but as that of the prophets. He explains everything accurately, and repeats the explanation, when required, with the utmost friendliness and patience. He teaches, not like the scribes whose interpretation followed the letter slavishly and killed the spirit, with a stiff, cold and haughty manner about it, mixing up human traditions with the words of God. The traveller's teaching is like that which the disciples had heard from Christ, when He interpreted the Scriptures: revealing the living spirit in the letter, casting light on the letter, and warming their hearts.

3. *With what result does He teach?*

The stranger goes on increasing the confidence of the hearers in Himself, clearing away their perplexity, reviving their hope, dispelling their sadness. From the Scriptures He draws a clear picture of Christ; He produces a most firm faith in the accomplished Resurrection, from a comparison of the women's and Peter's witness with that of the Scriptures. He kindles their charity and stirs up a keen desire to enjoy the presence of Christ; at the same time He persistently cherishes and purifies the disciples' love towards Himself, *i.e.*, the unknown traveller, so that they see in Him more and more the agreement of His heart and mind with the heart and mind of Christ; so that they love Christ in the traveller, and transfer all their love to Christ: thus they are prepared for the consolation to follow through the manifestation of Christ's presence.

THIRD POINT: Christ Manifests Himself.

I. *Christ.*

1. *He stays.*

As He wished to stay with the disciples, the traveller " acted as though he were going on" (Luke 24:28) in order that His presence might be the more eagerly desired and sought for. The disciples co-operate with the grace received, and constrain Him to stay, they do so not only to offer Him shelter for the night but also to enjoy His company and to progress in faith and love; they were loath to miss the conclusion of the exposition of Christ pre-figured in the Scriptures: they therefore begged, and insisted, and finally forced the traveller, who seemed reluctant to stay with them.

2. *He gives them Communion.*

Consider the feeling of close friendship with which the disciples sit down to table with the traveller: the fellowship of the previous journey, their perplexity and sadness now vanished in consequence of His conversation, the intimate affinity of their minds to that of Christ had created this restful feeling; they were living again in the happy past, when they used to be at table with Christ and the Apostles. Consider how this feeling was wonderfully increased, as the stranger, in exactly the same manner that was the Master's, took the bread, and blessed it in the same way and with the same words. Now they fix their look on Him, and suddenly they know the face of Jesus, His look, and His person, and they are flooded with the sweetest light. Consider how Jesus vanished from their sight at the very moment of Holy Communion, thereby confirming by a new miracle the truth of His Resurrection; He is now sacramentally present in their hearts, confirming all the previous instructions, strengthening their virtue, and increasing their consolation.

II. *The disciples.*

1. Consider how the sacramental presence of Jesus ripens immediately the fruit of generous action, in this case the resolution to go back to Jerusalem; " and rising up that very hour " (Luke 24:33) they carried it out. The motives of this resolve were these: a realization of the foolishness of their former departure and the necessity of being united to the Apostles; eagerness to make others share in the graces they had received and to strengthen their faith; only in the company of the Apostles could they hope to enjoy yet again the sight of Christ.

2. Consider how they now quicken their steps; how they hold eager conversation, as they review the instructions given them, and dwell on the gradual consolation imparted to them: " Was not our heart burning within us, while he was speaking on the road and explaining to us the Scriptures? " (Luke 24:32) Consider them entering the Supper Room: see their faith, eagerness, and joy, as contrasted with the doubt, faint-heartedness and gloom of the Apostles. They relate, as best they can, the conversation which Jesus had with them, also their feelings while they listened to Him, the proofs which went to show that He who spoke was Christ. At first they had not understood their full bearing; at the moment, however, when the traveller broke the bread, the whole character of the traveller: His face, eyes, wounds, the inner light of His sacramental presence: all these circumstances coalesced into a single evident proof that the traveller was Christ Himself, that Christ was come to life again, and that in Christ all the Scriptures were fulfilled.

3. Consider how all these show that Jesus is present by His grace and achieves all these happy results.

CHAPTER LIII

The Sixth Appearance

Cf. John 20:19-25; *The Exercises*, Sec. 304

★

First Point. *The disciples, except St. Thomas, were gathered together " for fear of the Jews."* (John 20:19)

Second Point. *Jesus appeared to them, the doors being locked, and standing in their midst said, " Peace be to you! "* (John 20:21)

Third Point. *He gives them the Holy Spirit, saying, " Receive the Holy Spirit; whose sins you shall forgive, they are forgiven them; and whose sins you shall retain, they are retained."* (John 20:23)

FIRST POINT: The Condition of the Disciples

I. *Its security.*

The disciples were the first-fruits of the Church; according to Christ's intention they were to become the spiritual Kingdom of Israel, the city of peace, ever victorious over the gates of hell, the ark of safety in the shipwreck of the world. Christ, the King of Israel, the helmsman of the ark, had been deprived of life through the treachery of the Jews. Yet, while the body lay in the sepulcher and the soul and descended into hell, the divinity remained near the Apostles, by omniscience knowing all their dangers, by omnipotence able to overcome every difficulty, by love ever watching over their safety. Now Christ has come to life again and is present visibly as a real man. From this you may infer the quite perfect security of the ark in that storm, of the Kingdom of Israel during that " interregnum."

II. *The fear of the disciples.*

Previously they had followed Christ faithfully; they had preached Him as the Messiah and led Him triumphant into the city. Afterwards presumption had led them to empty declarations, and they had pitifully fallen away from Him. At present they are overwhelmed with sadness at His death, at the sufferings He had endured, and at the unexpected change in their own lives. Nor did they derive any consolation from the Scriptures, since they did not understand them. They are in the grip of discouragement; their hope in the restoration of the Kingdom of Israel has been shaken; their courage has not been revived by the report of the women about the appearances to them, for " this tale seemed to them to be nonsense." (Luke 24:11) Fear, too, seizes the disciples and they are too frightened to move from their hiding place. Notice that the only thing which holds them together is fear of the Jews, whereas they should be indissolubly united by faith, hope, and charity.

SECOND POINT: Christ Appears to the Disciples.

I. *The appearance itself.*

1. The coming of Christ had been prepared by the appearances to Peter and to the disciples of Emmaus; the Apostles had not rejected these, as they had done in the case of the appearances to the women.

2. The features, the looks, the wounds, the voice show clearly that Christ is again alive; the brightness reveals the glory of the Risen Life; the closed doors bear witness to His omnipotence. By standing in their midst, He proclaims Himself to be the unshaken center of the Kingdom of Israel. The words, " Peace be to you! " are the motto of the Messiah-King, the Prince of peace. The angels had announced this at His birth and Christ had approved it in His last discourse. These words, then, are most appropriate, and help the disciples recognize Christ. By adding, " It is I, do not be afraid " (Luke 24:36), Christ tries to revive the faith of the Apostles by their memory of those same words, spoken before when He walked to them on the waters. He gives them to understand that He is their Lord, and that there is no reason to fear with Him present.

3. The immediate effect of the appearance is confusion and fright. The Apostles imagine that they see a ghost, as had been their reaction previously, during the storm on the lake.

II. *The confirmation of the appearance.*

1. Christ allows the disciples to examine His glorious hands and feet, in order that His identity might appear more clearly: " See my hands and my feet, that it is I myself. Feel me and see; for a spirit does not have flesh and bones, as you see I have." (Luke 24:39) He allows Himself to be touched so that the Apostles may convince themselves that it is no ghost they see. He speaks and eats in the same way as He did before so that the Apostles may become convinced that it is truly He. He dispels the darkness of their minds: " He opened their minds, that they might understand the Scriptures." (Luke 24:45) Note that the difficulty of understanding who Christ is does not come so much from the Scriptures as from the dispositions of men, who are unwilling or too lazy to discover the meaning of Scriptures.

2. The effect of all this is that the faith of the Apostles is renewed; they confess, implicitly, " Indeed, thou are the Son of God," as they did when Christ walked on the water and saved Peter. In place of fear, dejection and sadness there is joy: " The disciples therefore rejoiced at the sight of the Lord." (John 20:20)

THIRD POINT: Christ Gives the Power to Forgive Sins.

I. *The preparation.*

1. Christ repeats the words: " Peace be to you." (John 20:21) This is the condition and purpose of all Christ's actions: " As the Father has sent me, I also send you." (John 20:21) Reflect on the lowliness of those called, and the loftiness of the calling: it begins from the Father, it is the work of the Son, it bestows the Holy Spirit, and brings about the sanctification of the world. Reflect on the special gifts required for this calling.

2. The Holy Spirit is given to the Apostles: the same who proceeds from the Father and the Son; who overshadowed Mary; who was sent down on Christ at the baptism in the Jordan. The Holy Spirit is given by the Lord's breathing on the disciples, just as the soul was given Adam by God's breathing in paradise. The Holy Spirit is life, and the source of all supernatural life in us. On this occasion the Holy Spirit is given to enable the Apostles to have the fulness of divine power, and that, too, forever, and for transmission to others.

II. *The power is conferred.*

1. The worst of evils is sin; all other evils are only consequences of sin. The power to remit sins belongs to God alone, and it can be exercised only through the power of the Holy Spirit. Now this power is given in the largest sense, for all sins of all

men, however great those sins may be; the power is given to be administered quite freely, but it is given only to the Apostles and their successors.

2. Endowed with this power the spiritual Israel is guarded safely against all enemies. The gates of hell are cast at the feet of the Apostles; the heralds of Christ's banner are made stronger than the followers of Lucifer. It cannot be that Christ should deliver to the fury of the Jews or of hell those on whom He has conferred the power to remit sins.

3. Reflect on so easy and so sure a consolation, ever ready for you in the sacrament of penance: it is the remedy against the death of the soul, the cleansing of the most foul stain, the strength of the spiritual life. Reflect also on the consolation to be gained from the exercises connected with the sacrament of penance: the general and the particular examination, spiritual direction, and the practice of penance, internal as well as external.

CHAPTER LIV

The Seventh Appearance

Cf. John 20:24-29; *The Exercises*, Sec. 305

★

First Point. *Since St. Thomas was not present at the preceding appearance, he would not believe and said, "Unless I see . . . I will not believe."* (John 20:25)

Second Point. *Eight days after, Jesus appeared to them, the doors closed, and He said to Thomas, "Bring here thy finger, and see . . . and be not unbelieving, but believing."* (John 20:27)

Third Point. *St. Thomas believed, saying, "My Lord and my God."* (John 20:29) *Christ said to him, "Blessed are they who have not seen, and yet have believed."* (John 20:29)

FIRST POINT: St. Thomas Refuses to Believe.

I. *Exposition of the fact.*

The condition of Thomas was, on the whole, the same as that of the other Apostles: he was overwhelmed with sadness at the Savior's sufferings, and he was despondent about the work to be achieved by Christ. Yet, owing to his boldness, Thomas was less under the sway of fear of the Jews. This very boldness, however, became the occasion of his deplorable fall. Daring and stubbornness led Thomas to refuse to accept the testimony of the first witness of the Resurrection; of Magdalene: "They . . . did not believe " (Mark 16:11); of the other women: " this tale seemed to them to be nonsense " (Luke 24:11); of St. Peter and the disciples who had come back from Emmaus: " even then they did not believe " (Mark 16:13); possibly even of the Blessed Virgin when she related the appearance to herself. Next he refused to believe the testimony of the Eleven, when they told him the several proofs of the Resurrection given by Christ Himself. Thomas relied more on the witness of his own senses than on the combined testimony of all the rest; he demanded that he himself must see and feel all those proofs; nay, he demanded a further proof, to which he had not the least right, namely, to be allowed to " put my finger into the place of the nails, and put my hand into his side." (John 20:25)

II. *Analysis of the fact.*

1. Consider the origin of his error. St. Thomas had been absent at the first appearance; if he had been present, he would have seen and felt; by being absent he was deprived of this experience of the senses, and he lacked efficacious grace to believe without it. Reflect what great graces are given within the Church: the pardon of sins, etc. . . . ; wilfully to withdraw from the Church means also to miss all these graces.

2. Consider the guilt of the error. Thomas destroys the foundation of faith, namely the authority of testimony; owing to presumption he lays down unfair conditions for giving his consent.

3. Ponder the *consequences*: the wrong done to the other Apostles, and possibly to the Blessed Virgin; the sin of scandal, and the danger for his own salvation.

SECOND POINT: Christ Appears to St. Thomas.

I. *The appearance was delayed.*

Consider, in the heart of Jesus, His love for Thomas, and the long forbearance, trying by His grace to reclaim the straying disciple. At the same time the consolation of the others is delayed, that their faith and love may be put to the test, and because the fault of one delays the joy of many. Reflect on the feelings of trust and patience in the hearts of the Apostles. As for Thomas, in his heart stubbornness and a sense of triumph grow the more the longer the appearance expected by the others is delayed; at the same time, however, Thomas feels some remorse of conscience when he sees the confidence of the others becoming ever stronger.

II. *The appearance is granted.*

The sight of Christ present, " the doors being shut," and the words, " Peace be to you," convince Thomas of the Resurrection, and fill him with confusion. By now directly addressing Thomas, Christ shows His readiness to pardon. The Lord fulfils the condition which the disciple had rashly demanded; simultaneously grace enlightens the understanding of Thomas and moves his will. In return Christ asks for nothing more but that Thomas should believe.

THIRD POINT: St. Thomas Believes.

I. *St. Thomas.*

Following the promptings of grace, the repentant apostle says: " My Lord, and my God." Thus he acknowledges that the person before him is the same as Christ, and Him, too, come to life again, and so he professes his faith; he recognizes the gravity of his unbelief, and withdraws publicly, before all, and unconditionally the doubts he had uttered previously; he also professes his certainty of the pardon received, and the greatness of Christ's charity. By the same words he expresses his gratitude and his love.

II. *Christ.*

1. The risen Lord most gently reproves Thomas by mentioning his behavior: " Because thou hast seen me, thou has believed." (John 20:29) He contrasts this behavior with others: " Blessed are they who have not seen, and yet have believed." (*Ibid.*)

2. Christ teaches that we must not ask for signs and sensible consolations; but we must place our greatest consolation in believing the Church; thereby we are even more blessed than the Apostles whose faith was also based on the immediate testimony of the senses. In fact, it is just as reasonable, and just as obligatory, to trust witnesses of marked number, honesty, knowledge, so consistent in their profession as to shed their blood for their beliefs. This is all the more true when their testimony is continually confirmed by the Holy Spirit through the holiness of life which He inspires, and through various miracles performed by Him, and related in a trustworthy manner. Add to this the consideration that, other things being equal, faith without the witness of the senses is more meritorious.

3. Consider that all the consolations of the Risen Christ may become yours by faith, and that they are to reach you through the Church. Accordingly you should aim at the greatest conformity with the Church in doctrine, the greatest subjection to her in action, and the faithful reception of her sacraments.

It is suggested here that we read the rules given by St. Ignatius for thinking with the Church. (Cf. Secs. 352 sqq.)

The Eighth Appearance

Cf. John 21:1-17; *The Exercises*, Sec. 306

★

First Point. *Jesus appeared to seven of His disciples who were fishing. They had fished all night and caught nothing. But casting the net at His command " they were unable to draw it up for the great number of fishes."* (John 21:6)

Second Point. *Through this miracle St. John recognized Him, and said to St. Peter, " It is the Lord."* (John 21:7) *St. Peter cast himself into the sea and came to Christ.*

Third Point. *He gave them bread and part of a broiled fish to eat. After He had first tested three times the love of St. Peter, He recommended His sheep to him with the words, " Feed my sheep."* (John 21:17)

FIRST POINT: Christ Appears.

I. *The Disciples.*

1. *They go a-fishing.*—The sea is the world, the shore is the next life, the fish are souls. It is absolutely necessary for those fish to enter the net by faith and obedience, and to be thus drawn to the shore. God has called the Apostles to this sublime fishing, and they are strictly bound to apply themselves diligently to this work. The foremost part in this work is assigned to Peter: he leads, the rest follow.

2. *They take nothing.*—The fish, *i.e.,* the souls, are kept in the water through the deceits of the devil, the inborn corruption of nature, and natural helplessness to do any salutary work. They cannot be caught, except with the help of Christ's grace: " Without me you can do nothing." (John 15:5) Furthermore, God

has arranged things so that the Apostles' life is full of labor, and that often without fruit. This may be due to the faults of some, or it may be in order that the Apostles may learn that they can do nothing of themselves. Not even Peter, if left to his natural resources, is able to achieve anything.

II. *Jesus.*

1. The Lord *is at hand* with His presence, wisdom, kindness, and power; He is near on the shore, without being recognized; nevertheless His voice and power reach both the Apostles and the fish.

2. The Lord *commands,* and in doing so promises His help. Through superiors in the Church, Christ Himself directs us and gives efficacy to our labors.

SECOND POINT: Christ Is Recognized.

I. *St. John.*

1. By this miracle he knew the Lord. In the miracle he sees almighty power; from the affinity of this miracle with the former miraculous draught of fishes, John infers that the author in both cases is the same. The memory of the words spoken on that occasion, " I will make you fishers of men " (Matt. 4:19), brings more vividly to his mind the memory of the apostolic calling—hence, as he now strains his eyes eagerly on the man standing on the shore, he can, he thinks, make out the size and look of the Lord.

2. What really leads John by these signs to the knowledge of the Lord is his love: he loved Christ, he wished to find Christ, there was in his heart the pious inclination to believe. This inclination itself was a gift of Christ, the author of every salutatory action; it was a spark from the Sacred Heart, whence comes all the life of the Church.

3. Consider how all these sentiments of faith, joy, trust, and love find their expression in the words: " It is the Lord! " (John 21:7)

II. *St. Peter.*

1. In consequence of his fall and the previous appearances of Christ, Peter was burning with a great love for the Lord; he no longer seeks anything for himself, and only wishes to be with Christ; hardship does not deter him from going to Christ. He loves Christ more than his ship, his net, and the other Apostles; accordingly he leaves all this behind, and casts himself into the sea. On this occasion at least he does love Christ more than all the Apostles, more even than St. John, and that is why the passage of the laden ship seems too slow to him.

2. Consider how his love ever increases as Peter draws nearer to Christ, until at last, ablaze with love, he falls at the Lord's feet. Examine yourself, where you find yourself to be at the end of the retreat: have you at last seen clearly in what Christ is to be sought? Are you of the number of those who are going slowly nearer to Christ, or are you hastening to Him with Peter, throwing aside all obstacles.

THIRD POINT: Christ Confers the Primacy on St. Peter.

I. *A meal is offered.*

1. The meal on the shore is an image of the eternal banquet of the lamb, the reward of all apostolic labors after this life's hardships. The meal is also an image of the intimate union between Christ, His Apostles, and the members of the Church, a union begotten of charity. It is, moreover, an image of spiritual consolations. Christ indeed is always refreshing you with the daily bread of His grace, and the bread of trials; but at the time of His own choice He feeds you with the solid and sweet food

of consolation. The fish is Christ; the broiled fish may signify the Passion.

2. Work on earth, that you may one day sit down at the heavenly banquet. Increase your love especially by union with Christ through Holy Communion.—Before approaching the banquet of consolation, be sure that " It is the Lord " who calls you, lest you be deceived by some snare of Lucifer: you are sure if you approach with Peter, if you are led by obedience.

II. *Charity is recommended.*

1. The question, " Do you love me? " proceeds from the love of Christ for men; for only he who loves is wont to address such words to another; therefore this question makes St. Peter, and ourselves also, quite sure about Christ's love for us. This also proves that *the primacy is an institution due to Christ's love.*

2. The question, " Do you love me? " implies that the Primate in the Church must be united with Christ by charity, as the branch is united with the vine: it is but right to expect that the Primate's love for Christ is sincere and surpasses the love of others: for this reason the question was repeated three times, and the words " more than these " added. (Cf. John 21:15)

3. The Primate must feed the flock for the love of Christ, and in the spirit of love. The flock must cling to the Primate for the same love with which they follow Christ.

4. *Charity is made the fundamental law of the Church.*

5. This question also confirms Peter in humility. As humility is the foundation of the whole of salvation, so it is of every pastoral care. The threefold question recalls the threefold denial; the words " more than these " allude to Peter's presumptuous comparison of himself with the other Apostles. Now if Peter must be humble in his Primacy, how much more so must the rest, who are under Peter.

III. *The sheep are entrusted to Peter.*

1. St. Peter is given the power to rule all the faithful of Christ in all things. On the faithful is imposed the obligation to obey Peter in all things. Thereby is also promised to Peter the strength to do this efficaciously, to guard the sheep against the wolves, to strike down the gates of hell. The sheep entrusted to Peter's keeping remain nevertheless the sheep of Christ, " My sheep "; they must be fed in the spirit of Christ, and Peter must, one day, give to Christ an account of the administration of his charge.—Peter feeds by teaching, by commands, and by the sacraments. Christ feeds through Peter by giving him infallibility in teaching, holiness in his commands, and grace in the sacraments. Accordingly the sheep, under Peter, may well go on with the same joy, trust, and security as if they were being fed by Christ immediately and alone.

2. We partake *in the Church, through Peter,* in every true consolation which Christ has won for us by His Resurrection. From this it can be seen that now the Kingdom of Israel is solidly established.

IV. *The cross is pointed out for the future.*

Peter will exercise the Primacy, and receive the cross in addition. Therefore the flock, too, must walk the " Way of the Cross "; for the sheep are not above the shepherd. We partake of every true consolation in the Church, through Peter, *by the Way of the Cross.* The cross is a special gift, the granting of which Christ has reserved to Himself, with the exclusion of Peter; St. John will be led in a different manner, according to the Lord's good will. The cross is the more intimate conforming with Jesus, a closer following of Christ.

CHAPTER LVI

The Ninth Appearance

Cf. Matthew 28:16-20; *The Exercises*, Sec. 307

★

First Point. *The disciples at the command of Christ go to Mt. Thabor.*

Second Point. *Christ appears to them and says: " All power in heaven and on earth has been given to me."* (Matt. 28:18)

Third Point. *He sent them throughout the world to teach, saying, " Go, therefore, and make disciples of all nations, baptizing them in the name of the Father, and of the Son, and of the Holy Spirit."* (Matt. 28:18-19)

First Point: The Journey to Thabor

I. *The disciples go.*

The Apostles are not now, as they were at Gethsemani, sheep without a shepherd; they have again found their divine Shepherd, and they have His visible vicar. Peter is leading, recognized as the head of all; all follow him willingly, even James and John; they no longer quarrel, asking " which of them was the greatest." (Luke 9:46) They go, not as the two disciples on the way to Emmaus had done, lacking faith and hope; now they believe firmly that Jesus is the Son of God, that in Him is the fulness of life, and that the Church is the Kingdom of Israel.

II. *By the Lord's command.*

The Apostles were presently to enjoy the appearance which had been promised immediately after the Resurrection; the truth of this promise had been confirmed by all the appearances that followed, and at those appearances the same promise will have been repeated by the Lord Himself.

Since the Apostles had received such great graces in the previous appearances which paved the way for this one, they looked forward to still greater graces from this one: they were consequently going forward with the greatest joy and hope.

III. *To Mount Thabor*.

Sts. Peter, James, and John recalled the words of Christ: " Tell the vision to no one, till the Son of Man has risen from the dead." (Matt. 17:9) On this journey in particular they will have told the rest their vision on Mount Thabor. All acknowledge the meaning of the mystery: that Jesus is the Son of God, the Master, the end of the Law and the Prophets, represented by Moses and Elias; lastly, that the cross is necessary for salvation.—Now they have set out for the same mountain, in the hope of seeing there a more universal and complete manifestation of Christ's divinity and authority; yet they are aware that this time, too, the consolation will be passing, that they may not make tabernacles, and that the glory of Christ will again be overshadowed by a cloud. From experience they have learned the connection between the transfiguration and prayer: accordingly they watch and pray.

SECOND POINT: The Sovereign Power of Christ

I. *The person of Christ*.

Consider the royal authority of the Lord as He now appears, an authority sealed with the striking triumph of the cross; see His majesty and glory such as become the Son of God; see His friendliness, as He mingles in a most kind manner with the disciples, talking with them, and allowing Himself to be touched.

II. *The power of Christ.*

1. Consider that this power is given by the Father who has all power; that it is given irrevocably to the only-begotten Son, and therefore in a generous measure. It is given with the view of gaining glory for God and peace for men. The power is most comprehensive, including the whole extent and duration of the world; it includes heaven, to be opened or closed, all graces coming down from above and drawing hearts upwards; it includes all the angels, every creature on earth, all men, nay, the very devils, in so far as they try to ensnare men on earth.

2. Consider how few were at that moment actually subject to Christ's power: the angels, the saints delivered from limbo, and a handful of followers on earth, while the rest of the human race was held in bondage by Lucifer. From the height of Mount Thabor take in the view of all the kingdoms of the world, and all their pomp, shrouded in the darkness of ignorance, and overwhelmed by the death of sin.

3. Notice with what truly royal disposition Christ desires the salvation of all, and presently prepares the means for this salvation; behold all the graces acquired by His blood, gathered in His hands, soon to be entrusted to the Apostles, who are to distribute them to the whole human race.

THIRD POINT: The Sending of the Apostles

I. *They are to go.*

1. Consider how Christ decreed to use the Apostles in bringing about the salvation of mankind; He chose, called, and in-

structed them for this purpose. Ponder the words: "*Go there-fore*" coming from the heart of Jesus as the result both of His love and His power. See how great is the authority of this word to make Apostles use their talents well; how greatly it honors the Apostles, as sharing in the work of Christ; what great graces are connected with these words.

2. Consider that the Apostles are sent "to all nations," and "even unto the consummation of the world." (Matt. 28:20) This means, therefore, the most extensive mission as to place, persons, and time.

II. *They are to teach.*

By their teaching the Apostles shall help the intellect, so that, after removing the ignorance of the mind by the light of faith, the will may be moved to observe all things whatsoever Christ has commanded. This teaching is divine in its origin and dogmas, and with it goes the grace to be-lieve.—Christ will assist them in all their teaching, giving them infallibility: "Behold, I am with you." (Matt. 28:20)

III. *They are to baptize.*

To baptize means to wash or cleanse from sin, and to confer grace, life, and peace. Baptism is at the same time the renunciation of Satan, and his works, and his pomps. Accordingly by baptism they shall enlist the faithful un-der the standard of Christ, to fight against Lucifer; by baptism the faithful must profess at least the spiritual poverty and humility of Christ: they are to do so in the name of the three divine persons, who have sanctioned this as the military uniform of Christ's companions.

CHAPTER LVII

The Ascension of Christ Our Lord

Cf. Acts 1:1-12; *The Exercises*, Sec. 312

★

First Point. *After He had manifested Himself for forty days to the Apostles, and had given them many proofs, and worked many miracles, and had spoken to them of the Kingdom of God, He commanded them to await in Jerusalem the promise of the Holy Spirit.*

Second Point. *He led them to Mt. Olivet " and . . . was lifted up before their eyes, and a cloud took him out of their sight."* (Acts 1:9)

Third Point. *While they were gazing up into heaven, the angels said to them: " Men of Galilee, why do you stand looking up to heaven? This Jesus who has been taken up from you into heaven, shall come in the same way as you have seen him going up to heaven."* (Acts 1:11)

FIRST POINT: The Last Recommendations of Christ

I. *Christ converses with the Apostles.*

1. The Lord appeared to the disciples cheering them by His sight. He " showed himself alive after his passion by many proofs " (Acts 1:3), allowing His wounds to be touched, eating with His disciples, explaining the Scriptures to them. He gave them signs, coming through closed doors, granting the miraculous draught of fish, and many others which were not written (Cf. John 21:25). By all these manifestations He proved His resurrection more and more solidly; by these He showed that He

was truly the Son of God and the source of all life; by these He filled the disciples with solid, and never failing *consolation*.

2. Moreover Christ " was speaking of the kingdom of God." All the consolation obtained by the Resurrection is deposited in the *Church;* to the Church Christ entrusted His teaching and the sacraments. During those forty days He lovingly and patiently explained to the Apostles the nature of His Church; at the same time He stressed the necessary connection between living as a member of the Church, God's kingdom, and the cross.

II. *The Apostles must wait for the Holy Spirit.*

1. The Church has been founded, but she must be perfected by the Holy Spirit, the *Paraclete,* or Comforter, because He is the " Spirit of truth," and " the power from on high." (John 14:17; Luke 24:49) He will change the desert of the earth into a paradise by renewing the face of the earth; He will consecrate the bodies of men into His temples; He will complete the Kingdom of Christ in their hearts. Christ once again promises that He will send the Holy Spirit, and He tells them to wait at Jerusalem in humble retreat and assiduous prayer.

2. Review here Christ's loving conversation with you during the whole retreat: He has revealed Himself day after day, to be better known and loved by you; He has made known to you your state and calling in His Church. Observe that you too must persevere in recollection and prayer, in order to obtain the full effect of this calling.

SECOND POINT: The Ascension of Christ into Heaven

I. *The journey to Mount Olivet.*

Scarcely seven weeks had elapsed since that other journey to Mount Olivet, and how everything has been changed:—*The persons:* Christ is glorious and bears the marks of the glorious wounds; the faces of Mary and the disciples are beaming with joy.—*Their sentiments:* then Christ was sad at leaving the Apostles behind, now He is going to the Father, but He will not leave them orphans; then He was filled with horror of the Passion, now He is impassible and overjoyed at the fruit of the Passion; then He was solicitous about the Apostles, now He will presently send them the Holy Spirit. Mary and the disciples are filled with faith and charity.—In company of these holy persons make yourself the journey from the City through the valley of Cedron, past the Garden, where each step brings to mind the former sorrows; but now their remembrance produces sweetest consolation.—The city of Jerusalem is doomed, but its place will be taken by the spiritual and heavenly Jerusalem.

II. *The arrival on the mountain.*

Behold Christ as with one glance He surveys the whole world, a desert wrapped in darkness; the kingdom of Lucifer, with all its pomps, has now been shaken to its foundations; death, " the wages of sin " (Rom. 6:23), has been overcome in the person of Christ, and He hears the words of the Father: " Ask of me, and I will give thee the gentiles for thy inheritance." (Ps. 2:8) How very different are these words of the Father from the words of the tempter promising the whole world: Look once more at Christ, how His glance rests on the Apostles, the *seed of the Church!* They shall renew the face of the earth, and change it into a paradise by the power of the Holy Spirit; and so Christ beholds the fulfilment " of every word that comes forth from the mouth of God." (Matt. 4:4). Watch Christ as He raises His eyes upwards, where the Most Blessed Trinity calls Him to His crown: " Come to me." " Throw thyself down " was what the tempter had prompted! (Cf. Matt. 4:6)

III. *The ascension from the mountain.*

1. Consider the Sacred Heart of Jesus rejoicing in His triumph, and overflowing with kindness. Behold the hosts of angels hovering about, ready for service, and the saints of the Old Testament invisibly present there. With hands spread out Jesus blesses the new-born Church. This blessing is not only a prayer for good things but also the confirmation of all the goods granted and promised. Jesus ascends by His own power, and, as He rises higher and higher, His blessing embraces ever more and more worlds. The angels, to whom the Father has given charge over Him, accompany Him; the saints sing to Him " Hosannah " as the Son of David and the Son of God. Consider the feelings of glorified humility in the Sacred Heart of Jesus: the Lord's " Magnificat."

2. Behold Jesus, escorted by the angels and saints, entering the heavenly Jerusalem, the temple of the Blessed Trinity, and sitting down on the throne at the right hand of the Father. The hosts of heaven break forth in the shout: " Worthy is the Lamb who was slain to receive power and divinity and wisdom and strength and honor and glory and blessing." (Apoc. 5:12) Compare the glory, sweetness, and eternity of this triumph with the shame, pain, and brief duration of the cross.

3. Consider how a *cloud* veils the sight of this glory. We are separated from glory by the mist of our natural dullness which prevents us from seeing that glory; yet at the same time it is under the sacramental appearances that we draw near to God. Only a mist separates us from Him, and it will one day be scat-

tered; this mist, however, leaves a free passage to the light of God's omniscience, to the warmth of His love, and to the power of His omnipotence.

THIRD POINT: The Admonition of the Angels

I. *The disciples are looking upwards.*

The look of the disciples remains fixed on heaven, where faith seeks the home, hope the reward, and charity the Beloved. "Seek the things that are above, where Christ is seated at the right hand of God. Mind the things that are above, not the things that are on earth." (Co. 3:1-2)

II. *The disciples are admonished.*

1. It is not enough to look up to heaven, not enough to have chosen a state of life; the retreat is not an end in itself. We must labor with Christ. Thus, if we feel ourselves called to an apostolic life, we must go, teach, and baptize. We must labor by acting against our own sensuality etc. We must be clothed with the same garments and livery as Christ.

2. Jesus will come again to judge and reward our labor. He will come to be seen for eternity, and He will transform us into the likeness of His glory. We shall enjoy His sight to the extent in which we have labored for Him.

CHAPTER LVIII

A Contemplation to Attain the Love of God

Cf. *The Exercises*, Secs. 230 sqq.

★

THIS CONTEMPLATION stands apart from the fourth week, as the Principle and Foundation does from the first, and the Kingdom of Christ from the second. Yet it must not be separated from the other exercises as though it were a casual addition.

In order to understand the connection of this contemplation with the rest of the exercises, we must look back and see what we have accomplished thus far. In the Foundation we were persuaded to give God due service, on the motives of duty, honor, and self-interest, the salvation of our souls. The meditation on personal sins led up to perfect contrition, or sorrow out of love of God, for it contrasted our imperfections with God's infinite goodness and perfection. The meditation on the Kingdom of Christ, which was a preview of all the matter to follow, suggested a new motive, love of Christ, which was, from that moment on, constantly sought as the motive of following Christ and serving God.

Although, in the contemplation of the life of Christ, love was indeed the principal motive, it was by no means the only one; the motive of self-interest, which had been fostered by the Foundation, occupied a prominent role.

Christ the King drew us by the reward offered for poverty and humiliations; in the Nativity, the angels announced peace to men; in Christ was shown to us the fulness of true life, promised His followers; lastly, the whole fourth week celebrated the reward that had been promised.

Hence love has been found in the exercises which have already been made. The present contemplation does not touch new matter of which we have heard nothing. The point here is not to obtain disinterested love (*amor benevolentiae*) only to some degree, but to obtain it as the habitual motive of our spiritual life.

What is meant by the word " love "? St. Ignatius first excludes that pretended love, a love consisting only in words. Next he excludes that love which arouses some sentiments or affections in us, but does not lead to any actions. He says: " love consists in a mutual sharing of goods." (Sec. 231) Hence, where there is no mutual interchange, there is no love. The second prelude to this contemplation expresses affective love and its effects: That I " may in all things love and serve the Divine Majesty." (Sec. 233)

We are seeking disinterested love, or charity. From the points of the contemplation it is clear that we seek chiefly the love of God viewed as He really is in the life of the Blessed Trinity, rather than the love of God Incarnate, which had been stressed in the meditations on Christ's life.

In addition to the disinterested love common to all Christians, and based on our knowledge of God through ideas abstracted from sensible things, there is also the ecstatic love of the contemplatives, which is not based on that kind of knowledge. By ecstatic love the soul, altogether abstracted from the senses, enjoys God. This extraordinary grace was enjoyed by St. Ignatius; at that time of history many eagerly sought it. Shortly after the lifetime of St. Ignatius, Spain produced the masters of the contemplative life, St. Teresa of Avila and St. John of the Cross. Do you think that St. Ignatius can have wished to exclude this most sublime kind of love from the meaning of the words " to attain the Love of God "?

This contemplation is not on love, but to attain love. Consequently St. Ignatius outlines some means to acquire love.

There is a threefold way:

The first way consists in increasing our knowledge of God viewed in Himself, for love presupposes some knowledge; what is not known is not desired. Nevertheless here the proportion between knowledge and love is neither necessary nor equal: a theologian may have an excellent knowledge of God, but little charity, or even none at all. An illiterate man can have great charity. Since this deeper knowledge of God, viewed in Himself, is altogether speculative, it is not well suited to many minds. Therefore St. Ignatius does not follow this way. We will find in the points nothing to explain the excellence of the divine nature, nothing about God's self-existence, infinity, etc.

The second way to attain love is by the command of some other virtue. A virtue that is practiced easily by all, even by the illiterate, is gratitude, a virtue annexed to justice. Gratitude has also a special affinity with love. It is aroused by the receipt of a gift and tends to make a gift in return. It does so from the motive of justice or equity, whereas God bestows the gift from the motive of love. God's generosity prompts us to give something in return, not only service, but service with love. Gratitude of its very nature readily commends love.

St. Ignatius follows this way: "To ask for an intimate knowledge of the many blessings received, that filled with gratitude for all, I may in all things love and serve the Divine Majesty." (Sec. 233)

The third way to obtain love, and this the best and surest, is to ask God to give it to us. For this most pure love is, even more than all other things, a gift of God. St. Ignatius also follows this way, as may be seen by the words: "Give me Thy love and Thy grace." (Sec. 234)

Accordingly the means to obtain love, proposed by St. Ignatius, is this: Do you wish to attain to excellent love of God? Apply yourself eagerly to give God thanks for the benefits you have received; thence you will be led on with a grateful heart to give in return to God not only gifts for gifts but also love for love; at the same time pray earnestly that God may liberally bestow on you the gift of love.

This practical advice is a significant sign of the very great reverence in which St. Ignatius held this excellent love. He will have man labor on his part, first to serve God in all things from gratitude in a way free from illusions and from the mere sentiment of love that produces no effects. At the same time he will have man bear in mind that he is unable to reach this excellent good by his own strength, that he must pray constantly to God to grant him this gift: by doing so he will be free from pride. St. Ignatius does not give a method for practicing this love, nor does he explain that in his points: the chief master of this love is God; let the bridegroom teach the bride how to love. Like Moses on Mount Nebo, St. Ignatius points to a Holy Land, and shows the way that leads thither. He teaches how to knock, but does not himself open the door.

The gifts of God are the matter of this contemplation. We are to see what these gifts are and with what charity God bestows them: for this charity is one of the gifts, in fact, the greatest. Furthermore, the consideration of the divine gifts is divided into four points, not to separate the gifts themselves into four different classes, but to distinguish in all of them taken together four degrees of God's love toward us: *viz.*, God gives us so many and great gifts, He is present Himself to give them, He gives them with His own labor, and He gives them as so many communications of His own goodness. These four degrees of God's love toward us, by virtue of the principle which St. Ignatius puts at the beginning of this exercise, invite us to as many degrees of God's service: *viz.*, to serve God with all our goods and powers; to put our whole being into this service, being ever mindful of God's presence; to serve Him with labor; and in all things to recognize, seek, and love God alone.

It may be objected that in the actual text St. Ignatius hardly indicates these last three degrees of love toward God. For, after suggesting at the end of the first point that we should serve God with all our goods and powers, he tells us, for the following points, to reflect on ourselves " in the manner stated in the first point, or in some other way that may seem better." (Sec. 235)

We may first answer that the exercise can be made in such wise that the exercitant, pondering how many great gifts God has given him, insists again and again that his sole aim in life is to serve God with his entire being, proportionately as God has served him.

We can answer further that by the words " or in some other way which I may deem better " Ignatius indicates explicitly that there is a better way, more suited to the following points, of offering oneself to God. It is, however, not said expressly, perhaps because there is need to observe in this contemplation more than elsewhere the hint of annotation 2, that greater spiritual relish and profit is derived from something which the exercitant finds by his own reasoning. What this more suitable way is can be understood from what we said before. The proximate good, but not the chief one, consists in leading up to the generous offering of ourselves: " Take, Lord, and receive all my . . ." (Sec. 234) The chief, though remote good, consists in leading to perfect love. With the help of God's grace this good can be obtained in any point; as soon as it is offered, we must grasp it. We are to offer ourselves to God and ask for the grace to love Him perfectly.

Here I must " ask for an intimate knowledge of the many blessings received, that filled with gratitude for all, I may in all things love and serve the Divine Majesty." (Sec. 233)

First Point: The Benefits God Has Bestowed On Us

I. *Weighing the facts.*

1. *The benefits of creation:* In the beginning God created heaven and earth, and put into them laws by which they are permanently governed. He divided the darkness from the light, the water from the earth, so that the earth might some day be my abode, too; He created plants for my food and clothing,

animals to be used by me as food, for work, and for enjoyment; lastly, He created men, myself among them, with a nature including the perfections of all the lower orders.

2. *The benefits of redemption:* God not only restored to me the grace that was lost in our First Parents, but gave me, in the crucified Savior, an ever-flowing spring of all graces, which waters the paradise of the Church with the streams of the sacraments, and the tree of life *viz.,* the Holy Eucharist, the knowledge of God, and the gifts of the Holy Spirit.

3. *Special benefits:* God put me in this paradise, shortly after I was born, and made me share in all its pleasures; He assigned to me the state of life in which I should serve and please Him; He gave me the grace of going through this retreat etc.

II. *A closer examination of the facts.*

1. *The number and variety of God's benefits:* There are natural and supernatural gifts of every kind, and even uncreated gifts: the Son, and the Holy Spirit. They have been decreed from eternity, prepared from the beginning of the world, bestowed during my whole life, and they are to go on for all eternity. They are partly of God's creation, and partly essentially proper to God Himself. They were given without any merit of mine, in spite of my ungratefulness, altogether gratuitously.— I shall review all this, and " will ponder with great affection how much God our Lord has done for me, and how much He has given me of what He possesses." (Sec. 234)

2. *The ultimate aim of God's benefits:* I must see " how much, the . . . Lord desires to give Himself to me according to His divine decrees." (Sec. 234) God wishes to give me His whole self in heaven; accordingly all the gifts of this life are so many tokens of His love for me, so many pledges that are to bind my soul to Him for ever, so many presents setting now already the seal of my eternal union with God.

III. *A practical conclusion.*

1. I ought, on my part, " according to all reason " (Sec. 234) to give something to God: it is fair that I should make some gift in return, since God is showering, and will go on showering, so many gifts on me; He does so most lovingly and kindly, He the most High to me who am so very low.—I ought, on my part, " according to all . . . justice " (Sec. 234) to offer something to God: it is indeed just that I should make some present in return, since God has granted me these gifts not for arbitrary use, but for His service and glory. He could not have done otherwise, because the highest and innermost excellence of the creature consists in this service of God; and thereby man receives dominion over the whole visible world, exercises priesthood in the temple of material nature, and obtains his own true happiness both in the present life and the life to come.

2. *I ought to give all: all I have* and am, all my possessions.— *Myself with them.* It is not enough to offer what I have received and acquired, for God gave me not only His goods, but Himself as well. He gave me the Word, His uncreated understanding; then I will give Him " my memory, my understanding." (Sec. 234) God gave me the Holy Spirit, His uncreated will; then I will give Him " my entire will." (Sec. 234) God longs to give me His whole self in heaven; then I will give my whole self, offering Him my heart as a paradise or garden where God may take His delight.

3. *For what purpose shall I give?* " Dispose of it wholly according to Thy will." (Sec. 234) Let God withdraw, lessen, or increase His gifts according to His good pleasure; I will use them exclusively according to His will. In order that I may be able to do so, I need God's " love and grace." (Sec. 234)

4. *In doing this have I done enough for God?* No, because God has given me more, by giving me everything from the motive of pure love. All created things are proofs of God's love;

in the heart of the Son burns the love of God; the Holy Spirit is uncreated Love itself. I should not be acting with reason and justice should I not return to God love for love. This love, however, is God's choicest gift which He Himself must bestow; therefore I beg Him: " Give me Thy love," and in order to use it worthily and perseveringly I ask Him: " Give me Thy grace." (Sec. 234) I do not ask for anything else, for when I have the gift of love, and the grace to use it well, there is nothing more for me to seek: all comes to this alone, and all is contained in this, that I love, that I do nothing but love, in desire and in deed; this alone " is sufficient for me." (Sec. 234)

SECOND POINT: The Presence of God in All His Gifts

I. *Weighing the facts.*

Let me again remember that I am " standing in the presence of God our Lord and of His angels and saints, who intercede for me." (Sec. 232) Indeed, as Paul said, God " is not far from any one of us." (Acts 17:27) The thought of God's presence moves me with joy.

1. God is not only near me, standing before me or at my side, but He is present within me, and within all things, for " in him we live and move and have our being " (Acts 17:28); hence I must rejoice at so intimate a presence.

2. God is present in all things as the first cause of their existence, " upholding all things by the word of his power." (Hebr. 1:3) The same act of God's will by which He created all things still persists, keeping all things in existence.

3. God has become present to us in a special manner in the Incarnation, and as a consequence of it, by the indwelling of the Holy Spirit; this twofold presence persists in almost numberless places by the continuation of the work of the Son of

God through His ministers, when they say: "This is My Body"; "Receive ye the Holy Spirit"; "I absolve thee."

4. God is present by His grace in my soul which becomes His dwelling, His temple and His bridal chamber. Consequently my soul by this presence becomes beautiful, intent on the worship of God, and full of love.

II. *A closer examination of this fact.*

1. Consider that God is present with you interiorly and exteriorly, always and everywhere, that He is present in every way possible: by His omnipresence, by the hypostatic union, by the indwelling which sanctifies us.

2. Since His creatures are a manifestation of God's presence, He shows Himself the more as the creature is of a higher order: "in the elements giving them existence, in the plants giving them life, in the animals conferring upon them sensation, in man bestowing understanding. So He dwells in me and gives me being, life, sensation, intelligence, and makes a temple of me." (Sec. 235) In the Incarnation He shows Himself present in human flesh, in the Holy Eucharist under appearances other than human, in the indwelling of the Holy Spirit through the testimony of faith. By nature He is present in me as in His image, and by grace as in His temple.

3. What is the ultimate purpose of this most manifold and marvellous presence? God wishes to become ever more and more present to my understanding by my acknowledging Him, to my will by my loving Him, in order that He may at last be intimately and inseparably present in heaven, He with me, and I with Him!

III. *A practical conclusion.*

1. It is indeed meet and right that I should always and everywhere be *mindful* of God's presence, because this presence is

worthy of notice, because He is present for my sake, because He is constantly mindful of me.

2. It is meet and right that I should always and everywhere *acknowledge* God's presence in all my actions, doing what pleases Him who is present, and abstaining from what displeases Him who is present.

3. It is meet and right that I should endeavor to pass from the knowledge of His creatures to the knowledge and praise of God who is present in them; that I transfer all my love from His creatures to God who is present in them.

4. It is meet and right that I should acknowledge God's presence in my neighbor.

THIRD POINT: The Working of God with All His Gifts

I. *Weighing the facts.*

Turning my mind once more to the first prelude of this meditation, I behold the angels and saints interceding for me, and I reflect how they are active for me with God, and bring it about that God is active for me.

1. God is not only working in all things, serving me, and doing me good; He also co-operates with me in all I do.

2. God was working for me from the very beginning of the world, creating heaven and earth, establishing the laws of nature, directing the events so as to prepare a pleasant home for me on this globe, bringing about the propagation of plants and animals, that they might one day be useful to me, procuring the propagation of the human race, in particular in my ancestors, that I might be born, endowed, and overwhelmed with such gifts, and others even greater.

3. *The Son of God* was working for me from the beginning of His Incarnation, during the whole of His mortal life; He is

continually working for me in heaven as Mediator, on earth, concealed under the Holy Eucharist, and living in the Church.

4. The Holy Spirit is working in me, enlightening my mind, stimulating my will, co-operating in every supernatural act, increasing in me graces and virtues.

II. *A closer examination of the facts.*

1. The one indivisible and eternal act of the divine energy has been made available to me: God had me in view from eternity, when He willed my existence; He had me in view at the creation of the world, when He prepared for me a home; He will have me in view throughout eternity, when He shall keep me in glory and overwhelm me with gifts.

2. God is producing for me works of every kind: all the orders of natural creatures, my own natural powers, and the supernatural life by means of His grace. Put together the cries of the Holy Babe, and the tears and sighs of the Lord in His agony, His words of instruction, His steps in search for souls, His longings as He is hidden in the Blessed Sacrament. See how much you owe Him. Reckon up the inspirations of the Holy Spirit, and see how good He has been. What shall you do for such a loving God?

3. And what is the ultimate purpose of all God's gifts? God wants to make me share in His happiness which is the love and knowledge of Him " as He is."

III. *A practical conclusion.*

1. It is indeed meet and just that I should do all I can for God and with God, having His praise and glory as my goal.

2. It is meet and just that I should work for the God-Man, and with Him, that I should sanctify myself as a member of

His body, and sanctify others, becoming a fellow-worker with the Son of God.

3. It is meet and just that I should work for the Holy Spirit, and with Him, both in myself and in others.

FOURTH POINT: God Communicates Himself in His Gifts.

I. *Weighing the facts.*

Yet again shall I consider the first prelude and gaze with reverence on God. In God's face I can trace the features and dispositions I must acquire if I am to be truly a man " in His image and likeness."

1. All goodness and beauty of the lower creation is an ever so remote imitation of the divine goodness and beauty, descending from it as rays come from the sun, the waters from the spring, displaying a true likeness, together with on absolute dependence.

2. Man, who occupies the highest grade of visible creation, displays not only similarity but is a true image of God: his frame imitates God's majesty, his mind and will resemble God's knowledge and volition; the same may be said of man's virtues and immortality in comparison with God's holiness and eternity; he is also a true image of God's liberty, though it does not, in the case of man, mean absolute independence.

3. By the supernatural gifts man is a child of God, springing from God like the flower from the seed, the child from the father, displaying a true community with the divine nature, yet with absolute dependence from God.

II. *A closer examination of the facts.*

1. Accordingly I am raised to the highest kinship possible for any creature with the Son of God, who is begotten of the Father,

to the perfect likeness and image of His nature. The Holy Spirit, who proceeds from the Father and the Son, proceeds also in me, and by grace He makes me share in the nature and life of God. The Father embraces me with truly paternal feeling, raised as I am from being His servant to His adopted son.

2. What is the ultimate purpose of this divine sonship? " If we are sons, we are heirs also." (Rom. 8:17) All this is done with the view that I may at last, when this mortal life is over, be received into heaven, and admitted into the household of the Father, and of the Son, and of the Holy Spirit.

III. *A practical conclusion.*

I shall raise myself to a sense of piety or filial love, which is the noblest blossom of justice and gratitude, making due return to God, the Author of my being.

1. Accordingly I shall strive to become ever more like *God*, seeking to acquire His perfections and conforming my will to His. As Scripture has it: " Be ye holy, because I am holy! " (Lev. 11:14)

2. I shall strive to become ever more like the *Christ*, the Son of God. I shall seek to share His sentiments and sufferings; I shall seek to live more and more *the life of the Holy Spirit* and show myself as a child of my Father who is in heaven.

3. In my neighbor, too, I will reverence the image of God.

End with a colloquy, and the Lord's Prayer, which is the prayer of children to their Father.

APPENDIX

PRELUDES AND COLLOQUIES

As THE *Matter* of the Ignatian Retreat includes preludes and colloquies, we shall add here a brief explanation of these features.

I. *Preludes*

After the vocal preparatory prayer, which precedes and prepares for mental prayer, St. Ignatius sets down *Preludes*, two of which are essential and integral to the entire work (the second and third preludes), one of which is accidental or accessory (the first prelude).

Beginning with the mystery of the Incarnation the accessory prelude is composed of contemplations and meditations; the only exception occurs in the contemplation on The Love of God. The purpose of this accessory prelude is to call to mind " the *history* of the subject I have to contemplate." (Sec. 102) Hence it is clear that there is no solid objection against beginning even the preceding exercises, those of the first week, with such a prelude. Indeed, every meditation and contemplation should have its *history*, as St. Ignatius remarks in his " Introductory Observations." (Cf. Sec. 2)

The accessory prelude consists in examining the points given at the end of the book on the mysteries of our Lord's life. In the meditations this prelude merely recalls the " history " or fact that serves as the basis of the meditation, leaving out of consideration any conclusions we should draw from the meditation. The purpose of the prelude is always that the *memory* be applied to the exercise.

If we compare the first preludes set down for certain mysteries with the text of the same mysteries at the end of the book, we can see that St. Ignatius practices what he stated in his introductory observations, namely, that the retreatant should cover the history only in a summary and brief manner. (Cf. Sec. 2) There is given, not the plain history as found in the Gospel or in the Points at the end of the book, but only a brief summary, just enough to enable us to see the scope of the meditation.

The first of the essential preludes is the " mental representation of the place." (Cf. Sec. 47) The theory behind this is given in the first exercise of the first week. The " representation " should be made with the sight of the " imagination." (Sec. 47) Perhaps one may ask if there is any difference between this prelude made with the sight of the imagination, and the contemplation on hell, which is made by the use of the five senses. Though there are similarities between the two, there are two basic differences. These are: 1. In the contemplation we must always reflect upon ourselves and draw profit from our contemplation (Cf. Sec. 2) ; in the prelude such a reflection would be out of place. 2. The composition of place does not view things in particular; it does not consider the persons and the circumstances surrounding them but only the place, indeed the material place. The composition or representation of place " consists in seeing in imagination the material place where the object is that we wish to contemplate. I said the material place, for example, the temple, or the mountain where Jesus or His Mother is, according to the subject matter of the contemplation." (Sec. 47)

The place is nearly always viewed in its most obvious proportions: " It will consist here [in the contemplation on the Nativity] in seeing in imagination the way from Nazareth to Bethlehem. Consider its length, its breadth; whether level, or through valleys and over hills. Observe also the place or cave where Christ is born; whether big or little; whether high or low; and how it is arranged." (Sec. 112); " Here it will be to consider the way from Bethany to Jerusalem, whether narrow or broad, whether level, etc; also the place of the Supper, whether great or small, whether of this or that appearance." (Sec. 193) " It will be here to consider the way from Mt. Sion to the Valley of Josaphat, likewise the garden, its breadth, its length, and appearance." (Sec. 202) Many other examples could be given.

St. Ignatius does not try to place before our eyes some picture of the mystery, its persons and actions, which we should view; he does try to transfer us to the very place of the mystery, to meet there the persons, to hear their words, to look at their actions and to profit by their company.

The special feature of this accessory prelude becomes clearer by considering those meditations " where the subject matter is not visible, as . . . in a meditation on sin." (Sec. 47) In such meditations we are " to see in imagination [our] soul, as a prisoner in this corruptible body, and to consider [our] whole composite being as an exile here on earth, cast out to live among brute beasts." (Sec. 47) This prelude, taken from the meditation on the Three Sins, of course also states the condition of our First Parents, when the rebellion of the flesh against the spirit broke out, and they were cast out of paradise into this

" vale of tears " etc. Nevertheless the prelude is not re-stricted to our First Parents. It proposes that we consider the state of our own souls in regard to sin. We must look at ourselves.

The prelude is, therefore, a true " representation of place." Since sin injures the soul, the prelude shows us the place of the soul, and consequently of sin itself.

In the Three Classes of Men the composition of place is: " to behold myself standing in the presence of God our Lord and of all His saints, that I may know and de-sire what is more pleasing to His Divine Goodness." (Sec. 151) The purpose of this meditation is, therefore, to en-able us to know and desire the Will of God. The *place*, so to say, of this knowledge and desire is ourselves, stand-ing in the presence of God and His saints. In such august presence the dispositions desired can easily spring into being.

The prelude to the Love of God is almost the same as that of the Three Classes of Men. Here, too, the *place* of love is the lover, that is, ourselves, not kneeling, but standing, ready to do all that our Lord may suggest, begging His saints to be our coadjutors in His labor. (Cf. Sec. 252)

The prelude to The Kingdom of Christ is not quite so plain. It suggests to us a certain place, yet not one di-rectly corresponding to the imagination of Christ the King. In many ways this prelude is akin to that of the Two Standards. St. Ignatius tries, in these medita-tions, to put before us Christ standing in a definite and limited place. We are to " see a great plain, comprising the whole region about Jerusalem, where the sovereign Commander-in-Chief of all the good is Christ our Lord."

(Sec. 138) We are " to see in imagination the synagogues, villages, and towns where Jesus preached." (Sec. 91) The preludes in these meditations do not correspond to an image, but to a fact. They display all the places where the outward call of Christ the King was actually and successively made. Thus it seems that its aim is to fix our minds in contemplation and at the same time to warn us that the question is not about some imaginary thing, but about a real and historical call.

The second essential prelude is the *petition for grace* according to the matter under contemplation. There is some diversity in these petitions. Sometimes grace is sought, either for the intellect alone, or for the will alone, or for both. Thus in the Three Kinds of Sin we seek " shame and confusion " (Sec. 48); in the Kingdom of Christ we beg God for the "grace not to be deaf to His call, but prompt and diligent to accomplish His holy will." (Sec. 91); in the Three Classes of Men we " beg for the grace to choose what is more for the glory of His Divine Majesty and the salvation of my soul " (Sec. 152); in the Last Supper we ask " for sorrow, compassion, and shame because the Lord is going to His sufferings for my sins " (Sec. 193); in the Resurrection we ask " for the grace to be glad and rejoice intensely because of the great joy and Christ our Lord." (Sec. 221) And so on for other mysteries.

As examples of preludes which seek grace both for the intellect and for the will we have the meditations on the Incarnation, when we " ask for an intimate knowledge of our Lord who has become man for me, that I may love Him more and follow Him more closely " (Sec. 104); on Hell, when we " beg for a deep sense of the pain which the lost suffer, that . . . at least the fear of these punishments will keep me from falling into sin ". (Sec. 65); on the Love of God, when we " ask for an intimate knowledge of the many blessings received, that filled with gratitude for all, I may in all things love and serve the Divine Majesty." (Sec. 233)

In the meditation on the Two Standards petitions are set side by side: " to ask for a knowledge of the deceits of the rebel chief AND help to guard myself against them; . . . for a knowledge of the true life exemplified in the sovereign and true Commander, AND the grace to imitate Him." (Sec. 139)

An altogether peculiar petition occurs in the First Way of Making a Good and Correct Choice. Two coordinate graces are sought: one to stir up the will, " beg God our Lord to deign to move my will "; the other to help the intellect as well as the will, " to bring to my mind what I ought to do to promote His praise and glory." (Sec. 180)

Note that in those preludes where only an affection of the will is sought, there is also implicitly sought corresponding knowledge for the intellect. But the chief petition usually is for an affection of the will, as contrition, pain, joy, etc. In the Two Standards knowledge and affection are equally sought; knowledge of Satan's deceits and Christ's goodness; desire to flee Satan and follow Christ. In the mysteries of the second week and in the Love of God knowledge alone is asked for directly, and indirectly the affection subsequent to such knowledge. For knowledge must not remain barren, but must beget love and service.

As the first prelude fixes the attention of the mind, so

the third prelude usually seeks to give an impulse to the will.

II. *Colloquies*

The colloquy is closely related to the petitions for grace. The petition points out before the contemplation the goal to be reached; the colloquy rests in the same goal as one attained. Yet there is some difference. The petition is adapted to the points, preparing for them; the colloquy is adapted to the meditation, being its fruit and crown. Meditation and points, therefore, stand in the same relation as colloquy and petition. Therefore the petition should be short, the colloquy more extended. On the whole the colloquy goes further than the petition, for example, in the third exercise of the first week the prelude seeks for sorrow for sins, whereas the colloquy extends to sorrow not only for sins, but for any disorders of life. (Cf. Secs. 55 and 63)

The petition is about some general grace, the meditation about some particular one, and the colloquy, by making us reflect on ourselves (Sec. 53), adapts the particular grace to the particular retreatant. We can see here a general progression from the less perfect to the most perfect. At the beginning of the meditation (the preludes) particular things are not assumed to be understood very clearly. It is the task of the meditation to suggest them, and the work of the colloquy to perfect our knowledge of them. At the beginning of the meditation it is enough to ask for a general good, *e.g.*, love. The meditation makes this love concrete in the actions of our Lord. The colloquy seeks to make us imitate Christ in the practice of love.

The theory of the colloquies is fully treated by St.

Ignatius. We shall give a few quotations from him to show what the nature and work of the colloquies is. " The colloquy is made by speaking exactly as one friend speaks to another, or as a servant speaks to a master, now asking him for a favor, now blaming himself for some misdeed, now making known his affairs to him, and seeking advice in them." (Sec. 54) " In the colloquy, one should talk over motives and the present petitions . . . He should ask for what he more earnestly desires with regard to some particular interests . . . . he may engage in only one colloquy with our Lord, or, if the matter and his devotion prompt him to do so, he may use three colloquies, one with the Mother of our Lord, one with her Son, and one with the Father." (Sec. 199) In short, the colloquy is a reverential talk with God, with Christ, or with the Mother of God. In it heart speaks to heart, and special graces are to be asked relative to the matter previously considered in the meditation.

The colloquy is either simple or manifold. After the first and second exercises of the first week (Secs. 53 and 61), only one colloquy is mentioned; the structure of these exercises does not seem to admit several. The same holds true of other exercises, such as that on Hell. On the other hand St. Ignatius at times requires three colloquies: *e.g.* the third exercise of the first week " is a repetition of the first and second exercises with *three* colloquies " (Sec. 62) ; " the same three colloquies should be used at the close." (Sec. 64)

The same holds true in regard to the meditations on the Incarnation (Cf. Sec. 101), the Nativity (Sec. 117), and other mysteries of the life of our Lord. Liberty is granted to address the colloquy to the Three Divine

Persons, or to the Word Incarnate, or to His Blessed
Mother. (Cf. Sec. 199) During the fourth week we are
given full liberty: " Close with a colloquy, or colloquies,
as the circumstances suggest." (Sec. 225) The same advice
is also given at the end of other mysteries. Why this
variety in the number of colloquies? The reason becomes
in some way clear by a consideration of the aim sought
by the colloquy. Where several colloquies are made, the
progress is always ascending, from the Blessed Virgin to
Christ, to the Father. It is easy to see that we are to ask
the Blessed Virgin to intercede for us with Christ, and
Christ to intercede for us with the Father. It is clear that
some colloquies are multiplied with good reason when some
grace, such as the choice of a way of life is to be made, etc.

Occasionally an exercise intends to gain not so much
some grace to regulate our life as some affection, already
felt during the course of the meditation. In this case it is
more suitable to make only one colloquy, issuing from the
heart of the meditation: the mind can then yield quite
freely to that affection.

Lastly, the colloquy may start directly, not from the
desire of some definite grace, nor from the intention of
some definite affection in preference to others, but simply
from the fact that the soul is inflamed during spiritual
contemplation by the intercourse with holy persons and so
proceeds to address them devoutly in the order of their
dignity.

Since the " colloquy is made by speaking exactly as one
friend speaks to another " (Sec. 54), its essence consists
in a heart to heart talk with some holy persons. When the
persons were already present to the mind in the course
of the exercise, as is true of the exercises on the mysteries

of our Lord's life, the colloquy flows of itself from the exercise. Things are a bit different, however, in the exercises of the first week, in which the persons addressed in the colloquies were not mentioned in the meditation. In this case the person must first be introduced by acts serving as a kind of prelude. For example, in the colloquy of the meditation on the Three Sins we are told to imagine Christ our Lord present and placed on the cross, and on the other hand to look at ourselves. (Cf. Sec. 53)

Although the memory and the understanding are employed in the colloquy, the chief faculty concerned is the will. " What have I done for Christ? What am I doing for Christ? What ought I to do for Christ? " (Sec. 53) In the colloquy the memory and understanding are directed to an *affectionate* conversation.

Every exercise that has a colloquy should end with the *Our Father*. Already the explanation at the end of the Three Sins concludes by saying: " Close with an *Our Father*." (Sec. 54) The reason for St. Ignatius' insistence that every colloquy close with an *Our Father* is that it is the prayer taught us by Christ Himself (Cf. Matt. 6:9) However when several colloquies are made, the one to the Blessed Virgin should end with a *Hail Mary* and the one to our Lord should end with the *Soul of Christ*, a prayer of St. Ignatius' own composition, one so dear to him that he thought it right to place it at the head of his book.

We must distinguish from the colloquy the *oblation* of ourselves, which is of a very solemn nature, made in set words, not in words of our own choice. The Kingdom of Christ (Cf. Sec. 98) ends with such an oblation and no colloquy is to be made, nor is any vocal prayer to be said. The oblation itself is the final vocal prayer. Another oblation occurs in the contemplation on the Love of God. It is introduced at the end of the first point with the words: " I will reflect upon myself . . . I will make this offering of myself: Take, Lord, and receive etc." (Sec. 234). At the end of the second point St. Ignatius suggests that we repeat the offering (Sec. 235). In this contemplation, the last one to be made, we have an exception to the rule that no exercise containing an oblation should end with a colloquy and an *Our Father*. St. Ignatius has us end with a general colloquy, in which we can talk to God about all the graces we have received during the entire retreat and our plans for the future, and an *Our Father*, as the perfect prayer of a follower of Christ.

A NOTE ON THE TYPE

IN WHICH THIS BOOK WAS SET

This book is set in Linotype Garamond, a type face considered by many as one of the most successful ever introduced. Claude Garamond, the designer of these beautiful types, was a pupil of Geoffroy Tory, a leader of the Renaissance in France, a university professor, artist, designer and printer who set out to place French on an equal footing with Latin and Greek as a language of culture. Garamond's evenness of color throughout the font is highly appreciated by book designers. The moderately strong fine lines tend to soften the effect, which is decidedly agreeable to many. One thing is certain, Garamond is unusually pleasing and will distinguish much good printing for many years to come. This book was composed and printed by the Wickersham Printing Company, of Lancaster, Pa., and bound by Moore and Company of Baltimore. The typography and design of this book are by Howard N. King.